Bridgw

# Suffolk

*Mechanisms of the windpump at the
Museum of East Anglian Life, Stowmarket*

# Bridgwater's
# Suffolk

*St. Edmund*
*Bury St. Edmunds*

Beth Bridgwater

Encompass Press    Norwich

*For Richard*

First Published 1996

© Beth Bridgwater (Text) 1996

© Beth Bridgwater (Photography) 1996
except those on p. 138, p.152, and p.159 which are from the
author's collection, copyright unknown, and on p. 195 courtesy of
Ipswich Borough Council

© Richard Green (Maps) 1996

Encompass Press, 45 The Street, Alymerton, Norwich NR11 8AA

A CIP catalogue record for this publication is available from
The British Library

ISBN 1 897924  09 7

Printed in Great Britain by
Broadgate Printers, Aylsham, Norfolk

# *Preface*

My first weekend foray into Suffolk at the beginning of the 1980's was little short of a disaster. The weather was lousy, a bitingly ice cold wind blowing its trumpet of hail, the company no better, the accommodation barely adequate and my return to London desperately awaited. No wonder my reluctance then when a few years later, by now living in Norfolk, my husband checked us into an hotel on the Suffolk coast. My fears though were unfounded. Not only was the accommodation and company first class, but I was amazed that what I had previously found loathsome was nothing short of beautiful. How fickle then can we be! Thankfully though I have not had to reverse my views again and visits into neighbouring Suffolk from across the Norfolk border are now looked forward to with much relish.

Remote from the rest of the country, though less so than Norfolk, Suffolk is something of a barely undulating lowland. Its skyline one of its most dramatic features and especially as there is little else in the landscape to divert your attentions. For here you can see as far as your eyes can tolerate and then sometimes a little further still. It is a place of great majesty, of learning to appreciate how small we are in the overall scheme of things, of taking pride in ones countryside, and of marvelling at the achievements of those who have trodden here before us. It is a county characterised by rolling farmsteads, small hamlets, straggling villages, medieval market towns, lush meadows, meandering rivers, an eerie and evocative coastline, and a wealth of historic architecture. Its people are always warm, friendly and helpful and its cultural traditions remain very much alive. All in all, Suffolk is one of those rare places which eludes a quiet charm not easily displaced and best returned to whenever opportunity presents itself. In what follows, I hope the visitor too will find and enjoy what I so nearly missed.

*Beth Bridgwater*
*April 1996*

## Acknowledgments

A great many people have helped in the making of this title and to all those I offer my sincere thanks and appreciation. Particular thanks must however, be extended to Simon, Barbara, Richard, Caroline, Kirk and Luke. Love and thanks to you all.

# Using This Guide

In an attempt to help visitors get the best out of any stay in Suffolk the bulk of this Guide has been broken down into area Chapters. Wherever possible these Chapters follow a particular feature of the landscape - for example, Breckland, The Waveney Valley and High Suffolk all have Chapters in their own right. The coast has been split into two Chapters - North and South - and these also provide coverage of those inland areas falling within their ambit. Bury St. Edmunds and its dormitory villages rightly deserve a Chapter all their own, as do the west Suffolk Wool Towns and Villages. Finally, Ipswich, and The Orwell and Stour Estuaries are covered in the concluding Chapter and this also provides a decent section on what is popularly known as Constable Country on the Suffolk-Essex borders.

By arranging the Chapters thus, you can quickly decide where you want to go within a radius of only a few miles i.e. by using the maps accompanying each Chapter, a tour of that particular locality can easily be put together, and places to spend time identified. Additionally, as the countryside is best enjoyed and understood on foot, 31 walks have been included, spread across the various Chapters. These walks vary in length from two to nine and a half miles and can be enjoyed by anyone who is reasonably fit. Good footwear is always advisable (especially as many of the paths can be a little muddy) as are local maps: the Ordnance Survey Landranger series being more than adequate. Walks around Bury St. Edmunds and Ipswich have also been included.

In addition to identifying local attractions - anything from stately homes to museums, gardens and unusual leisure activities - we have included as many pubs, restaurants, hotels and the like, as we have been able to sample, and consider good in terms of value for money, service and quality. *At no time has hospitality or payment been accepted in return for these establishments' inclusion in this Guide. They have been sampled independently and anonymously by our own team and are included on a merit only basis*. In this way, the visitor should have a greater degree of confidence in what is reported.

Finally, your comments on what you find are welcome, just as are suggestions for what might be included in later editions. Please use the following Freepost address for these purposes only: The Editor, Encompass Press Guides, Encompass Press, Freepost, 45 the Street, Aylmerton, Norwich NR11 8BR.

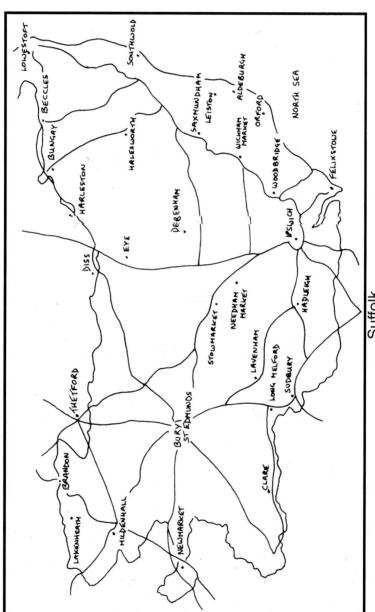

Suffolk

# Contents

# List of Illustrations

All photographs by Beth Bridgwater except p. 138 Herring Catch at Lowestoft (author's collection); p. 152 Scottish Fisher Girls (author's collection); p.159 Garrett Showman's Engine (author's collection), and p. 195 Bronze Statue of Carl Giles cartoon creation *Grandma* (Ipswich Borough Council)

## Colour Plates

## Illustrations in the Text

# List of Walks

All maps by Richard Green

# Introduction

Whilst there is nothing immediately spectacular about the Suffolk landscape, it is, however, extraordinarily easy on the eye and soothing on the soul. It is an undemanding rolling countryside, at once both remote and timeless, and not that dissimilar from its northerly neighbour Norfolk. Suffolk and Norfolk have always formed East Anglia's core and until King Egbert united England into a single kingdom as late as 829 AD, the region literally was comprised of only *Southfolk* (Suffolk) and *Northfolk* (Norfolk), bounded by the River Cam to the west, the River Stour to the south, and north and east by the indomitable North Sea.

Suffolk's geological structure is both young and relatively simple, formed from a substratum of chalk which is only immediately obvious in the north-west of the county around Breckland. Elsewhere, this chalk is covered by sands, clays and crags, making the county virtually stoneless and, therefore, giving it a mainly flat appearance. The county is consequently not rich in natural building materials other than flint in the north and north-west, and bricks made from an abundance of suitable clays. Nonetheless, as we shall see, the county's architecture has much to offer the discerning visitor in terms of its variety and simple beauty.

Water, as in Norfolk, is however a key feature of the landscape. For Suffolk is bordered from Norfolk in the north by the River Waveney, from Essex in the south and west by the tidal estuaries of the Rivers Orwell and Stour, by the Cambridgeshire Fens further to the west and of course by the sea to the east. Another two main rivers run through its heartland, namely the Deben and the Alde, plus there are a great many smaller rivers to account for including the Blythe, Butley, Dove, Gipping, Lark and Ore.

The River Waveney takes a meandering course alongside lush woodland, pasture and water meadow and at Oulton becomes Oulton Broad and beyond there, at Gorleston, it flows out to sea. Oulton Broad is the most southerly of what are collectively called the Norfolk Broads and like the rest of that landscape is man-made, a consequence of the huge peat-digging industry of the medieval period. The Waveney is navigable as far as Beccles and along its tranquil banks a significant 19th Century hemp growing industry once flourished.

The River Orwell is the most important waterway linking Ipswich via the sea with Continental Europe. Felixstowe too nestles snug within Harwich Harbour and the mouths of the Orwell and Stour. But it is the Stour though which is the county's largest river, in places over a mile wide and over 50 miles long, the last ten of which are tidal. Sudbury is the largest town along its banks but its course takes us first via Harwich and Manningtree, the latter both in Essex. Although immortalised by the likes of Constable and Gainsborough, it is to the wool industry that we should look for explanations of the prosperity of the towns along the Stour's course.

The River Deben rises in the pretty village of Debenham but it is not until it reaches Woodbridge that one can truly say it accords full river status. From Woodbridge it too becomes tidal, bordered by mud flats and marshes and following a course along the ancient settlements of the Anglo-Saxons and finally out sea. It is an evocative river, haunted by the Wuffinga's, the ancient ruling house of East Anglia, their ancient burial sites - not least at Sutton Hoo - and their once great open wool port, *Goseford*, of which nothing now remains.

As for the Alde, it rises just to the north of Framlingham, once an important fortified town, and weaves a wonderful course south-east to Snape. Beyond here it snakes its way through the marshy creeks and reaches to join the River Ore as also the Butley until they all eventually find their way out to sea beyond Orford Ness and Halvergate Island at Orford Haven.

Suffolk's coastline is over 45 miles long, much of it rightly designated a Heritage Coast and only occasionally marred by the likes of the nuclear power station at Sizewell, north of Aldeburgh, and to the south by Felixstowe's vast container port. It is a fairly uniform coast with few bays or premonitories but one which has seen much change over the centuries not least as a result of heavy storms, periodic floodings, and the consequent erosion of the few scattered cliffs along its shores. The North Sea inevitably determines the destiny of all along its wake and whilst some have prospered others have done so only later to be tossed aside into historical obscurity. Witness for example that vast port once to be found at Dunwich and now little more than a small backwater bravely awaiting its sad, final demise which will come, it only being a question of time.

Suffolk's beaches are a mix of sand and shingle, the latter formed by what is now commonly known as North Sea or Longshore Drift. In the north, this erosion of the shingle bed has caused the closing of estuaries and the consequent formation of meres as at Benacre Broad, Covehithe Broad, and Easton Broad. Further south though the southerly direction of the shift means that Orford Ness is continually extending its reach, and so the rivers have so much further to run before they find their eventual release into the North Sea.

Running adjacent to the coastline and bordered to the west by the A12 are the sandlings, known for their sandy soil and dependent upon heavy irrigation for successful harvesting. Interspersed within this area are the Suffolk heaths and forests which support a vast array of plant and wildlife. In earlier times, the sandlings were renowned for their sheep and rabbit farming, the heaths carefully maintained to preserve these practices. The decline in both being testament to changing farming techniques, land reclamation for forestry production, and more recently for housing and commercial developments. The last decade has however seen some return to sheep and swine farming in this area, and we can only hope that more rather than less land is given over to grazing instead of being swamped by further development and the over-production of cereals.

> Swine breeding has always been part of the Suffolk agricultural scene and even today there is nothing more sumptuous than a *sweet-cure black Suffolk ham*. These hams are traditionally cured with black treacle, brown sugar and hot beer and can be bought freshly prepared from a number of outlets in the county. Cooking methods though have no doubt advanced considerably but at one time they would have been boiled in copper with hay; this to stop the meat from sticking to the pan bottom but also to impart a unique rural flavour. Brick bread ovens were also sometimes used to bake the ham in and here the meat would have been covered in a layer of dough or 'huff pastry' so as to keep it moist. Whatever the methods used now, and all producers employ their own 'secret' recipes, it is certainly a treat not to be missed.

So now to High Suffolk, to the rich chalky boulder clays of west and central Suffolk, and in essence forming the county's rich arable heart with its rolling landscape, valleys and scattered woodland. Not for nothing were these lands once referred to as England's Granary and today they remain an arable kingdom dominated by huge prairie like open fields and the necessary mechanisation attendant with them. This area also supports a number of significant boulder clay woodlands especially noted for their carpets of oxlips. To see these at their best, explore the ancient woodlands at the Bradfields, just south-east of Bury St. Edmunds.

The most geometric part of the Suffolk landscape is to be found in Breckland, in the north-west, and which was once very sandy and a mass of wild heaths. Today this is impressively afforested with some of the largest coniferous plantations in England. During pre-historic times, the area was densely populated resulting in the lands conversion from deciduous woodland to open heath. At Grimes Graves (just inside Norfolk), a network of over 300 pits, dug by our Neolithic ancestors in search of flint, have been revealed. Much of this flint finding its way into axe heads to fell the trees and so clear the land for growing crops.

By the Middle Ages though the poor quality of the land had ensured sparsely populated villages, all concentrated around the fringes of the heath and in river valleys. Even before this the importance of these valleys is attested to by the large Anglo-Saxon settlement excavated at West Stow on the northerly banks of the River Lark. After the medieval period, the population declined even further and by the 18th and 19th Centuries much of this heathland was enclosed with long lines of Scots pines planted to shelter what few enclosures were left and to stabilise the light, sandy soils. During our own 20th Century, more and more of this heathland has been given over to forestry production and hence the environment we can now see.

Despite its shortage of natural building materials, architecturally Suffolk is as diverse a county as any you will find. First to those ingredients which are abundant and in this context let us consider flint, employed most heavily in the chalky uplands of the north-west, around the Breckland towns and villages of Mildenhall, Lakenheath and Brandon. Whilst very few flint cottages have survived, and these mostly post 17th Century, there is nonetheless a large quantity of medieval churches whose primary material is flint and this usually knapped, i.e. where the stone is split in half and the flat surface exposed. Brandon itself was the foremost home of the flint-knapping industry as one of the town's pubs, the Flintknappers, serves to remind us. Only occasionally in Suffolk though is the blending of flint with freestone, known as flushwork, to be seen and perhaps most gloriously in the beautiful remains of Butley Gatehouse and the churches of Eye and Southwold.

Suffolk's chief claim to fame, however, is for its timber-framed dwellings found further to the south though there are many variations in the structuring of the same. Whether plastered over or infilled and colour washed these timber-framed dwellings are exceptionally well refined, from the lavish specimens to be found in medieval Lavenham, to the more simple but equally exquisite cottages dotted all over the countryside. Such typically Suffolk buildings are usually of a long structure with complex roof gables or jetties which project over the ground floor. Generally, only pre-16th Century buildings reveal their timbers, usually oak, infilled with wattle and daub and the frames arranged decoratively. With timber thereafter becoming scarcer and more expensive, there was a move to increasing use of plaster with horsehair from the Suffolk Punch used in place of straw for extra protection and support around the doorways and windows. Colour wash would then be applied and in Suffolk you will find a whole range of hues from the yellow-apricot embellishments to be seen in Lavenham to the truly Suffolk pink so evident in neighbouring Cavendish, and reputedly once achieved by a mix containing bull's blood.

Many of these timber-framed properties also display the technique of pargeting, raised plaster facades of geometrical patterns and figures, and perhaps best known from the Ancient Houses of both Clare and Ipswich. The earliest examples of such decoration are quite elaborate - deploying, for example, extravagant foliage and figurative designs - and date from the late 16th Century through to the second half of the 17th Century. By the 18th Century, however, the technique fell out of favour and where it was employed simpler, more stereotyped swirling patterns or 'combing' were the norm and occasionally the raised panels were even left plain. Nonetheless, pargeting is little known or practiced elsewhere in England and Suffolk remains its artistic home.

Clay lump is another Suffolk speciality, where the clay is mixed with straw and then formed into large building blocks jointed with mud and later plastered. These buildings too are nearly always colour washed and it is extraordinarily difficult at times to tell a clay lump building from a timber-framed one, especially when both are plastered. Like timber, clay lump requires a deep overhanging roof to protect it from the elements and hence also the preponderance of thatch in the county.

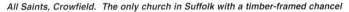

Although not as common as in neighbouring Essex, **weatherboarding** can also occasionally be seen but mainly as a cladding material for light-weight timber-framed structures. It is rarely employed in Suffolk's domestic architecture, unlike in Essex, and can more commonly be found in buildings serving an agricultural or commercial need. For example, there are many weatherboarded barns in the county and there is also that glorious tidal mill, so constructed, on the banks of the River Deben at Woodbridge.

Thatch is a relatively light, malleable material and as such does not require a particularly massive roof structure to support it. It thus lends itself well to Suffolk's clay lump and timber-framed dwellings. The principal materials of thatch are either reed or straw, the best reed to be found in neighbouring Norfolk although Suffolk's own tidal estuaries do afford some indigenous beds, and the straw usually wheaten as combed wheat straw bears some similarity to reed. The ridges of these thatched roofs are then given an extra protective thickness which is frequently scalloped at the edge and brought to a decorative peak. Such is the nature of thatch that it allows a building's valleys and dormers to be incorporated into the total roof structure and it is this which gives off a soft embracing line unparalleled by other materials. A scene at once in harmony with Suffolk's gently rolling countryside.

*All Saints, Crowfield. The only church in Suffolk with a timber-framed chancel*

Suffolk is also one of the best counties in which to see Tudor brickwork often adorned with fine ornamental motifs and huge moulded chimney stacks. Although the Romans were known to have established a number of brick kilns in the county, the technique was somehow lost and even in the Middle Ages what bricks there were were usually imported from the Continental Lowlands.

Suffolk though is rich in its own natural clays and once the use of bricks achieved some popularity again, not least because of the scarcity of good timbers, local brick manufacturing was not far behind. Perhaps the best known being the relatively white output of the kilns around Woolpit, but all manner of colour variation is to be found from the apricot tinges of Little Wenham Hall to the dark blue so obvious at Helmingham Hall. An early elaborate instance of such English brickwork is to be found at Hadleigh's Deanery Tower but examples of the skill are evident everywhere. Continental Lowland influence on the Suffolk architectural scene is at its most obvious in brick built structures. Note for example the frequency of Dutch or crow-stepped gables and the use of pantiles, the latter too once imported before local manufacturing got under way.

> **Crinkle-crankle** walls are another Suffolk speciality and are usually to be found enclosing large wealthy estates with their continuous serpent like curved lines. Most were erected in extravagant Georgian times and one of the best examples is to be found in the village of Easton.

A great number of moated properties, mainly farmsteads, can also be found in Suffolk and although they serve as reminders of a once very wealthy middle class past few today are little more than cottages standing isolated in the middle of open countryside. A number of explanations can be put forward for their popularity not least their obvious advantage in keeping unwanted visitors out but most are practical adaptations of the countryside to everyday needs: from land drainage, keeping the top soil for the dwelling dry and as a source of daub for infilling the walls, to a good source of water supply which also provided fresh fish for the table. Most moats though only ever enclosed about an acre of land and usually the farm buildings lay outside the area.

> To a large extent **windmills** characterise the East Anglian landscape though are perhaps less evident in Suffolk than in the other counties which make up the region. The most impressive examples in Suffolk today are the tide mill at Woodbridge, the post mill at Saxtead Green and the tower mill at Thelnetham

Architectural diversity then is not something Suffolk is short of. Nor can it be said to be short of churches and this will become all too apparent in the Chapters that follow. Most of these churches were financed by the many fortunes made in the county's wool industry, and a great number of them are especially lavish in their interiors, despite the heavy handed attempts of William Dowsing and Cromwell to rid them of the same. Popish relics may be no longer but the roof timbers in these buildings are unsurpassable, no other county richer or enjoying such variety. The most basic categorisation is between single and double framing, but further qualifications are needed for strengthening by tie-beams, as at Lakenheath and Mildenhall, and for hammerbeams as at Earl Stonham and Badingham. Sometimes these hammerbeams are hidden by a further dimension, namely ribbed coving, as at Framlingham, but all are superb. Let us suffice the subject of churches, for now at least, with the words of Sir John Betjeman:

> *'What would you be, you wide East Anglian sky*
> *Without a church tower to recognise you by.'*

You may well appreciate that great laureate's words as you endlessly search your direction in this labyrinth of country lanes!

Of great country homes too Suffolk has been heavily endowed and even today very few of these are open to the public; most hidden behind the working agricultural estates they contain. Of those that are open, Ickworth, Melford and Helmingham are amongst the most interesting. Let us not forget though Daniel Defoe's (*Tour Through the Eastern Counties*) 1724 account of the same which serves to remind us of the once great wealth to be found in these parts:

> *'Any traveller from abroad who would desire to see how the*
> *English gentry live and what pleasures they enjoy should come to*
> *Suffolk ... and take but a light circuit among the county seats of the*
> *gentlemen ... they would soon be convinced, that not France,*
> *no not Italy itself, can out do them.'*

A wealthy aristocracy and an increasingly rising and prosperous middle class needs a large populous to support them and in this respect Suffolk was once well endowed. It was after all once one of the most densely populated counties in England. *Domesday* (1086) records 70,000 inhabitants, exceeded only by Norfolk's 95,000. That same scrutable document also listed some 500 parishes and nine market towns, including in the latter category Blythburgh, Dunwich, Ipswich, Kelsale and Stowmarket. 7,460 freemen were also identified; more than half the total of the rest of the country put together. Suffolk was clearly then both a wealthy part of the country and one which was economically strong.

By the early 16th Century, it was the fourth wealthiest county and Ipswich the sixth richest town. Much of this can be attributed to the hugely successful wool industry supporting not only the farmers, but also an elaborate array of manufacturing industries and merchants plying their various trades to other British ports as well as to Continental Europe. Many of the weavers who first began this enterprise were Flemish refugees and not only did their influence leave its mark on the county's architecture but also engendered much trade outside our own shores. By 1547, Suffolk had no less than 98 towns and villages granted Charters to hold a market/fair, and by the 18th Century the number had even risen slightly. By the early 20th Century though this had somehow dwindled to less than a handful and even that once famous event at Bury St. Edmunds was no longer. Furthermore, by the 1850's the population had shrunk considerably, only made worse by agricultural changes of the 1880's.

The slump in the cloth industry had followed the rise of a newly industrialised northern England and Suffolk was only able to maintain its prosperity via its agricultural prowess, supplying a significant element of London's ever increasing demands for foodstuffs as also for malting barley for the capital's burgeoning breweries. Industrialised agriculture followed this early success, spurred on by the new practice of land enclosure.

Via this new ingredient in the age old landowning recipe, large landowners were able to concentrate their holdings at the expense of small farmers and labourers, the latter in effect losing their rights to common land grazing. With little means to support themselves they had no option but to uproot themselves seeking work in the factories and mills of the newly industrialised North and hence the decline in Suffolk's once large population. Today, most of Suffolk's rich agricultural land remains in the hands of a small group of people and their farming techniques are as mechanised as technology allows but lest we forget those that lost out in those enclosure reforms a delightful snippet of Suffolk verse (anonymous) suffices:

> *'They hang the man and flog the woman*
> *Who steals the goose from off the Common;*
> *But let the criminal loose*
> *Who steals the Common from the goose.'*

As for Suffolk's population today, generally there is a large proportion of those who have retired here, as of second-homers and commuters; those for whom an idyllic country retreat far surpasses the struggles and strains of polluted and over crowded cities, and let's face it who can blame them. Aside from farming, trade with Continental Europe remains as important as it always was only now concentrated around the container ports of Felixstowe and Ipswich rather than the likes of Orford and Dunwich before them.

Fishing, once the mainstay of all coastal towns and villages, is little more than a part-time operation although Lowestoft still hangs on to the most sizeable trawler fleet in East Anglia, its North Sea industry perhaps only superseded by the activities of off-shore gas and oil companies. Animal feedstuffs, sugar and flour are still produced in large quantities in the county and other important industries include the British Telecom Research Station at Martlesham Heath, and, regardless of one's persuasion, the nuclear power station at Sizewell.

In essence the Industrial Revolution by-passed Suffolk, and it remains much as it has always done: a county of farms, large manorial styled houses, small market towns and an abundance of villages. Aside from changes in agricultural practices - seeing the introduction of prairie like techniques - and during World War II the stripping away of large tracts of land for a phenomenal array of air-fields - at one time as many as 750 of them most now thankfully hidden beneath gorse and heather - little has really changed since ancient times. The Romans only enlarged on what their predecessors left behind and by the time the Normans arrived the general outline of the county was set.

Today, there are very few railway lines and those that were erected served only to expand the already well established towns of Bury St. Edmunds, Felixstowe, Ipswich and Lowestoft. Similarly, main roads are just as scanty serving once again the same larger commercial centres as above. As for the rest of Suffolk it is a maze of country lanes leading this way and that, and in the coastal areas of Aldeburgh, Dunwich, Orford and Southwold you need to drive down spurs miles long to visit these gems and then only to retrace your steps back again.

Perhaps it is this free roaming landscape though which is responsible for the large numbers of political radicals, religious dissenters and free thinkers which have sprung from Suffolk's womb. For it was here in Bury St. Edmunds that the first seeds of British democracy were sown; the feudal barons in cahoots with Archbishop Langton forcing King John's hand by their declaration of civil rights in 1214, and its eventual manifestation in the Magna Carta signed the following year.

Characters for whom religion and politics seemed inseparable and who in their own ways also made a lasting impact upon the national scene include Ipswich born Cardinal Wolsey and Cromwell's axe-man William Dowsing. One the epit-ome of lavish high church for his own ends and the other determined to be done away with all such popish nonsense.

Then there is Bartholomew Gosnold who, in 1607, organised the voyage of *Goodspeed*, to establish England's first successful colony in Virginia, USA, and this a remarkable 13 years before the Pilgrim Fathers set out on the *Mayflower*. This was just the first such enterprise from these parts and before long the Puritans were of sufficient numbers to create a second Suffolk in Massachusetts.

Among the free-thinkers, Arthur Young would also have to be included and he an agricultural pioneer. Spending much of his life at Bradfield, he was one of the first to elevate agriculture to the ranks of a science, and during the 1760's he is recorded as having conducted no less than 3,000 experiments on his Suffolk farm; incidentally, none of them were successful, but Young's dedica-tion is there for us all to respect. Then there is George Ewart Evans, a unique chronicler of the East Anglian countryside and way of life. Two of his better known works are the *Pattern Under the Plough* (1966) with its detailed account of the region's folklife and *Where Beards Wag All* (1971) which records its oral tra-ditions, drawing heavily upon the memories of those living in the region at the end of the 19th Century. Of a more artistic bent, but nonetheless equally con-cerned with the land, is Humphrey Repton, the well known landscape gardener and designer of whose work vestiges can still be seen and enjoyed in East Anglia.

Moving ever more firmly into the arts, Suffolk was once the proud home of musician and composer Benjamin Britten. Here he wrote many of his finest works and here is where a great many of them received their first public hearing. Britten together with his long standing companion Peter Pears were also responsible for the Aldeburgh Music Festival, still one of the best known concert venues outside London. Other musicians who continue to leave their mark, albeit in glorious rock fashion, include Bill Wyman of the Rolling Stones, a band which continues to hold sway over the contemporary music scene.

Yet it is to the likes of native born John Constable and Thomas Gainsborough that perhaps the most alluring and enduring of all Suffolk's images are gained. Suffolk after all is the home of English landscape painting, and it is they, their contemporaries and their successors, who have caught the unique and quiet majesty of the place. By virtue of their broad and lofty skies, their graceful rural, pastoral scenes, people have been made to realise - if they did not know already - what beauty is to be found here.

# Bury St. Edmunds

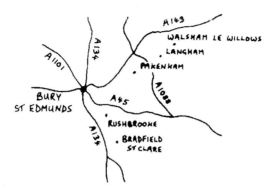

Situated on the confluence of two tiny rivers, the Lark and the Linnet, Bury St. Edmunds is Suffolk's most charming market town, one rather more graceful and alluring than the county's principal offering at Ipswich. Indeed, Bury was until as late as the 1970's Suffolk's county town only then being replaced by the more affluent and commercially geared Ipswich. Bury's relative decline can be attributed to the fact that, unlike Ipswich, it did not rise to undue prosperity in Victorian times and has thus retained its 11th Century lay out, its quaint narrow streets, open squares and market places.

From the 11th Century through to the Reformation, Bury was a town of the greatest importance as also a renowned cultural centre. But even before this its importance was first accorded to by the Anglo-Saxons. For as early as the 7th Century, Sigebert - a descendent of Wuffa, founder of the Wuffinga dynasty of Sutton Hoo fame - established a small monastery here with the town then known as *Boederics*. This was followed by King Canute sanctioning a Benedictine community here in 1021. Ironically, it is to Canute that Bury owes its importance for it was he who established the monastery in honour of St. Edmund and to which pilgrims from all over the world came to pay their tributes. The town's name then changed to St. Edmundsbury and is known more popularly today as Bury St. Edmunds, or simply as Bury.

It was left to the Normans however, under Abbot Baldwin, to lay the town out following their Roman predecessors in grid-like fashion - the first such Norman planned town, similar but larger than that to be found at New Buckenham in neighbouring Norfolk. The streets run north to south, parallel to the west side of the Abbey and are crossed by the two main streets of Churchgate which runs through the Norman Gate to the Abbey Church and high altar, and Abbeygate which once led to the Abbot's Palace. In this way both the Abbey and the town seemed inseparable - linked not only architecturally and spiritually but also economically by virtue of the Abbey's commercial holdings.

By the time of the *Domesday* (1086) reckoning, 342 houses in Bury fell under the jurisdiction of the Abbey alone. *Domesday* also recorded 30 parish priests, 28 nuns, 34 knights, 75 bakers, brewers, tailors, shoemakers, cooks and the like, as well as 13 monastic administrators. Inevitably though it was the Abbey's huge concentration of power and wealth which led to the many conflicts with the townspeople. One such riot, in 1327, saw the Abbey Gate pulled down but as penance the townspeople were ordered to rebuild it.

The English monarch **King Edmund** was killed at *Haegelisdun* in 869/870 AD (some believe this to be the present day Hoxne, others prefer Hellesdon) by pagan Danish invaders. He was reportedly stood up against a tree and executed by a volley of arrows all the while refusing to denounce his Christian faith. Eventually pronounced dead, his decapitated body and head were flung into a nearby wood. Legend has it that a wolf later led Edmund's followers to the spot where his remains lay and where the animal was seen to hold the King's head. When the head was subsequently placed correctly against the body, the two miraculously re-united, and it was this occurrence which largely gave rise to the cult which was later to see the Abbey at Bury St. Edmunds so hugely enriched; the Abbey being the guardian of his relics as also his shrine.

St. Edmund's corpse, however, was reburied on a number of occasions and at each such time claims were made to the effect that the body had not suffered any decline; on the contrary St. Edmund's nails and beard were said to have continued growing. All of this was of course welcome news for the Benedictines, at least until some time around the 13th Century when St. Edmund's remains were stolen and taken to Toulouse in France. These were only returned, some say minus the head, at the beginning of the 20th Century, and are now held at the Duke of Norfolk's seat, Arundel Castle.

This miraculous tale of St. Edmund's death and the subsequent retrieval of his body is depicted in a great many carvings in and around the town. In fact the town's coat of arms also bears testimony to the same depicting as it does two gold crowns, two silver arrows and of course the wolf. These represent the emblems of the old Kingdom of East Anglia and the insignia of St. Edmund. In our own times, we should note the beautiful bronze statue of the Saint by Elizabeth Frink (1976) which stands proud in the Abbey Gardens.

Historic Bury was not just a place of significant religious proportions but also one of huge political importance as well. It was here that the Charter of Liberties, later to become the Magna Carta, was endorsed by the country's leading feudal barons in an attempt to control the roguish King John. This was followed, in 1447, by the holding of a Parliament in the town. The outcome of this though not so fortuitous as it was on this occasion that Humphrey Duke of Gloucester, regent during Henry VI's minority, was murdered. This action was to set in motion that lengthy and devastating war between the Houses of Lancaster and York and which embroiled the country in what later became known as The Wars of the Roses.

On the 20th November 1214, St. Edmund's Day, under the leadership of Stephen Langton, Archbishop of Canterbury, 25 barons took an oath to adhere to a proclamation of 61 Articles which in effect constituted a **Charter of Liberties**. As can be gleaned from a couple of these Articles everyone was to enjoy equal rights before the law and receive protection from Crown abuse:

*'To no one will we sell, deny or delay right or justice.'*

*'No freeman shall be taken, imprisoned or outlawed ... except by the legal judgement of his peers or by the Law of the Land.'*

In reality, however, the barons really only aimed at protecting themselves from the injustices of monarchs like King John and ordinary people were essentially excluded and left to their own devices. Nevertheless, the barons move did provide the starting point, the basic foundation, for civil rights in this country. As will be recalled, King John was forced the following year to sign the **Magna Carta** at Runnymede, thus endorsing for all times the barons Charter. Appropriately enough, Bury St. Edmunds motto remains *Sacrarium Regis, Cunabula Legis*, or Shrine of a King, Cradle of the Law.

In his *Tour Through the Eastern Counties* (1724), Daniel Defoe leaves us with some of the best and most informative descriptions of life in 18th Century Bury. He tells us for example that the River Lark was navigable as far as Mildenhall and from there via Mildenhall 'Dreyn' as far as King's Lynn and beyond to London. It was by this means that Bury sought its coal, iron, wine, lead and other heavy goods requirements.

The Fair here, granted by an early Charter, was also known for its excellent trade especially during the reigns of the Plantagenet Kings through to the 15th

*Elizabeth Frink's St. Edmund,*
*West Front of the Abbey Ruins*

Century. Henry III, for example, is known to have sent his tailor to the annual event to buy cloth imported from as far away as Ghent. But by Defoe's time it had become like Bartholomew Fair, a fair '... *for diversion more than for trade*' (Defoe.) By this we can assume an abundance of freak shows recalling entertainment from the likes of 'The Smallest Man' - a dwarf little more than two feet tall - 'The Giant of Norfolk', and the Duke of Grafton's players. The Fair was finally disbanded in 1871, by then considered to be too rowdy and squalid an affair.

Bury's prosperity continued through the 18th and early 19th Centuries and this saw many of its half-timbered buildings faced with the locally manufactured grey - white Woolpit brick. In this way most of the buildings were allowed to survive instead of being cleared away to be replaced by whatever was vogue at the time. Later, with the rise of Ipswich as Suffolk's alternative town, Bury's buildings were further saved the onslaught of everything Victorian and thank goodness this was so as it is an immensely attractive and soothing place to wander around. Nothing austere here, just simple good taste.

Among the town's more illustrious individuals, we find that **Humphrey Repton** (1752-1818), the landscaper gardener, was born in Bury. He is noted for completing the change from the more formal landscaped gardens of the early 18th Century to the more favoured 'picturesque' types of his time. Another famous son was **Henry Crabb Robinson** (1755-1865), a diarist and lawyer who was originally articled to a Colchester attorney in 1790. He was later engaged by *The Times* as a war correspondent - the first of his kind - to operate out of Spain. A known Dissenter and Liberal, Robinson was also one of the founders of London University (1828). Another interesting character originating from Bury was the novelist **'Ouida'** or Louise de al Ramee (1840-1908). In 1874 she moved to Italy where she later died in poverty but not before having completed two of her better known romantic works *Under Two Flags* (1868) and *Strathmore* (1865).

Even as late as 1843 though Thomas Carlyle in *Past and Present* was able to describe Bury as '... *a prosperous, brisk town, beautifully diversifying.*' Such prosperity did not as we have seen continue into the second half of the 19th Century nor has it truly raised itself today. For even though Bury is one of East Anglia's more prosperous towns, it is an old money firmly grounded in agricultural success and, as is the norm with this section of the community, such wealth is rarely lauded nay more usually denied. We can infer today then a wealthy farming community supporting and depending upon the largest cattle market in the county but one also determining to some extent at least the activities of allied industries, indeed the only industries to be found hereabouts. The town still boasts, for example, the largest sugar beet factory in the country, as it does the largest factory for the manufacture of malt extract, a principal ingredient in beer making. Perhaps not surprisingly the town is also home to one of the regions largest independent breweries, Greene King, originally founded in Bury in 1799 by Benjamin Greene.

The best way to appreciate Bury is to follow the walk described below as it wanders around the streets taking in all of the town's principal sites. Features which have not received full documentation elsewhere but which nonetheless deserve brief mention here include the general and most picturesque area of Angel Hill, with its varied architecture and where at No. 1 scientist William Hyde Wollaston invented the 'camera lucida', the bronze statue to a wounded soldier of the Boer War in Market Square, the former Guildhall with its 13th Century door and 15th Century porch, the unusual shop fronts especially along Abbeygate Street, the three-storeyed 17th Century Cupola House in the Traverse originally built for Thomas Marco - a wealthy apothecary - in 1693 and which still retains its elaborate brackets supporting the balcony, and we should not forget the little Nutshell which claims to be the smallest pub in England.

## Walk 1: Bury St. Edmunds

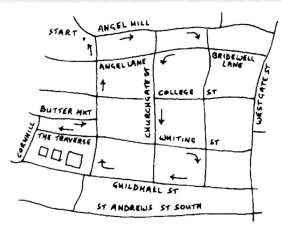

### Directions:

1. Start your walk at Angel Hill to walk past the Abbey Gateway on your left, Angel Corner and the Angel Hotel on your right, and then to the Athenaeum. 2. Go through Athenaeum Lane to Chequer Street with the Cathedral and Norman Tower on your left. 3. Continue along Crown Street to St. Mary's Church. Cross the road into the narrow street known as Tuns Passage. 4. Turn right on the corner with Bridewell Lane and continue along there to Churchgate Street where you go left. Pass the Unitarian Chapel on your right and turn left into Whiting Street where you come to the United Reformed Church. 5. Turn right just after the Church and at the next junction go right into Guildhall Street to pass the Guildhall on your right. 6. With the Corn Exchange in front of you, go right into Abbeygate Street and then left into The Traverse to pass the smallest pub in England, the Nutshell, and Cupola House. At the end of The Traverse, on the left, is The Market Cross Gallery and then you bear right into Cornhill (formerly 'Beast' Market). Note Moyses Hall on the left. 7. Go right into Skinner Street and then left into Abbeygate Street. 8. Once back at Angel Hill, go through Abbey Gate to explore the gardens and wander down to the River Lark before returning back to the town proper.

**Approx. Distance: 2 Miles  Approx. Time: 1.5 Hours**

# *Places to Visit*

## *Museums:*

*Manor House Museum* *(01284 757072), Honey Hill, Bury St. Edmunds* was originally built in 1738 by John Hervey, 1st Earl of Bristol (Ickworth) for his wife and was designed by Sir James Burrough. It is now an excellent museum of art and horology and where special exhibitions are held in the splendid former Ballroom. The Museum is home to the collection of old time pieces dating from the 16th Century onwards and which was until recently held at Angel Corner. A visit here at 12 noon will ensure a memorable experience. The collection, one of the best in the world, was originally put together by Frederick Gershom Parkington and was bequeathed to the town in memory of his son killed in World War II. Amongst the more important elements of the collection can be included a glorious 1690 longcase by Windmills of London, a Tompion bracket clock, and a 'nocturnal', the latter so constructed that the time is told in accordance with the relative positionings of two star constellations - the Great and Little Bear. *Open daily. Admission charge.*

*Moyses Hall Museum* *(01284 757072), Cornhill, Bury St. Edmunds,* overlooks the Butter Market and is a Norman flint and stone dwelling which now houses the Bury Museum. The Hall, Bury's oldest domestic structure, was probably built around 1180 as a merchant's house and still retains its vaulted ceiling and Norman windows. Note also the stone carved wolf guarding Edmund's head at the entrance way. As a Norman house, the living quarters to the Hall would have been on the first floor with animals tethered below. But sometime during the 15th Century through to the 17th Century it is thought to have been used as a hostelry and subsequently as the town jail, a house of correction and as a parcel office for the Great Eastern Railway Company. It was purchased by the

*Cupola House, The Traverse*

Borough Council in 1899.

The Museum's Collection is mainly Suffolk in orientation and includes firearms made by local gunsmiths, and a good range of Bronze Age, Iron Age and Anglo-Saxon objècts. Perhaps the most popular exhibits are the gibbet cage and relics of William Corder hung in Bury's Butter Market in 1828 for the murder of Maria Marten. These items seem rather macabre today and include Corder's pistols, death mask, severed ear and scalp together with an account of the trial bound in the culprit's own skin! *Open daily. Admission charge.*

### Ecclesiastical & Public Buildings:

*The Abbey.* Founded in 945 AD by the Benedictine Order, later enjoying the support of King Canute, and rebuilt in the 11th Century by Abbot Baldwin around 1080 but not completed until a century later under Abbot Samson, the Abbey was once one of the greatest religious buildings in the Kingdom. Originally 500 feet long and nearly 250 feet wide - the widest in the country -the Abbey was built to house the shrine of the martyred King (later Saint) Edmund, killed by Danish invaders in either 869 or 870 AD, and it soon became an important place of pilgrimage. Furthermore, it is from Edmund that the town derived its name.

History accords the Abbey special place as it was within the Church here that on the 20th November 1214 that 25 major English barons met Stephen Langton, then Archbishop of Canterbury, and vowed at the high altar to force King John to ratify a Charter Of Liberties later to become the Magna Carta. On the northeast pier of the presbytery a plaque records this historic meeting.

In 1538, John Leland, Henry VIII's librarian described the Abbey as '... *one of the greatest architectural glories of the kingdom ... verily it were a city; so many gates there*

*Abbey Gate*

*are in it ... so many towers and a most stately church upon which attend three other churches also standing gloriously in the same churchyard.'* But only the following year, 1539, saw Henry VIII's dissolution campaign dismantle most of the Abbey buildings along with thousands of other places of worship around the country. In effect the Abbey became little more than a quarry, its stones used in the town's houses but fortunately some fragments of its former glory remain. Foremost amongst these are the Norman Gate and what is commonly called the Great Gate. The latter dominates the eastern end of Angel Hill framing the beautiful Abbey Gardens (open to the public) which lead down to the River Lark and the Abbot's Bridge, the latter dating from the late 12th Century. The Norman Gateway is a beautiful example of decorated work of the time, thought to have been built by Abbot Anselm sometime after 1120; it later served as a free-standing bell-tower for St. James Church. Originally the Gate would have had battlements, making it one of the first so fortified buildings in England, but these were somehow removed around the late 18th and early 19th Centuries.

The Abbey's monks were noted for their finely **illuminated manuscripts,** not least Master Hugo's *Bury Bible*, which dates from the mid 12th Century and which is now held in Corpus Christi College, Cambridge. Also attributed to Master Hugo is the Bury Cross, of circa 1155, made from walrus ivory with exquisite relief work. It was purchased by the New York Metropolitan Museum in the 1960's for the then princely sum of $600,000. Other highly regarded religious writings emanating from the Abbey's monks include Jocelyn de Brakeland's Diary in which he paints an extraordinarily detailed picture of monastic life in the 12th Century.

The Great Gate which was begun sometime after the 1327 riots, and which is now managed by English Heritage, is a broad and embattled structure about 60 feet high and richly decorated with carvings, niches and panels - all of it 14th Century. One of the shields carved onto the walls is thought to bear the arms of Edward the Confessor. It was mainly erected for defensive purposes, the archer sections and port cullis grooves still visible, after the townspeople, resentful of the Abbey's power over the town and the exorbitant taxes imposed upon them, destroyed the original. As fate would have it, the townspeople were ordered to build its replacement as penance for their misdemeanour. This was a time as Defoe (1724) reminds us in his *Tour* when the monks were '*... absolute lords of the town and governed it by their steward for many ages.'*

Of the Abbey Church itself little remains save parts of the west front - incorporated into later houses - and parts of the cloister buildings, notably the parlour, refectory and chapter house. Do take time though to walk around the Abbey grounds, especially the Old English Rose Garden donated by an American, John Appleby, who served in the area with the US Air Force during World War II. Catch this Garden during the summer months and you cannot help but be intoxicated by the glorious scents which seem to permeate the whole air hereabouts.

*The Cathedral Church of St. James* was originally built in the perimeter of the old Abbey during the late 15th and early 16th Centuries in Perpendicular style, but was heavily restored by Sir Gilbert Scott in 1862 and further extended during the years 1960-70. In 1914, a bishopric was created at Bury encompassing the diocese of St. Edmundsbury and Ipswich, and St. James was designated as the Cathedral, hence the more recent additions to its structure. These additions have included new side chapels, a new choir area and a new chancel by Stephen Dykes Bower to replace that by Gilbert Scott. Of the interior, note especially the early 16th Century Flemish window in the south aisle which depicts a Tree of Jesse and the story of Susanna and the Elders. Note also the more recent iron screens emblazoned as they are with gold, silver, red and blue, and the roof shields which bear the armorial banners of the Magna Carta barons and donated by the American Society, The Dames of Magna Carta Finally to the tapestry covered hassocks given by Suffolk schools and parishes and worked with local emblems to a set framework - one even depicts the nuclear power station at Sizewell!

*St. Mary's Church*, *Crown Street*, is actually the fifth place of worship to be built on the same site. Building of the current structure began in 1424 and St. Mary's claims to be the finest parish church in England. Note in particular in the nave the superb original hammerbeam roof complete with angels - this is rightly famous - and in the chancel you cannot miss the blue and gold, single-framed panelled roof with its carved bosses depicting a fox in the guise of a priest preaching to his chickens, two dogs fighting each other and another dog carrying two water-bottles.

*The Cathedral Church of St. James*

Note also the tomb to the left of the altar which belongs to Mary Tudor, Henry VIII's sister and Dowager Queen of France; after the French King's death she later married Charles Brandon, Duke of Suffolk. Mary died in 1533 and although she was originally buried in the Abbey Church, her remains were removed to St. Mary's after her brothers successful campaign to dissolve the monasteries. Furthermore, the east window of the south wall depicts scenes from her life and was presented to the Church by Queen Victoria.

Look also, halfway along the north side of the Church, for the mid 15th Century porch with its fan tracery bequeathed by John Notyngham, a local grocer - obviously a very wealthy one - in 1437. Known as the Notyngham Porch it commemorates John and his wife. Finally, to a memorial remembering several hundred men who lost their lives when HMS *Birckenhead*, a troopship, went down after hitting a reef off Danger Point, South Africa.

**St. Edmund's (RC) Church**, *Westgate Street*, was built in 1837 by Charles Day, and is reportedly one of the earliest buildings erected for Roman Catholic worship in England since the Reformation. The interior, although remodelled in the 1870's, is heavily Grecian and where Ionic columns abound.

**The Unitarian Chapel** built in 1712 was originally intended for Presbyterian worship. Nonetheless it is considered one of the best surviving examples of an unaltered town chapel in the country. Note the old English bond red brickwork, where alternate layers of stretchers and headers are set using only a minimal amount of mortar between each, and which gives the building its decorative effect. Also note the original double-decker pulpit. Today it is very much a working venue - concerts, receptions, art and antique fairs - and is only open when not being used for functions and usually late afternoons.

**The Athenaeum** at the southern end of Angel Hill is a superb example of a Queen Anne styled Assembly Room (in 1853, becoming the Athenaeum Club) hiding a Regency interior. Built in Palladian fashion by Francis Sandys (also responsible for nearby Ickworth) but sometimes also attributed to Robert Adam, it shows some elegant stucco detail together with a superb double staircase. Charles Dickens is known to have given readings of *David Copperfield* in the elegant Ballroom here which was also once used to hold lavish banquets.

**The Corn Exchange** was built by Ellis and Woodward in 1861 and has a superb roof supported by massive cast iron trusses. The external pediment is decorated with figures representing agriculture, engineering and commerce. A further floor was manipulated from the interior in 1970 and this provided space for the shops which trade on the ground floor.

**The Market Cross** was originally designed as a market hall and theatre by Robert Adam in 1774 and is probably the finest post-medieval building in the town. Standing on the site of a former Market Cross which consisted of a cornstead below and a clothiers hall above, the playhouse was converted from the latter and continued in use until 1819 when it became the Town Hall; the corn market on the ground floor, however, continued in its intended capacity until as late as 1836. Restored in 1970, it is now an Art Gallery.

## Stately Homes:

Three miles south-west of Bury St. Edmunds at *Horringer* is the grand neo-classical home of the Earls of Bristol and known as *Ickworth*. The Hervey's (pronounced Harvey) have lived on this site since the 16th Century though the current incumbent's continued residence is in doubt following his recent prosecution and heavy fine for drug offenses. The place is in any case managed by the National Trust so access to the property is not, however, in doubt.

The Hall was originally begun in 1796 by the 4th Earl but was not finished before he died in 1803. The architect was Francis Sandys again. The Earl's successor completed the east wing and did enough to the Rotunda to enable the family to move in at the beginning of the 1830's but by 1956, in lieu of death duties, the Hall passed into the hands of the Government and so to the National Trust.

There is much to see including a considerable art collection and perhaps the most important pieces are the portraits by Gainsborough and that by Hogarth depicting the Whig Cabal that ran the government of the day and which included John Lord Hervey. Look out for two 18th Century commodes, some fine Regency furniture, the collection of Bristol silver, and the Majolica earthenware plates. The Rotunda is the library and its unusual elliptical shape, connected by two curved corridors to the flanking wings, is dictated by the unusual nature of the building and is quite splendid. The gardens are also delightful and there are several waymarked woodland walks around the estate lands.

**Ickworth House**

The Hall *(01284 735270)* is *open most afternoons (excluding Monday - but including Bank Hols - & Thursday) from the end of March to the beginning of November, and the gardens are open daily during the same months. Admission charge for the Hall but there is only a car park fee for access to the large parkland which surrounds it.*

*Horringer* village is an attractive place, one dominated by the flint-built St. Leonard's Church on the green. A number of thatched, timber-framed cottages line one side of the street and on the other side is the former Guildhall now converted into domestic residences.

### Live Entertainment:

*Theatre Royal (01284 769505), Westgate Street, Bury St. Edmunds* is a beautifully restored Regency theatre, owned by Greene King Brewery, and the only Regency theatre still extant in England complete with pit, boxes and gallery. It was originally built in 1819 to the design of William Wilkins, architect for the National Gallery, and was especially famous in its early days showing for example in 1892 the premiere of *Charley's Aunt*. Closed in 1925, it was used by the brewery as a warehouse until restoration in 1962. It is now managed by the National Trust who secured a 999 year lease from the owners in 1974, and is home to an excellent range of shows.

### Sports Venues:

*Golf: Bury St. Edmunds Golf Club (01284 755979), Tut Hill, Fornham All Saints, near Bury St. Edmunds.* Visitors are welcome at this 18-hole parkland course though there are some weekend restrictions.

*Horse Riding: Linkwood Equestrian Centre (01284 386390), Bradfield St. George, near Bury St. Edmunds* offer a full range of courses by qualified tutors. Also try *Hardwick Stables (01284 766570), Horsecroft Road, Bury St. Edmunds.*

*Ten Pin Bowling: Bury Bowl (01284 750704)* can be found on *Eastgate Street, Bury St. Edmunds.*

# Food & Accommodation

### Hotels:

*The Angel Hotel (01284 753926), Angel Hill, Bury St. Edmunds.* A friendly welcome awaits any visitor to the Angel and one much less stuffy than perhaps its imposing frontage may lead one to suspect. Situated in the centre of historic Bury, perhaps no better base can be found for exploring the town's many sites.

The general decor is interesting and relaxed, the upper restaurant for example is hung with oil paintings and the bedroom accommodation is mostly luxurious and furnished with some sizeable antiques. The building's cellars are the oldest part of the structure and now house a crypt styled restaurant with a less formal arrangement than that to be found upstairs.

An inn since the 15th Century and rebuilt on its original site in 1779 by Redgrave, The Angel will no doubt have seen its fair share of eccentric visitors not least Charles Dickens who stayed in Room 15 on two occasions, namely during his 1859 and 1861 reading tours, and which is still furnished as it was then complete with four-poster bed. Dickens has Mr. Pickwick in *Pickwick Papers* receiving notice of the commencement of the breach of promise action taken against him by Mrs. Bardell here, and on another occasion he has Pickwick enjoying a roast dinner at the Angel. Whilst the menu today for sure offers greater variety and sophistication, who are we to argue with such a grand literati.

> In *Pickwick Papers*, Dickens narrates the arrival of Pickwick at the Angel Inn thus:
>
> > *'The coach rattled through the well paved streets of a handsome little town of thriving and cleanly appearance and stopped before a large inn situated in a wide open street nearly facing the old Abbey.'*

Other well-known literary visitors to the inn include the likes of Harold Pinter and Ruth Rendell and the owners have ensured a continuing relationship with their kind by means of the annual Angel Literary Award. The only hotel in the country to offer such a prize and which first began in 1982.

*Ravenwood Hall* (01359 270345), *Rougham Green, near Bury St. Edmunds.* A few miles to the east of Bury, Ravenwood Hall Hotel is a Tudor manor set in several acres of woodland. It is tastefully decorated and furnished throughout and where the owners have employed antiques and old prints to good use. The bedrooms in the main house are the more cosy and characterful - oak beams, panelled walls and four-posters - and the restaurant is geared towards English fare. *Note one bedroom is especially equipped for disabled visitors.*

### Bed & Breakfasts:

*The Glen* (01284 755490), *84 Eastgate Street, Bury St. Edmunds.* A short stroll from the centre of Bury, this 17th Century listed building provides traditionally furnished and well decorated en-suite accommodation and where guests can also enjoy their own sitting room. If you stay here, do take a look at the lime kiln in the garden, it is reputed to be the oldest in the country.

*Ounce House* (01284 761779), *Northgate Street, Bury St. Edmunds.* At the top of the hill, this pair of former merchants' houses just a short distance from Bury centre offers a friendly and relaxing stay for those who want first rate facilities without hotel formalities and bills to match. The owners have ensured the ground-floor rooms - drawing room, library and dining room - have retained their spaciousness and are enhanced by oil paintings, antiques and etchings. The bedroom accommodation is equally smart and you cannot but appreciate the owner's attention to detail. Evening meals.

*Twelve Angel Hill* (01284 704088), *12 Angel Hill, Bury St. Edmunds.* A smart Georgian establishment in the heart of historic Bury. The bedroom accommodation is of a good-size and well furnished. General areas, although small, are very comfortable, with antique furniture, paintings and porcelain together with carefully selected fabrics and bold colour schemes providing much ambience.

## Self-Catering:

For self-catering in well above average standard accommodation try *Purton Green, Stansfield,* just a few miles to the south of Bury. Restored and managed by the Landmark Trust *(01628 825925),* Purton Green is a former medieval hall parts of which date back to the 13th Century. The living accommodation makes use of some early 17th Century additions but all is set in the midst of splendid, isolated countryside. (*Sleeps 4.*)

## Restaurants:

*Mortimer's* (01284 760623), *30 Churchgate Street, Bury St. Edmunds.* If fish is your passion then go to Mortimer's but don't always expect too leisurely an evening for the pace is brisk, the restaurant always busy, and the opening times rather short. Nonetheless it is a consistently good house and one not that dissimilar from its sister operation in Ipswich.

*Bradfield House* (01284 386301), *Bradfield Combust, near Bury St. Edmunds.* An attractive 17th Century part-timbered house which operates as a restaurant - with-rooms; whatever your purpose you won't be disappointed. The kitchen offers consistently good quality fare, much of it English though some French inspiration is evident, and is complimented by well chosen wines. The house is furnished with antiques, warmed by open fires and wood burning stoves and cheered with fresh flowers. An expansive, two acre garden, complete with kitchen allocation, can be enjoyed to the back of the house and some of the trees are even subject to special protection orders.

In a 400 year old barn adjoining the gardens to *Wykan Hall, Stanton,* just outside Bury is the *Leaping Hare Cafe* (01359 250287), where you can enjoy imaginative and well prepared light lunches and stylish afternoon teas, and on Friday evenings even opt for dinner here. The proprietors also have their own vineyard nearby so expect to sample some of their own production.

## *Pubs:*

*The Beehive* (01284 735260), *Horringer, near Bury St. Edmunds* offers some very good food and well kept ales in a convivial atmosphere. The newly and tastefully redecorated rooms are small and rambling with the alcoves and low beamed ceilings making it altogether snug. Well furnished throughout in cheerful country style it is a good place to begin or end a visit to Ickworth Hall.

*The Mason's Arms* (01284 753955), *14 Whitling Street, Bury St. Edmunds.* Dating from the early 18th Century, the pub is noticeable for its weatherboarding; a feature more typical of vernacular architecture in southerly neighbour Essex. Go here for good real ale, above average food - seafood especially well featured - and interesting items of folk decor. Occasional music evenings are another plus.

*The Plough* (01284 789208), *The Green, Rede, near Bury St. Edmunds.* Standing close to the village pond, this pink-washed, semi-thatched pub was originally built around 1610. Period details, including timber beams and a superb inglenook, have been retained, and the rest is well decorated with copper measures, plates, tea-pots and pewter tankards. An excellent choice of good value home-cooked food and fine ales.

# *Out & About Near Bury St. Edmunds*

Specialist nurseries seem to abound in this part of Suffolk. First to *Caroline Holmes* (01284 810653), *Denham End Farm, Denham,* for over 170 different varieties of culinary, medicinal and aromatic herbs as well as an interesting selection of alpines, shrubs and trees; alternatively, *Netherfield Herbs* (01359 270452), *37 Nether Street, Rougham* offer over 200 varieties of culinary, medicinal, cosmetic, aromatic and decorative herbs in a cottage setting; and if you have a penchant for gooseberries go to *Rougham Hall Nurseries* (01359 270577), *Ipswich Road, Rougham,* where an incredible 250 plus varieties are grown. They also offer an extensive selection of hardy perennials, including over 100 varieties of Delphinium.

Also at Rougham is *Blackthorpe Barn* ((01359 270238), an ancient timber-framed, thatched building dating from the mid 1500's. Over 100 feet long and 30 feet wide, it was used as a grainstore until 1985 but more recently is home to a varied programme of exhibitions, lectures and craft-makers.

Then there is *The Rake Factory, Little Welnetham*, three miles south of Bury. Dating from the last century, this factory continues to make rakes and scythes in the traditional way. Tours can be arranged by appointment only, otherwise just take a look.

For organic meat - beef, pork, lamb and poultry - try Soil Association member **Longwood Farm** *(01638 717120)* at *Tuddenham St. Mary.* The official shop days are Monday, Wednesday, Friday and Saturday and other times are by appointment. For a treat of a different kind, go to **The Manor Farm Creamery** *(01359 230208), Thurston* for dairy ice cream using fresh cream and pure fruits. Alternatively, try **Giffords Hall Vineyard** *(01284 830404), Hartest* where you can enjoy a tour of the winery and tastings of their harvest.

Just south-east of Bury is **Rushbrooke**, probably the last estate village which will ever be built, and one which was financed by Lord Rothschild and completed in 1963: John Weeks and Richard Llewelyn Davies were the designers. Each cottage, all of them brick brick built, enjoys a unique ground plan and siting and all are joined by continuous high walls. Wells House, the only property with an earlier history, forms the centre of the village. The former home of Lord Rothschild, Rushbrooke Hall, though is sadly no longer and was once a splendid 16th Century Tudor manor; it was destroyed by fire in 1961 and subsequently demolished. Take the trouble to visit the charming, if small, St. Nicholas' Church. Inside you will find a rare carved rood beam and above it an equally rare typanum with the arms of Henry VIII clearly depicted.

Further south sees us in **Bradfield St. Clare**, the largest of the three Bradfield villages, the others being St. George and Combust. St. Clare takes its name from the Norman family who once occupied the former 13th Century moated Hall here, and the Church, also called St. Clare, is the only church in England to bear her name. If you look carefully north of the Church you will notice another small moat - this part of Suffolk replete with them - and which is believed to have been the site of a retreat for monks of the Abbey.

But it is to **Bradfield Woods**, managed by the Suffolk Wildlife Trust, that we should make our way towards. Part of this woodland, Monk's Park Wood, is still the original which belonged to the former Abbey and because of its rare fauna and flora is considered to be of national importance and contains in any case the finest range of plantlife to be found in East Anglia. All in all, over 350 flowering plants can be seen - anything from primrose to bluebell, wood anemone, oxlip and purple orchid - and more than 42 native shrubs and trees have been identified. Many breeding birds, including the great-spotted woodpecker and tawny owl, also share the environment as do the deer. These woods have been continually worked and coppiced for over 700 years and by looking at the woodland pattern it reveals you can see how English woods have both evolved and been maintained since those early medieval times.

Also here is **Maynard House Orchards** *(01284 386264),* a relatively new producer of English apple juices with a variety on offer from Bramley to Cox, Russet and Discovery.

This time going north-east of Bury sees us in **Pakenham** to find two fine mills, one water-powered and the other wind, and unusually both in working condition. The five-storey brick built tower mill, used originally for grinding corn, was built in 1816, one of the last of its kind to be erected. Restored in the 1950's, it has regularly been featured in television programmes, the latest being in *Campion*. It is only open by appointment.

On its *Domesday* site (1086), the 18th Century **Pakenham Watermill** *(01787 247179)* was completely restored by the Suffolk Preservation Society in 1978, only this time equipped with an oil engine. Also used for grinding corn, which can be bought on the premises, it is **open from Easter to the end of October. Admission charge.**

Go to the village Church, St. Mary's, as it has a rare octagonal tower situated midway on the crossway, and added sometime during the 14th Century. Built from flint with Barnack stone dressing, the rest of the structure is cruciform and dates from the early 12th Century. Try also to catch a glimpse of the window in the former rectory next door which was painted by Rex Whistler, reputedly in just over an hour, and which depicts an 18th Century be-wigged vicar sitting at his window looking out over the countryside. Whistler was stationed here for a short while during World War II and just before his untimely death on the Normandy battlefields.

Also of architectural interest is Nether Hall built around 1600 and the Jacobean Newe House with its Dutch gables, two-storey porch complete with triangular pediments and built in 1622. This was the home of the notorious American-Englishman Reeve.

Reeve was a Pakenham smallholder who eloped to the USA with a young village girl. Operating out of Dodge City, he ran a team of buffalo hunters and flayers and having made his fortune from these wild beasts hides he returned to England. Before long though his wanderlust returned leading him to buy a herd of Aberdeen Angus cattle which he then shipped out to America. Reeve then drove these himself down the Chisholm Trail selling them to ranchers to improve the stock of their Spanish Longhorns.

So successful was the operation that Reeve repeated it several times. On one occasion he even attempted to ship over a flock of sheep but these had to be jettisoned overboard when the Captain made it clear it was sink or sheep! Although a famous and well respected figure in America's West, Reeve chose to return home to Pakenham where he purchased Newe House for the princely sum of £10,000. Reeve settled down to live the life of a country squire, but he was never accepted by the Suffolk 'county set' finding popularity only amongst his fellow villagers.

## Walk 2: The Mills of Pakenham

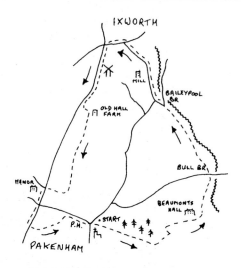

### Directions:

1. From your car park at Pakenham Church, go to the road junction near the Church and walk a few yards along the road to Stowlangtoft (i.e. by going right). Look for a path on your right leading along the edge of Pakenham Woods. Follow the woods round to the left and at their north-easterly fringe, where the path swings sharp left, pick up a track on your right leading to Beaumont's Hall. 2. Pass the barns at the bottom of the hill keeping to the winding track, and kept left towards Bull Bridge when another track comes in from the left. 3. Cross the road and bearing slightly left to pick up a path on your right (signed) which leads across fields to Baileypool Bridge. Go slightly left at the lane towards Grimstone End following it round to the left, and where it joins another lane go right to Pakenham Watermill. 4. Continue along that lane until you come to the Ixworth By-pass. Cross this carefully and go between the posts which have closed the road in front to traffic. At a T-Junction, go left along the lane leading to Pakenham Windmill. 5. Go straight ahead at the road junction along what was an old Roman road. When you come to a handful of houses, go left on a track towards Old Hall Farm. Just before a pond, go right along a path and over a field. 6. At the next meeting of paths, go right and follow this round as it snakes back to the old Roman road. 7. At the road, go left to pass Pakenham Manor (ignoring a road off to the right). At the junction, go straight across (signed Thurston and Beyton). After a few hundred yards, look for a track on your left which curves its way back into Pakenham village proper, Nether Hall can be seen in the distance to your right. 8. At the road, turn right to return to the Church.

**Start: Pakenham Church**
**Approx. Distance: 6.5 Miles**
**Approx. Time: 3 Hours**
**Map: Landranger 155**

*Pakenham Watermill*

Finally to **Walsham-le-Willows** still further north-east and as pretty as its name suggests, and yes there is a belt of willows down by the Little Ouse. A number of old styled buildings have survived, including the 15th Century priory, now the rectory, a tiled 14th Century cottage and two inns - the 16th Century Six Bells and the Blue Boar. The weatherboarded houses opposite were formerly a work-house. St. Mary's Church, if you have time to visit it, is home to a rare medallion or 'crant' in memory of young Mary Boyce who died unwed in 1685.

Up until 1911, a Gala of the Ancient Order of Foresters' was an annual event. That year though an ugly scene developed between the villagers and the travelling showmen, the former claiming that they had been short-changed on one of the Galloper rides. The net result was a shoot out between the two groups leaving many injured and an innocent passer-by dead. It is said to rain in the village on the anniversary of this grave day, every 3rd July.

If you need any groceries, in this case meat, then a visit to **D.J. Rolfe** *(01359 259225), Hatchmere House, Walsham-le-Willows* is a must. This small butchers shop attracts custom for miles around and no wonder when you can buy stuffed saddle of lamb, boned birds one stuffed inside the other, Suffolk-cure bacon, dry-cure beef and much more besides.

## *Walk 3: Rural Villages: Badwell Ash and Langham*

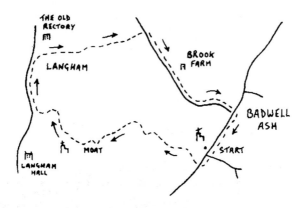

### *Directions:*

1. From your park on the street running through Badwell Ash, head for the Church and a little way beyond that look for a path (signed) on your right just before the village green. Continue along here, over a meadow, following the yellow waymarker signs. Cross a bridge over a stream and go along the edge of a field. 2. Bear left at the trees with Langham Church immediately in front of you and pass the moat of an old castle on your left. 3. At the Church, follow the path round to a gate. Go right here, and over a bridge to go left along a path which leads you past a stud. At a junction, go left, and at a minor road go right. 4. After a short distance, near a grass triangle, go right along a track which leads past the Old Rectory. Continue along this track to a minor road. 5. Go right here to walk along the lane leading past Brook Farm and back into Badwell Ash. Go right at the road to return to your start.

**Start: Badwell Ash**
**Approx. Distance: 3 miles**
**Approx. Time: 1-1.5 Hours**
**Map: Landranger 155**

# Breckland

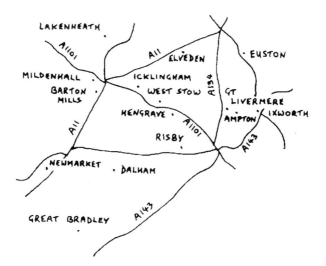

Our tour of Breckland begins in the typically Breck village of West Stow, just north-west of Bury St. Edmunds. From here we move on to explore Mildenhall, Lakenheath and Brandon, a fine hall at Euston and a series of villages which bring us back at Ampton almost full circle before we dart off to Newmarket in the far west of the county on the Cambridgeshire borders.

## West Stow

The lands around West Stow are replete with Iron Age, Roman and Saxon remains and an Anglo-Saxon village has been authentically reconstructed on the original foundations of a site dating from around 400- 650 AD. Excavations in fact revealed over 80 dwellings as having been extant at West Stow, the most complete Anglo-Saxon site in the country - plus over 2,000 supporting objects were unearthed ranging from bone combs to weaving implements. It is known to have been a typical Breckland farming community, breeding cattle, sheep and goats. *The reconstructed village is open daily (excluding Monday) April to October. Admission charge.*

*West Stow's Village Sign*

For those finding this a little trite then take the walk described below which does in any case afford reasonable sight over the village and which makes good use of the beautiful 125 acre Country Park which embraces it. As for West Stow village proper, you cannot help but notice the great brick built Gatehouse of the Hall, put up in the 1520's by John Crofts, Master of Horse to Mary Tudor, and which would originally have spanned a moat. Three-storeys high, it has polygonal turrets and Mary Tudor's coat-of-arms. The rest of the building is timber-framed, and of the Hall itself very little has survived.

*West Stow Gatehouse*

# Walk 4: Anglo-Saxon Tracks Around West

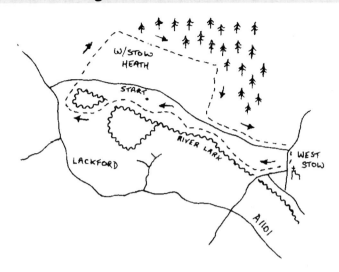

## Directions:

1. From your park at the Anglo-Saxon Village Visitors Centre, follow the footpath (signed) down to the River Lark (by going right at the end of a field and then following the path round to the left) 2. At the River, bear right following the Lark Valley Path signs. Where the path forks, continue straight on keeping the river on your left and walking round the edge of the lake (on your right). Follow this path to a kissing gate, and turn right for a few yards onto a tarmac lane, and then right along a grassy track (outside the Country Park boundary). 3. Once at the lane, cross straight over onto a track (signed Icknield Way) and after a short distance pass a flint bungalow on your left. 4. Take the first wide track on your right through West Stow Forest and continue along here for approx. one and a half miles. As you see the track ahead of you bending sharply right, look for a bridleway on your right (a tree on your left is numbered 111 and the opposite tree on your right is 117). Go along this bridleway to the lane and turn left to walk through West Stow village, passing West Stow Stud and West Stow Gatehouse on your left. 5. At the junction, go right to walk past the entrance to the Church and take the first right hand lane after it. Continue along here until you come to a small bridge crossing the River Lark. Take the footpath (signed) on your right just before the bridge and which follows the course of the River. 6. Walk along the River bank, using the Lark Valley Path signs as your guide; there is a slight detour into the forest to by-pass private land and a house and which also skirts an old pumping station but all is well signed. 7. Once the diversion is complete and the Anglo-Saxon village is in sight, take the path on your left to regain the River bank. After approx. a quarter of a mile bear right again to return to your starting point.

**Start: West Stow Anglo-Saxon Visitors Centre**
**Approx. Distance: 6 Miles  Approx. Time: 2.5 Hours**
**Map: Landranger 155**

Close to West Stow and although only open by appointment *Hengrave Hall* and its adjoining Church are certainly worth the effort. Considered one of the most important Tudor mansions in the county, it was built in 1525 for wealthy London clothier Sir Thomas Kyston. The front is in grand Tudor style complete with mitred turrets. Inside is a courtyard enclosed by cloisters on three sides but perhaps the most beautiful is the oratory which is still used by nuns. The Church of St. John Lateran in the grounds has a Saxon tower although the rest is 14th Century and commissioned by Sir Thomas de Hengrave. As this was a private chapel it did not suffer the fate of other religious houses during the dissolution and consequently the monuments to be found here are many and all of them heavily decorated. The Hall *(01284 701561)* is now run as an Ecumenical Conference and Retreat Centre and to arrange a visit contact: The Hengrave Hall Centre, Bury St. Edmunds, IP28 6LZ.

On your route along the A1101 to Mildenhall, take the trouble to enjoy the traditional Breckland environment at *Cavenham Heath* with its mix of woodland, varied shrub and vast sweeps of gorse, bracken and heather. A wide variety of fauna and flora shelter here not least the grayling butterfly which is rarely found so far inland. The Heath is managed by the Nature Conservancy Council and a nature trail can be followed around the area.

A little further along at *Icklingham* the mix of Norfolk and Suffolk architectural styles is at its most apparent - flint structures standing alongside whitewashed and thatched ones. Somewhat unusually, the village has two churches, the large thatched All Saints which is 13th and 14th Century in origin, and the earlier flint built St. James (12th Century). Icklingham is thought to have once been an important Roman settlement - *Camboricum* - and the frequency of Roman finds in the area adds weight to this theory; a villa has been partially excavated near the village and other finds include coins, jewellery, pewter and kilns.

Situated on the banks of the River Lark, *Barton Mills* today is little more than a sleepy backwater. It too was once a busy waterway where a daily passenger service to Norwich operated and where the barges would unload coal for the village and reload with stones collected from nearby Chalk Hill. If you have time to explore the village, look for a property called 'The Dhoon', once Sir Alexander Fleming's country home; it is thought he first discovered penicillin in his shed at the bottom of the garden.

Other interesting snippets of local history include the village's 13th Century rector, none less than Jacobus de Scabellis who later went on to reach the heady heights of cardinal, papal prefect and ultimately Pope Honorius IV. By the time the last honour was granted him he is said to have been so afflicted with gout that a mechanical contrivance was erected to assist him raise his hands at the moment of the Elevation of the Host! If no sympathy can be found for Scabellis, then perhaps a little can be felt for Elizabeth, Oliver Cromwell's mother, who was born into the Steward family who held the manorial rights to Barton Mills.

# Mildenhall

Now to Mildenhall and although it is today primarily associated with the American Air Base here it was, in medieval times, a royal manor of Bury St. Edmunds. It also once supported a highly regarded fish market. The Church of St. Mary & St. Andrew is majestic both inside and outside; following a spate of vandalism access is no longer automatic and details of how to gain entry are posted on the door. Look for the unusual 14th Century window in the east end and the clipped wings of the angels on the hammerbeams of the north aisle - clipped by avid Puritans during the 17th Century. Under the tower is the altar-tomb commemorating Sir Henry de Barton, once Lord Mayor of London and the person reputedly to be thanked for London's street lighting.

Today though Mildenhall's real claim to fame is its celebrated treasure now in the British Museum, London; in 1946 a farmer, discovered an incredible collection of 4th Century Roman silverware near Thistley Green. The 34 pieces so revealed included a huge dish over two feet in diameter and depicting Bacchus' triumph over Hercules. Two unusual baptismal spoons engraved with Christian symbols were also unearthed. Only a decade earlier at Thistley Green a two bedroomed Roman building was discovered on West Row with pottery also dating from the 4th Century.

The Eastern Counties Transport Co. kept the River Lark at Mildenhall navigable until 1892 and that it was heavily relied upon for the transportation of essential commodities - coal, corn and iron - is documented by Defoe (1724). Now, the River is shut off by a fixed weir. The town does however retain its Market Cross, an hexagonal timber structure thought to be 16th Century craftsmanship and still home to a lively market.

## Food & Accommodation

**Riverside Hotel** *(01638 717274), Mill Street, Mildenhall.* A pleasant and efficiently run hotel with a Georgian facade. Although the River is not immediately obvious it does add a quiet charm and for the energetic there is always opportunity to go for a row along the Lark. The ceilings throughout seem extraordinarily high but as this is a popular business/conference venue perhaps this is to the guests advantage. Bedroom accommodation is individually furnished and Laura Ashley style predominates.

At nearby *Eriswell* you will notice the initials NEC (New England Company) on some of the houses. NEC was originally set up by Puritans in an attempt to propagate the Gospel in New England, USA, and especially to North American Indians. The Eriswell Estate was bought by the monies so raised and its revenues invested in the NEC's propagation programme. Its operations lasted for over 200 years until, in 1869, the Charity Commissioners sold the Eriswell lands to Duleep Singh, the new owner of the nearby estate at Elveden.

## Walk 5: The Brecks Around Mildenhall and Eriswell

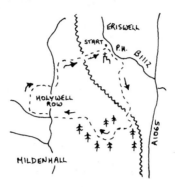

### Directions:

1. From your park near Eriswell Church, walk a short distance south along the B1112 looking for a track on your right, on the bend, between the Old Rectory and School. Continue along this track until you come to the Cut-Off Channel. 2. Cross the bridge over the sluice, and go left along a track on the western side of the Channel. After approx. 200 yards, go right along a narrow path heading up a sandy bank and down the other side into the woods. 3. Cross over another bridge, and at the end of a line of pines on your right, go left beside a ditch which you keep to your right. At Mildenhall Woods, ignore the path leading through the trees and instead bear right along a track leading round the wood's edge. 4. At a bungalow ,follow the track round to the left and so down the lane. Cross the lane going straight ahead into another one for approx 400 yards. 5. As this bends right, look for a sandy by-way, Fen Lane, also on your right. At a junction of paths, go right into a field and cross this diagonally aiming for the right hand corner of farm buildings in front of you. Join the road again just before a belt of trees. 6. Cross the lane and go left into a field following the field edge as it runs parallel with the road for a while and at the field corner go right to get back to the Cut-Off Channel. 7. Cross the footbridge over the Channel, and continue straight ahead to return to Eriswell bearing right at the B1112 to find your way back to the Church.

**Start: Eriswell Church**
**Approx. Distance: 4 Miles**
**Approx. Time: 1.5 Hours**
**Map: Landranger 143**

# Lakenheath

Lakenheath stands next to East Anglia's largest American Airbase though the latter's future is somewhat uncertain; the collapse of the Cold War seeing most western countries defence budgets significantly reduced. Nonetheless, it was from here and from nearby Mildenhall that President Reagan's 1986 Tripoli

*St. Mary's Church, Lakenheath*

Campaign against Colonel Ghaddafi was launched using F111's from the two bases and no doubt craft from both were also used during the more recent Gulf War.

As for the village, like others along this stretch of Breckland, it is built from a mix of brick, chalk, flint, church, carstone and limestone. Evidence of Neolithic, Iron Age, Roman and Anglo-Saxon settlements in the area is also considerable. A dragonesque brooch (now in the Ashmolean Museum), coins and kilns have all been unearthed. Check out St. Mary's Church though noted for its fine hammerbeam roof decorated with 60 angels, some rare bench ends depicting amongst other things acrobats and a giant fish, the wall Painting of St. Edmund and another depicting scenes from the Life of Christ. A number of members of the Kitchener family are also buried here, note the memorial tablet to Earl Kitchener of Khartoum (1850-1916) who was lost at sea when HMS *Hampshire* was mined off the Orkney Islands in 1916.

# Brandon

Brandon on the Suffolk-Norfolk borders was for centuries the home of Britain's oldest industry - flint knapping; inevitably much of the town is also built from flint. Although it is not the most attractive of places, Brandon's history and surrounding countryside more than compensates. In the early days, arrowheads and prehistoric tools would have been hammered out of mined flint slabs. Later, flints from Ling Heath were brought to a yard behind the Flintknappers Pub and here chips would be struck off for gun-flints or knapped for building materials. Local records reveal a wealth of specialist flint knapping families, notably the Snares, Fields, Edwards and Carters, who supplied amongst others the British Army with gun flints during the Napoleonic Wars. Indeed, flint knapping was at its height during the Napoleonic Wars when there were as many as 200 flint knappers in Brandon alone. Incredibly, a flint knapper could produce as many as 300 gun flints per hour. The practice went out of fashion during the mid 19th Century more than anything else because of the adoption of percussion guns but a small number of flints are still in demand today, especially for American collectors of muzzle-loading, flintlock guns.

The oldest part of Brandon however was originally the site of the Remembrance Playing Fields and in recent years this has been excavated to reveal a former moated Iceni village. Archaeologists have even found the actual markings of several items of adornment.

The Suffolk-Norfolk county boundary follows the line of the Little Ouse which flows through the town to Thetford. Although the lighters which once plied their way along the River ceased commercial carrying after 1914, canal boats and pleasure cruisers can still occasionally be seen negotiating holiday makers along its banks.

**Brandon Country Park** can be found just outside the town and is a small element of what was once a large 2,500 acre estate owned by Edward Bliss during the early 1800's and now owned by Suffolk County Council. It is an ideal place to see some of Breckland's wildlife; jay, long-tailed tit, feral golden pheasant, red squirrel, deer and adder. There is a **Visitors Centre** here equipped with a small shop and toilet facilities, as well as providing details of the history and natural history of the area. Enjoy your picnics here, take a waymarked forest walk or just explore the grounds - the former Brandon Park House is now a nursing home but provides a beautiful backdrop to the lawn and lake. There is also a recently restored mausoleum and walled garden in the grounds.

Although in Norfolk, **Weeting Heath** a couple of miles north-west of Brandon should be visited as it is one of the best remaining heathlands in Breckland complete with its chalk grassland peculiar to the area. These dry stony soils support a host of rare plants including spiked speedwell. Others include hound's tongue and early forget-me-not. Additionally, the Heath is a well known haunt for green woodpecker, stone curlew, butterflies and rare spiders. A warden is on the site *from the beginning of April to the end of August* and the *hides can be used* during this time.

*Grimes Graves,* three and a half miles north of Brandon and again in Norfolk, and managed by English Heritage, are unique Neolithic flint mines comprising over 340 pits or shallows, almost circular depressions, on a 43 acre site. Visitors can go down one of the excavated shafts and see for themselves the mining gallery. Although the shafts were first discovered in 1869 by the Rev. Canon Greenwell of Durham, the main period for their exploitation was during the late Neolithic and early Bronze Ages, from around 3100-2200 BC. In the earliest pits, the chief mining tools would appear to have been the bones of red deer and flint wedges. **Open daily April to October, & Wednesday-Sunday November to March. Admission charge.**

Although much of Elveden's history - *Elveden* found just to the south of

Brandon - is not open to public viewing, it is nevertheless exotic enough to afford the reader some description of the place. The Maharajah Duleep Singh bought the house at Elveden after he had been banished from both his Lahore Court and from India by Queen Victoria for his part in the Sikh Wars. During the 1960's, he employed the Gothic architect John Norton to transform the original but modest Georgian mansion at Elveden into a vast oriental palace complete with copper dome.

Tons of Carrara marble were imported to support Norton's elaborate design, and the carving was performed *in situ* by Italian craftsmen. The walls, pillars and arches of this unparalleled extravaganza are covered with Indian ornamental detail. Even the doors were covered with panels of beaten copper. After the Maharajah's death in 1894, the Elveden estate was bought by the family that owned the Guinness Brewery. From 1899-1903, the first Lord Iveagh employed William Young to enlarge the palace giving it a new Italianate front and continuing the internal decoration along the lines of the Taj Mahal. Today, this lavish palace is not inhabited, the current Lord & Lady Iveagh living elsewhere on the estate profitably farming its agricultural holdings.

The Church of St. Andrew & St. Patrick affords some ideas of the elaborate notions of both men. The Maharajah was responsible for enlarging the basic Norman structure and Lord Iveagh employed Caroe, in 1904, to raise the standard of the Church to that of the Hall. All this new detail - a new north nave and chancel, and a new south tower - is of the most ornate Gothic style.

The remaining parts of the Elveden estate - the almshouses and estate houses - are much simpler in orientation. Built from red brick with timber-framed gables they have a peaceful and serene air. The towering Corinthian column, approx. two miles south of the village was erected in 1921 as a memorial to the men of the estate who died during World War I. 113 feet high with 148 steps, it was designed by Clyde Young. Although it is no longer open to the public, it is nevertheless worth a few minutes reflection from the outside. More recently, the Centre Parcs Elveden Forest Village Holiday Centre has been built around what was once Warren Wood.

*Brandon's Village Sign*

# *Euston*

The village of Euston to the east is rather more accessible and was essentially built for the aggrandisement of one family, namely the Dukes of Grafton. Their story begins much earlier with Lord Arlington, a notorious member of the Cabal Ministry (1667-73), who paid Charles II the sum of ten thousand guineas for the privileged position of Lord Chamberlain. It was Arlington in the 1660's who commissioned the Hall's building although it was substantially altered and enlarged a century later to bring it more in line with Palladian tastes of the time. The Hall then passed to the illegitimate son of Charles II, Henry Fitzroy, who had married Arlington's daughter. Initially 1st Baron of Sudbury, Henry was later and variously known as the Viscount of Ipswich, the Earl of Euston and finally as the Duke of Grafton.

We can only assume he was something of an eccentric for as a great huntsman he was known to keep one pack of hounds at Euston and another in London so that he could hunt whilst away from his home. A trip to the capital in those days would have involved crossing the Thames by ferry, so Henry, in one of his furies, pushed a Bill through Parliament facilitating the building of Westminster Bridge thereby easing his own journey to and from his Suffolk estates. Rather more eccentrically, he had the original village of Euston moved from where it is now because it spoiled the view. Henry was to meet his end at the Siege of Cork in 1690 but the estate is still owned by the Graftons, the 11th Duke one of the Queen's cousins and a Knight of the Garter and the Duchess the Queen's Mistress of Robes.

What is left of **Euston Hall** *(01842 766366) is open Thursday afternoons from the end of June to the beginning of September. Admission charge.* Amongst the more notable things to be seen include paintings by Van Dyck, Stubbs and Reynolds. Take time to wander around the grounds which run alongside the winding River Black Bourn, canalised such that it forms a wide ornamental waterway. William Kent and John Evelyn are responsible for the garden/park's design as is Kent again for the splendid domed Palladian Temple and the Garden House.

English poet **Robert Bloomfield** (1766-1823) born at nearby Honington was at one time granted an allowance by the Duke of Grafton to enable him to continue his muses. We can be fairly certain than that the following snippet of verse was written by way of tribute and thanks:

*'Where noble Grafton spreads his rich domains*
*Round Euston's watered vale and sloping plains;*
*Where woods and groves in solemn grandeur rise,*
*Where the kite brooding unmolested flies;*
*The woodcock and the painted pheasant race*
*And skalking foxes destined for the chase.'*

Given the village was moved in the 17th Century, the Church now stands alone in the parkland. The outer walls and tower of St. Genevieve's are medieval but the remainder was rebuilt in 1676. As can be expected, there are many memorials to the Grafton family, and a richly decorated pulpit and reredos said to be the work of Grinley Gibbons.

Continuing in a southerly direction sees us in *Ixworth* (not to be confused with Ickworth Hall to the south of Bury St. Edmunds) and which has enjoyed a long and ancient history being first a major settlement of the Iceni tribe, then an important station for the Romans, subsequently endowed with two Anglo-Saxon manors and then, under the Normans, enriched by a community of Augustinian Canons sometime during the 12th Century. The Abbey as this is now known is only open by prior appointment and incorporates what remains of the 12th Century priory and prior's 15th Century lodgings. The village is attractive enough and includes houses with over sailing frontages and pargeting. At nearby *Bardwell,* a Georgian tower *windmill (01359 251331),* built in 1825 and currently undergoing restoration, can be seen. *Open during the summer months.*

## Food & Accommodation

**Theobalds** *(01359 231707), 68 High Street, Ixworth.* A small cottage-type restaurant where seasonal produce translates into a menu of mainly French inspiration. Consistency and good service are the keys to this successful operation. Don't be misled by the buildings plain frontage, it has a great deal of charm.

Now to *Ampton,* a pretty Breckland border village, surrounded by good woods and close to the delightful Ampton Water. Note both the 1693 almshouses and the Hall rebuilt in Jacobean style during the late 1880's; the latter structure being destroyed by fire in 1885 and only its fine wrought iron gates in the wall towards the street a reminder of its existence.

The original Hall was once home to Captain Robert Fitzroy who sailed aboard HMS *Beagle*, in 1828, on the first of two voyages to explore the Magellan Straits. On his second expedition, Fitzroy was accompanied by Charles Darwin no less. We must not overshadow the Captain's own achievements, however, for he is the father of modern meteorology, the first official weather forecasts commencing in 1861.

*Great* and *Little Livermere* are thought to derive their names from the *laefer* - a flag-iris which grows around the mere, the latter known as a wildfowl haven. The Park itself was bought by a Baptist gentleman who won the state lottery in 1772.

# Walk 6: Ampton and Breckland

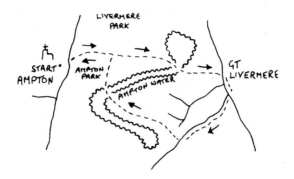

## Directions

1. From your start at Ampton Church, walk a little way north along the country lane passing the grounds of Ampton Hall on your right. Just after a belt of trees and between two buildings, take the track on your right which, after just over a mile leads, you to the two lakes forming Ampton Water. 2. Cross the bridge and continue along the track, ignoring left and right intersections, until you arrive in Great Livermere. At the lane, go right and where it is joined by another lane continue along the main village street. Ignore the first right lane leading off here, taking the second right as the road forks. Continue along here for approx. one mile. 3. Just after a track leading off to the left and near some white posts, go right along the edge of a field and down to Old Broom Plantation. 4. Take the path leading through the Plantation and onto the long footbridge over Ampton Water (approx. one mile). Once over the bridge, go along the track to your right which runs fairly parallel with a belt of trees. 5. At the track, bear left to rejoin your outward journey continuing along there to the lane where you bear left to return to the Church.

**Start: Ampton Church**
**Approx. Distance: 5 Miles**
**Approx. Time: 2 Hours**
**Map: Landranger 144**

If you decide to go west to Newmarket along the A14 then a visit to St. Giles' Church, **Risby** is well worth the effort. Inside is a beautiful 15th Century rood screen with its uncommon (at least for Suffolk) three-light division; it was restored by the Pilgrim Trust in 1966. Some early 13th Century wall paintings are also evident though their subject matter not always distinguishable but thought to depict the Story of the Nativity and the Lives of the Saints. Also in the village is an antiques centre housed in a 400 year old barn. **Risby Barn Antiques** can be contacted on *01284 810454*.

# *Newmarket*

On the Suffolk-Cambridgeshire border, Newmarket became new in 1227 when nearby Exning's old market was forced to close because of an outbreak of the plague. It is not the most attractive of places but Newmarket's pre-eminence in the world of horseracing make it deserving of a visit.

> The American novelist **Henry James** (1843-1916) in his *Portrait of Places* (1883) even accords Newmarket special mention:
> *'Newmarket is, in its own peculiar fashion, so thriving a locality. The country is like a board of green cloth; the turf presents itself as a friendly provision of nature ... amidst this gentle, pastoral scenery, there is more betting than anywhere else in the world.'*

James I was the first to appreciate the springy turf around here, arriving in 1605 to course hares. It was not, however, until Charles I patronage that horseracing really took over and has been more or less practiced without a break since. So influential was Royal support during those early days that the famous Rowley Mile was named after one of Charles II's horses.

Newmarket's High Street is rather disappointing dominated at the top by the 1887 Clock Tower erected in memory of Victoria's Diamond Jubilee but which many people, including the renowned architect Sir Nikolaus Pevsner, consider to be *'hideous'*. Those few buildings which do deserve our attention are limited to the Jockey Club, 101 High Street, originally founded in 1751 but not housed in the current building until 1840 and this heavily restored in the 1930's. Next door is the **National Horseracing Museum** *(01638 667333), 99 High Street*, which ably documents the history of racing since the times of Charles II. Here, all the great jockeys are portrayed in their racing silks and other exhibits cover breeding, owners and trainers. ***Open most days of the week, Easter to early December. Admission charge.***

> **The Jockey Club** is the most powerful horse racing institution in the country. Not only are its members self-elected and self-regulatory but theirs is the body which determines all laws and judgements relating to the sport. Jockeys themselves are not eligible for membership, The Club after all is their governing organisation but all fear being hauled before the 'Stewards' Room to account for some misdemeanour or another. Women too have only recently been awarded membership and this as late as 1977.

Tattersall's, the Sotheby's of the turf, are also to be found in the town, their motto appropriately enough *'Match the best with the best and hope for the best.'* Originally founded in 1766 by Richard Tattersall, the son of a Yorkshire wool merchant, Tattersall's have risen from their early beginnings selling horses at Hyde Park Corner to the multi-million pound operation they are today. Their Newmarket set up was not formerly established until 1939 but they had held auctions outside The Jockey Club during the 18th Century with George IV, both

*Mill Reef's Statue at the Newmarket Stud*

as King and earlier as Prince Regent, one of their better customers. The company remained a family operation until 1942 and is still the most illustrious of horse auctioneers the world over. There is some doubt however about whether Tattersall's will stay in Newmarket, indeed about whether they remain in the UK at all; much depending on the imposition of VAT on their activities. In any case the Irish Government's monetary policies with their greater flexibility towards horse racing many well see the company drawn across the Irish Sea with Newmarket by far the worse off.

Newmarket Heath remains an oasis of grassland and if you want to see the horses in training go up the heathland slopes to the north and north-west of the town. You will need to be up and around bright and early though. The Jockey Club itself owns 4,000 acres of this land and trainers pay The Club a 'heath tax,' applied per horse and per month, such that they can train there horses here.

> **George Stubbs** (1724-1806) recorded many vivid scenes of Newmarket's horseracing prowess in his memorable paintings and perhaps none better than *Gimrack on Newmarket Heath with a Trainer, Jockey and a Stable Lad* (1765). Stubbs was a formidable exponent of the sporting genre and many others have followed his lead including Sir Alfred Munnings who had a studio here during the 1930's. Stubbs is also known for his monumental work *Anatomy of the Horse*, published in 1766, and which is illustrated by his own engravings.

Alternatively you can visit **The National Stud** (*01638 663464*), near the racecourse, and where you must join a conducted tour (phone first to check availability). Better still perhaps is a visit to the races, and Newmarket has two courses, one the Rowley Mile Course used during the spring and autumn and on which both the 1,000 Guineas and the 2,000 Guineas are run at the start of the

May season. Other important races, both run in October, include the Cesarewitch and the Cambridgeshire. Then there is the July Course used during that month as well as through August. For a full programme of events contact *The Racecourse* direct on *01638 663482*.

Any drive around the outskirts of the town and its neighbouring villages reveals a wealth of Victorian and Edwardian houses standing in their own grounds. Many of these are private studs more often than not now Arab owned. The Arabs have invested enormous sums of money in the sport and perhaps one of the most influential has been Sheikh Mohammed el Maktoum of Dubai whose Stud at Dalham Hall ranks amongst the most important.

Many of the legendary jockeys including the likes of Fred Archer and Lester Piggott also made Newmarket their home at one time or another. Lester Piggott won his first Derby at the incredible age of 18. Aged 50, he had an amazing 4,389 wins under his belt including nine Derby's and 29 English classics. Supposedly retired in 1985, he made a come back and has only now decided to finally call it a day. Fred Archer's story is not so sweet. At the peak of his career, Archer rode more than 600 races per year, winning most major events and earning at the time the princely sum of £10,000 per annum. Then in 1886, just after his 5th Derby win, he committed suicide, using a friend's revolver. He was only 29 years old.

So what else to do in this land of horses? Perhaps do what the Queen Mother does and purchase some sausages from *Musks Ltd* (*01638 661824*), *1 The Rookery, Newmarket*. Particularly renowned are their Musk sausages made from a mix of pork, spices and bread and without the use of dreaded preservatives. Alternatively, a round of golf at the *Royal Worlington & Newmarket Golf Club* (*01638 712216*), *Worlington*, where visitors can enjoy a 9-hole course on sandy soil. You must take your handicap certificate and also note that weekends and Bank Holidays are strictly for members only.

Close to Newmarket, *Dalham* is something of a show village where thatch abounds and which uses both banks of the River Kennet over which little white footbridges aid resident and visitor alike. Two mills still stand though neither are in use; the five-storey smock mill complete with sails, pepper-pot cap and gallery is in especially good repair. The Church of St. Mary's is mainly 14th Century though the tower is a later 17th Century addition. Inside you will find many memorials to the Affleck family plus one commemorating Cecil Rhodes. Rhodes (1853-1902) had purchased Dalham Hall but unfortunately died before he was able to reach the village; the Village Hall, financed by his brother, is another monument to this great South African statesman.

> The **Icknield Way**, a long distance footpath stretching from Ivinghoe Beacon (Buckinghamshire) to Knettishall Heath (on the Suffolk-Norfolk border) passes through Dalham. Once linked with two other long distance paths, the Peddars Way to the east and the Ridgeway to the west, the Icknield Way thus completed a major route across Britain.

The Hall was originally built for Bishop Symon Patrick of Ely in 1704 with the strict command that it be built upwards until Ely Cathedral, across the Fens, could be seen on a fine day. Another illustrious occupier was Wellington. Today, the Hall is not so elevated being only two-storeys high after a fire in 1957 destroyed the top floor.

## *Food & Accommodation*

**The Affleck Arms** *(01638 500306), Dalham, near Newmarket* A pleasant thatched pub of Elizabethan origin with a lovely situation on the narrow banks of the River Kennet. Good home made food and real ales can be enjoyed, outside or inside, the latter especially welcoming in winter with a raging log fire and further sheared by flowers on the table.

**The Star Inn** *(01638 500275), The Street, Lidgate, near Newmarket.* Variously dated as between 400 and 500 years old, The Star is a typically characterful beamed building and one which is both busy and friendly. An excellent changing menu, much of it Mediterranean inspired, is to be thoroughly enjoyed as is the real ale and a good choice of wines. Note the spit-roasts cooked on a huge log fire are an excellent Sunday treat during the winter.

Finally, if you are in the vicinity of *Great Bradley*, a few miles to the south of Newmarket, then do visit St. Mary's Church. Yes, yet another Church but there are so many of interest and importance in Suffolk. The bricks of the south porch here are thought to have been made by Henry VIII's own brickmaker, and the fireplace in the Church is said to have been used for baking the Communion wafers. There is also some good stained glass in the east window and which depicts a young soldier, Rex Wilder, in the trenches of World War I where he lost his life.

# The Waveney Valley

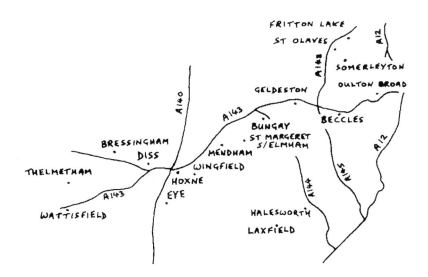

Our tour of the Waveney Valley begins in the quaint, sleepy estate village of Somerleyton, taking a look at the Hall there before heading south to Oulton Broad, the only true Broad to be found in Suffolk. As far as possible we then follow the course of the Waveney first through Beccles then to Bungay and Diss (Norfolk) collecting many of the interesting hinterland villages on our way through this lush and tranquil part of the Suffolk countryside.

## Somerleyton

Although Somerleyton Hall was built in Victorian times, in style it is mainly Jacobean, '... *more Jacobean than any original Jacobean house*' says the architect Sir Nikolaus Pevsner, and this around a Tudor shell. Sir Morton Peto commissioned its building in 1844-51 and it was designed by John Thomas.

Peto began his career as a builders' apprentice but by his early thirties could count Nelson's Column, St. James Theatre and railways in Argentina, Australia, Canada, France, Norway and Russia as among his many accomplishments.

**Somerleyton Hall**

Later an MP and a guarantor for the 1851 Exhibition, he was knighted in 1855. Peto was also responsible for developing Lowestoft into a seaside resort as also for extending its port. By 1861 however he had overreached himself and was declared bankrupt. The Hall and estate were subsequently sold to Sir Francis Crossley, 1st Baronet of Halifax, and is now home to his descendent, the 3rd Lord Somerleyton.

Interesting things to look out for include the unusual stable clock which was the original model of a clock designed by Vulliamy in 1847 for the Houses of Parliament. In the gardens, there is an especially fine yew maze planted in 1846 to a design by William Nesfield; at the centre of which is a small pagoda. Note also in the gardens the unusual glasshouses by Sir Joseph Paxton designer of Crystal Palace. *The Hall and Gardens are open variously between April and September. Admission charge.*

The somewhat irregular but pretty village of Somerleyton, with its combination of brick, mock timber-framing and thatch to a variety of shapes, is also attributable to Peto and Thomas. At nearby *Herringfleet* there is a unique timber-smocked octagonal *drainage mill* and built in 1830 its design is of the earliest type. Inside is a 16 feet diameter scoop wheel once driven by sail but now converted to oil. Also evident is the fireplace which the marshman would have warmed himself by should the mill have been worked round the clock. Today the mill is maintained by Suffolk County Council and *is open occasionally*.

Continuing to follow the most easterly course of the River Waveney, *Fritton Lake & Country Park*, owned by Lord and Lady Somerleyton, can be found a few miles north-west of Somerleyton village. Although the entrance is a rather unattractive collection of commercial paraphernalia, do not be misled by this as the large lake beyond is quite unspoilt as is the vast woodland. The half-acre

Victorian Garden is also an unusual feature with its irregular beds and clipped box hedges, all planted with a wide variety of herbaceous perennials and shrubs. Amongst the more commercial attractions are the craft workshops, putting green and boat-hire facilities. *Open daily, Easter to October* (01493 488208). *Admission charge*. Course fishing on the lake is also available.

> **Fritton Lake** was once a decoy for wild ducks, the latter lured onto the lake by handfuls of grain. Trained tame ducks would then swim out into a carefully placed funnel-shaped net, much like an eel catchers basket, followed by their wild duck counterparts. The net would then close, the tame birds retrieved and the wild ones wrung and sent to market.

The Church of St. Edmund at Fritton has an asymmetrical round Norman tower and a thatched nave. In the chancel though you will see a rarity for such a small church, namely the tunnel vaulting.

Now to *St. Olaves*, a pretty Broadland village to the north of which are the scanty ruins of an Augustinian Priory founded in 1216 and close by is a tiny timber-smocked drainage mill. This is also as good a spot as any from which to hire boats to explore the Broads: contact *Castle Craft* (01493 488675), *Reeds Lane, St. Olaves.*

# Oulton Broad

Heading south now along the Waveney takes us to Oulton Broad which stretches across an area of more than 1,300 acres and which is also the most southerly of the Broads. It is a major holiday centre crowded with pleasure boats, boatyards and boat builders. If you are in the area in August try to time your visit during Regatta Week when the spectacle is at its most colourful. The Lowestoft Museum is also here and for details of this see the entry on Lowestoft to be found in the North Coast Chapter.

Like all the other Broads, Oulton was created from the peat diggings of the 13th and 14th Centuries. In 1341, it is claimed that more than 300,000 turves were exported from Oulton alone.

The Broads are always best explored by boat and at Oulton motor launches can be hired from *Day Launch Hire* (01502 513087), *The Yacht Station, Oulton Broad.* Alternatively, you can take a half-day trip along the southern Broads aboard the *Waveney Stardust* (01502 712473), *Oulton Broad.* *Note this particular boat is especially equipped for disabled visitors and you must book in advance.* You may also enjoy a visit to *Boatworld* (01502 574441), *Harbour Road, Oulton Broad* where traditional wooden boatbuilding skills can be watched. The Centre also incorporates the world famous international Boatbuilding Training College. *Admission charge.*

# *Walk 7: Oulton Broad and the River Waveney*

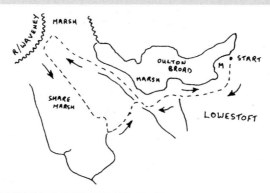

## *Directions:*

1. From your park at Oulton Broad Yacht Station, walk along the bank heading west along the Broad edge and past the Lowestoft Museum on your left. Go over a small bridge in the park and bear right staying with the Broads edge. Go through the boating yards to pick up a path with a bridge leading over it. Once over the bridge, continue round to the right. At the next boating yard you move slightly away from the Broad but bearing left along a narrowish track. At the end of that and as it goes round to the left, follow the marked footpath (signed Waveney Way & Angles Way) on your right instead. Continue straight along the path, following the signs and ignoring all left and right intersections.. 2. Go over a stile, and at the next stile follow the yellow waymarker signs round to your right round the edge of a field. As you start to go round the corner of the field edge, look for a path leading off to the right to a raised bank on the Broads edge i.e. do not continue along the field to a group of houses. 3. Once at the raised bank, go left along a path leading along the fringe of Oulton Broad and round to White Cast Marshes. Continue along here for approx. one mile ignoring any left intersections. At the end of this stretch, you come to a meeting of paths. Ignore the path leading north along the fringe of Oulton Broad, and instead go down the bank on a path to your left. Keep left for a few yards to pick up a public bridleway on your right. 4. At the next junction of pathways carry straight on, and at the next go over the stile and along a path which runs pretty well straight ahead and keeping the Cut-Off Channel to your left. Keep straight on when another track leads off to the right. After approx. 400 yards you join the banks of the River Waveney. Turn left here and walk to the disused pumping station ahead of you. 5. Just after the pumping station, go left along a signed public footpath which leads straight across Share Marsh. Continue along here for approx one mile without deviating left or right. 6. Once at Sprats Water Nature Reserve, managed by the Suffolk Wildlife Trust, go left along a formal walkway (signed). At the next main fork of paths, keep to the left and once through the kissing gate at the end go right to a farm gate, 7. Once through the farm gate, keep left along the edge of a field until you come first to the path on your left which earlier took you to the edge of Oulton Broad, and a little further along to a stile. Cross the stile and return the same way as

your outward journey and so back to Oulton Broad proper.
**Start: Oulton Broad Yacht Station Car Park**
**Approx. Distance: 5 Miles**
**Approx. Time: 2 Hours**
**Map: Landranger 134**

# *Beccles*

Now to our first main town in the Waveney Valley, Beccles, which is predominantly Georgian much of it rebuilt after several great fires destroyed earlier habitations during the 16th and 17th Centuries. Although it is a fairly small place today, the market area is an attractive square with streets running in all directions off it. Of those buildings which did survive the fires, note the Elizabethan brick and stone Roos Hall (1593) on the outskirts of town; it's walls and gables battlemented, and the corners pinnacled in keeping with the elaborate old chimneys. Other buildings of note include the fine 18th Century brick St. Peter's House which may well stand on the site of the pre-dissolution St. Peter's Chapel. Additionally, there is Ravensmere House (1694) comprised of blackish-blue and red chequerwork with its doorway formed of Roman Doric pilasters. Both Northgate and Ballygate also have good examples of 18th Century Georgian brickwork. As for St. Michael's Church, note the mid 15th Century double storeyed, 34 feet high, south porch complete with intricate embellishments and with a frieze of shields at its base.

That Beccles was once a thriving port is clear from *Domesday* records which reveal that the town yielded up 10,000 herrings per year to the Abbey of St. Edmund's (Bury St. Edmunds); William the Conqueror, himself, was shortly afterwards to demand 60,000 herrings every year in the way of rent to the Crown. With Broadland at this time still flooded, Beccles would indeed have been a seaport, and even once the Broads had been drained, the River Waveney continued to provide an outlet to the North Sea at Great Yarmouth and Gorleston. In more recent times, where we now see a plethora of pleasure craft,

*St. Michael's Church,*

**Pleasure Craft on the River Waveney, Beccles Quay**

wherries would have plied their trade up and down the River, tying up at the staithes, and their operators walking home along the 'scores' or narrow streets which lead back into the town itself. Today, motor launches for Broads use can be hired from **Arrow Boats** *(01502 713524), 32A Puddingmoor, Beccles.*

The town boasts a couple of small museums, first the **Beccles & District Museum** *(01502 715722), Leman House, Ballygate, Beccles.* Most of the items on display inevitably relate to the town's history. During the 17th Century, Beccles was important enough to have its own coinage. Rare examples of the 1670 farthing with the original dies from which they were first struck are among the most interesting artefacts. *Open daily (ex. Monday) in the afternoons, Easter to October. Admission is currently free but this may be revised.* The other museum is the **William Clowes Printing Museum** *(01502 712884), Newgate, Beccles.* Of particular note here are the countless woodcuts and books dating from the early 1800's, together with the extensive machinery used to produce them. More up-to-date equipment is also on view and factory tours can be taken by prior arrangement only. *The Museum is open afternoons during the week, June to August.*

Although in neighbouring Norfolk, the village of **Geldeston** marks the limits of navigation on the River Waveney and here a useful and attractive public footpath runs through Geldeston Dyke to Beccles (approx. three miles). The Lock here was in use until the mid 1930's and was amongst three such structures enabling wherry traffic to sail the few miles to Bungay. Although its original dating is unsure, it is certainly known to have been restored as early as 1670 by an Act of Parliament. Just south of Geldeston Lock is Holy Trinity Church, **Barsham,** noticeable by virtue of its spiked round tower. Of particular interest here is the exterior of the east wall with its superb stonework trellis. Although this is undated it is thought to be pre-17th Century and of further note is the late 1870's stained glass window by Kempe which it incorporates. Also of interest is the pretty rood canopy (1919) with its brightly painted cut-out figures contained within open arches, and the stuccoed chancel roof (1906).

# Walk 8: Beccles and Geldeston Lock

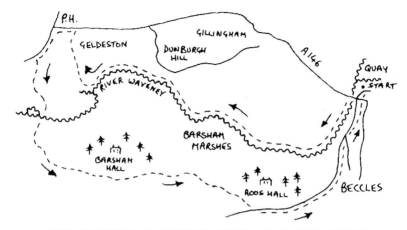

## Directions:

1. From the Information Centre on Beccles Quay, head back into town passing the Loaves & Fishes pub. At the top of Fen Lane, bear right to cross the bridge over the River Waveney. Look for a footpath marker pointing immediate left and go down steps onto the Riverside, and on through the boat and timber yard. Shortly after, you will come across the old railway bridge pier and from here the track now narrows to a footpath along the Riverbank. 2. Continue along this footpath, through the small stretch of woodland at Dunburgh Hill, and eventually on to the Dyke at Geldeston. 3. To get to the village, pass under the old railway bridge and through the boatyard. Reaching the street, via left until you reach a point where the road goes round to the right. At this point, turn left following the road into Dockeney. 4. Look for a track, Locks Lane, on your left which will take you over the marshes and to what was once the most isolated of all pubs, Lock Inn. 5. Before reaching the pub, bear right crossing the bridge over the dyke and then over the bridges at the Lock (three of them). Continue straight across the marsh until you reach a junction of pathways. 6. Go left, following the path around the edge of a copse of trees until it joins another pathway. Again, go left here along what is the Angles Way. Continue along this as it skirts another stretch of woodland, crosses the driveway leading to the remains of Barsham Hall, and as it crosses Barsham Dyke. 7. Just before Roos Hall, the track then joins the B1062. Use the footpath which keeps you off the worst of the road. Look for a road to your left, after the Hall, which provides a pleasant entry into Beccles. 8. Once at the Market Place, go left into Northgate and on into Bridge Street which will get you back to the Quay.

**Start: Information Centre on Beccles Quay**
**Approx. Distance: 7 Miles  Approx. Time: 3 Hours**
**Map: Landranger 134**

# *Bungay*

Nestling on the southern banks of the River Waveney, Bungay is only just a Suffolk town. It must however have provided an important river crossing for the Romans for when the Normans arrived there was already a Castle and settlement which they quickly turned into a stronghold. Again of pre-Conquest origin, and now unique to Bungay, is the office of Town Reeve and Feoffes. Dating back to Saxon times and still extant today, this is the only such ancient office held in England. As for the Castle, only a few ruins of a later post-Conquest structure remain. Running diagonally from the west to the south side of these ruins is a small gallery in the middle of which are two small cross cuts through the masonry. Theory has it that this is a sappers tunnel, which would have been reinforced with timber and set alight as a means of seizing the Castle. It is thought that Henry II's troops drove this sap into the keep in an effort to repel Hugh Bigod for his part in the uprising against the King; their efforts were halted when Bigod chose instead to pay a fine as punishment for his misplaced loyalties. Another Bigod, Roger rebuilt the Castle at the end of the 13th Century and it is primarily the ruins of this structure which can be seen today. The Castle is managed by English Heritage and is *open all year, free of charge.*

A network of paths, collectively know as the **Bigod Way** , begin at the Castle. Additionally, the section along the marshes, on the northern banks of the Waveney was well characterised in George Baldry's classic work of Suffolk-Norfolk country lore, *The Rabbit Skin Cap.*

As many people will know, Bungay is a famous printing town. The industry was originally begun in 1795 by John Brightly, a local school master who set up an early wooden press. He was later joined by grocer J.R. Childs, who was to marry Brightly's daughter. For years known as John & R. Childs, the company was later taken over by Richard Clay and the business continues to thrive today being one of the town's foremost employers. Nor should we forget that Bungay was once also an important wherry building centre and William Brighton, considered the most influential builder of these boats, worked from the town. Here he built the unconventional *Albion* which still sails the Broads; unusual in the sense that it was made as a carvel (smooth) rather than as a clinker (overlapping) built hull, probably so that she could navigate the shallow waters between Bungay and Beccles more easily.

**Wherries** were specifically designed for sailing the very shallow Broads and rivers and thus facilitated trade between the coastal and inland towns and villages. To many isolated communities, these boats were their only lifeline with the outside world and their only access to all but the most basic of local commodities. The wherries had to be able to tack in very narrow waters, drop their masts quickly to shoot the countless bridges along these waterways, be man-powered when the winds failed, be capable of negotiating reed beds and of carrying a heavy cargo, anything up to 40 tons, at great speed. Quite a tall order! Inevitably, there was much competition between the various building yards to produce the fastest and most efficient boats. Usually, however, they were about 58 feet in length, with a long, straight keel, and a 40 feet high adjustable mast.

Another Bungay industry is the working of leather sheep skins into clothing; **Nursey & Son Ltd** first began in 1790 and the same family continues this tradition in the town. Their retail outlet can be found at *12 Upper Olland Street (01986 892821)*. Furthermore, Bungay was once a well known weaving centre; until 1855, hemp was grown in the locality and many homes had their own hand looms. Indeed, 'Bungay Canvas' was a highly rated sailcloth.

The Butter Cross marks the town centre and a market is still held here on Thursdays. Its octagonal structure with tuscan columns and arches is surmounted by a dome crowned with a leaden figure of Justice (added in 1754) and was built to replace an earlier structure after the 1688 fire destroyed much of the town. The stocks were also here as was a large cage which held prisoners in the centre of the Cross; this was only removed in 1836. Near the Butter Cross is an electric light standard with a black leaden panel at its top depicting Old Shuck. It commemorates one Sunday in August 1577 when Old Shuck, the terrifying black dog of East Anglia, appeared in St. Mary's Church and wrought his havoc:

*'All down the Church in midst of fire*
*The Hellish monster flew; And passing onwards to the Quire*
*He many people slew.'*

Stories of Old Shuck abound in East Anglia generally and sightings of him are still supposedly common.

Other places to visit include St. Edmund's R.C. Church, built in 1892 and known for its very lavish statuary both inside and out. To the east of St. Mary's Church, known for its splendid buttressed and turreted tower, the ruins of a former 12th Century Benedictine Nunnery founded by Gundrede, wife of Roger de Glanville, can be found. **Bungay Museum** *(01986 892176)*, housed in the Waveney District Council Offices on *Broad Street*, depicts the history of the town mainly by means of old photographs and prints. **Open Monday to Friday.**

*Dutch Gables in Bungay*

*St. Edmund's Church, Bungay*

## Food & Accommodation

**The Chequers Inn** *(01986 893579), Bridge Street Bungay.* A 16th Century pub known especially for its excellent range of real ales and good conversational atmosphere to match. Food is not available Sat. evenings but otherwise all is home-cooked with good summer barbecues. The furnishings are in country style and note some interesting old jugs hanging from the beams.

Of a different bent is *The Otter Trust (01986 893470),* one mile west of the town, at *Earsham.* Here, otters live in conditions as close as possible to their natural habitat. The Centre is *open daily, April to October,* and riverside walks are a further plus. *Admission charge.* Earsham itself is an ancient village with Saxon, Viking and Roman beginnings. In a field opposite All Saints Church, evidence of a Saxon burial ground has been found, and although the oldest parts of the Church are Norman, it is nonetheless thought to have been built upon an earlier Roman encampment. During World War II, Earsham was an important centre for Allied Air Operations - much of the estate lands around here being used for storing bombs and armaments. It is now home to the *Norfolk & Suffolk Aviation Museum,* with its collection of warplanes and associated memorabilia.

Before we leave Bungay and its immediate environs, however, we should add that just north-west of the town is Bath Hills, the slopes of which in Roman times were a mass of vines. Furthermore, a cold-spring, considered as health improving as early as 1730, ensured Bungay achieved a reputation as a spa town long before the likes of even Bath.

# *Walk 9: Bungay and the Bigod Way*

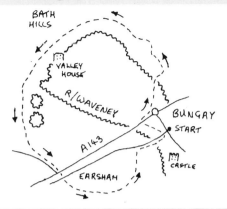

## Directions:

1. From Priory Lane Car Park in the centre of Bungay, continue along Priory Lane as it goes around Castle Orchard. Shortly, you will come across a bridleway on the left and follow this as it runs in front of the Castle. From the bridleway, a footpath leads into a pub yard and on into Earsham Street. From here, go left so as to pass the Post Office, and look out for Outney Road on your right. Follow Outney Road as far as the footbridge. Cross this bridge over the by-pass, and then take the track on your right. This track soon joins a footpath running along the side of a pond. 2. Before long, the path takes you away from the common and onto the marshland (via a kissing gate) and so along part of the Bigod Way across the marsh. Once at the banks of the River Waveney, bear right and so over the River and into Norfolk. 3. Once out of the trees, bear left, eventually going through another kissing gate and so into a meadow and on up a relatively steep hill. From the summit, continue westward, over the valley's top, and on underneath a wooden footbridge. 4. The path joins a farm drive at Bath Hills and now your descent is begun. After Bath House, the track continues through pleasant woodland and on through a gate (note the old ice house on your right). 5. The track continues just above Valley House from where it becomes a metalled road. To begin with the lane winds through some lovely woodland but later on a number of gravel workings somewhat mar the scene (a number of earlier workings though are now ponds which thankfully attract a wide variety of wildlife). 6. Eventually you will reach a road junction. Go left here into Earsham, crossing the main road onto a footpath, and leading into a blocked-off road. Walk past the Post Office and pub, and once again cross the road to a footpath. Turn left at the lane end passing the Church and over the humpback bridge. Continue over the the next footbridge but turn left to walk the Riverbank back to Bungay. 7. Once at the road, turn right at Roaring Arch Bridge, cross another bridge, and take the right turn into Castle Lane. From here take the left turn into Castle Orchard, then Priory Lane and so back to your starting point.

**Start: Priory Lane Car Park, Bungay**
**Approx. Distance: 5 Miles  Approx. Time: 2.5 Hours**
**Map: Landranger: 156**

## The Saints

The Saints, an area just south of the Waveney Valley proper, comprises 13 parishes: St. Mary South Elmham, St. Cross South Elmham, St. Margaret South Elmham, St. Nicholas South Elmham, St. James South Elmham, St. Michael South Elmham, St. Peter South Elmham, All Saints South Elmham, Ilketshall St. Margaret, Ilketshall St. John, Ilketshall St. Andrew, Ilketshall St. Lawrence and last but not least All Saints Mettingham.

This is good walking country - albeit very flat - and this has to be the best way to explore the numerous typical Suffolk farmsteads around here to best advantage. Do carry a map with you though as it is all too easy to lose your bearings in this part of the countryside.

The South Elmhams once formed a deanery in the manor of Almar, Bishop of East Anglia. Close to South Elmham Hall (not open to the public) the Bishops of Norwich once had a summer house, some of the ruins to which can still be seen across the fields. A short distance away though are the accessible remains of South Elmham Minster, dating from the 11th Century. The ruins include elements of the semi-circular apse, an aisleless nave and a tower, and all give off something of a desolate and mysterious air. Some of the churches are also worth a visit especially South Elmham St. Margaret with its 14th Century tower. The nave is crowned by a lovely arch braced roof and the rood loft has also survived. It is clearly a much cared for Church and quite different from the now redundant All Saints (South Elmham). This stands in the middle of a field, next to Church Farm, and is early 13th Century. Look for the huge font bowl standing on a large circular shaft, the Holy Water stoup near the door and two small 15th Century benches with their unusual carved ends including a dog with large floppy ears.

Little of the Ilketshall history is documented but during the 11th Century they are known to have belonged to the Earl of East Anglia, Ulfketle. Do though try the **Cider Place**, *Cherry Tree Farm, Ilketshall St. Lawrence*. This is a small family business which has revived the art of farm cider making. All the ciders and apple juices are produced using original wooden grinding mills and presses all dating from 1864. The cider is then matured in oak barrels for a period of two years. Choose from four different ciders, four apple juices (non-alcoholic), cider vinegar and mead. *Open daily.*

## Food & Accommodation

**The Huntsman & Hounds** *(01986 781341), Stone Street, Spexhall.* A pleasant rural pub with a huge oak beamed ceiling, large inglenook fireplaces and a tiled floor. Good generous food and well kept ales.

# Walk 10: Country Lanes Around The Saints

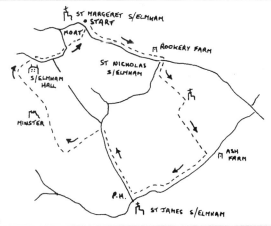

## Directions:

1. From your park at St. Margaret South Elmham Church, continue along the road in a south-easterly direction towards All Saints South Elmham. Just past Rookery Farm (after a mile and a quarter) on your left take the lane on your right (signed St. James). 2. Just after some farm buildings on your right, look for a raised patch of ground on your left leading over the ditch. Go over this keeping left and right round the edge of the field. Once over the next ditch, aim straight across the field in front of you which leads you to a farm track. At the track, go right and keep right of the entrance to Church Farm to get into the church-yard via a little wooden gate. 3. Leave the Church by its main entrance to where you see a footpath signed to your right over the field. At the farm track, bear left heading towards Ash Farm. 4. At the junction with the lane, go right to walk into St. James South Elmham (approx one mile). Continue along the lane through the village passing the church on your left, a pub on your right, and taking Mill Lane with its unusual circular brick building in the grounds on your left, past two public footpath signs on your left and past a concrete parking area with its old pill box. 5. Just before you come to a lane on your right after approx. one and a half miles (signed St. Nicholas South Elmham) take a grassy track on your left with a small pond now on your right. Continue along here and then beside the edge of a field to a group of derelict farm buildings. Keeping those buildings to the right, look for a stile in front of you and just to the right of a metal gate. 6. Once over the stile go right along the edge of a field and then aim diagonally left to a gate with three oak trees guarding the way. Once at the pond on your right continue through the next meadow, the beck (a tributary of the River Waveney) on your left. 7. Once through the next gate go immediate left over a little bridge across the beck and then bear right to pass the remains of the 11th Century Saxon South Elmham St. Cross Minster on your left. 8. Continue straight across the meadow the beck now on your right to a stile and gate. Once over the stile head down to the beck on your right and follow this straight ahead to anoth-er stile at the bottom right hand corner of the meadow. Go over the

footbridge and follow the red marker leading right, over the edge of a field. By the side of South Elmham Hall, note the scanty remains of the former Bishop's Palace. 9. At the lane, go right and then round to the left. Ignore the next right hand turn to St. James and follow the road round to the left. Immediately after a commercial orchard on your right, follow the public footpath on your right leading to a group of farm buildings. Go through the next gate and keep left of these buildings onto a drive. With the house on your right, look for a small gate on your left which leads diagonally right over a grazing area to a small stile and on to another small gate into the churchyard and so your starting point.

**Start: St. Margaret South Elmham Church**
**Approx. Distance: 6.5 Miles**
**Approx. Time: 2.5 Hours**
**Map: Landranger 156**

# Halesworth

Although situated on a tributary of the River Blythe, Halesworth is a busy market town not easily slotted into a distinctive area of Suffolk and as such not truly forming part of the Waveney Valley. There is not a huge amount to see here but what there is includes the late 17th Century Cary Almshouses which house the *Halesworth Museum* with its collection of local bygones and archaeology. *Open variously during the summer months.* Just east of the town is *Holton Post Mill* built in 1749 but no longer working; *open late spring and summer Bank Holidays.* A couple of miles just south-west of Halesworth is a real little treat in *Walpole Old Chapel.* Originally built in 1607 as a Congregational Church it was adapted as a Chapel in 1647. Inside, all the old pews, galleries and pulpit have been retained (access details are posted on the door).

*Chediston*, just west of Halesworth, enjoys a long history which can be be documented as far as back to Roman times. The old Hall which once occupied most of the parish was demolished in 1950 following a fire and a new building was erected in its place in 1960. Of greater interest perhaps is Chediston Grange, a 13th Century moated site, and until relatively recently the home of Harry Burroughs. Burroughs' Suffolk Punches together with his large collection of horse drawn agricultural implements were clearly featured in the writings of George Ewart Evans in the likes of *The Pattern Under The Plough.*

# Mendham

Back to the Waveney Valley proper now in Mendham and a good spot from which to explore the extensive marshes and wet meadows which hug this stretch of the River. It was also the home of Sir Alfred Munnings (1878 - 1959), born at the Mill, which ceased to operate in 1938. The Mill itself is now a private home but the lands around it now form a trout fishery. Munnings first studio was in the main street and his painting *Charlotte and her pony* was used as the inspiration behind Mendham's own welcoming sign. A specialist in the painting of horses, Munnings became President of the Royal Academy in 1944 and today his work hangs in most major galleries as it does at Dedham, his latter day home.

## Food & Accommodation

**Sir Alfred Munnings Country Hotel** *(01379 852358), Studio Corner, Mendham.* As is only right, prints of Munnings work decorate the walls of this spacious and comfortable 16th Century freehouse and restaurant. The atmosphere here is cheery, the ales well kept, and the bar food good. Some of the bedrooms have exposed beams, most are ensuite and all are characterful.

Henry Cabell at least in his formative years was a much less illustrious son. A convicted thief he was transported to Sydney Cove, Australia, being reputedly the first Englishman to set foot there having carried the ship's captain ashore. Nonetheless he went on to become a prosperous man, well respected by his new 'colonial' community.

## *Walk 11: Mendham Marshes*

### *Directions:*

1. From your start at Mendham Church, walk along the quiet lane heading east out of the village. Go straight over the crossroads, up hill looking for a path on your left. 2. Turn left along the track leading to a cottage, and just before the cottage go through a gate to cross a meadow diagonally right. Just after a pond go left through more farm gates aiming for a point to the right of Walsham Hall. 3. At the road, go right to pass Oakhill Farm and then Laurel Farm and a little further on go right into a field. Continue along the field edge to go through gates, keeping Moat Farm on your left. Follow the farm track down the lane. 4. At the lane, go right for approx. 15 yards and then left along a path over the field bearing diagonally right. You should be mid way between Botwrights Farm on your right and Kett's Farm on your left. Join a farm track and continue straight ahead to a lane. 5. Cross straight over the lane and walk along there for approx. half a mile until you join the B1123. Go right at the road to walk through Withersdale Street. Follow the road round to the right and just before the drive to Mendham Priory Farm on your left, go right along a wide track leading down to Mendham Marshes. 6. At the end of this, bear right along a narrower track and follow this path left and right over the marsh-

to a point close to the River Waveney. Where the River bends sharp left follow the path over to the right following a ditch. Keep on this as it swings round to the left and so into Mendham churchyard.

**Start: Mendham Church**
**Approx. Distance: 5 Miles**
**Approx. Time: 2 Hours**
**Map: Landranger 156**

# Wingfield

A little further south sees us in the straggling village of Wingfield now home to an excellent Arts & Music Festival. Throughout the 14th and 15th Centuries, the de la Pole's, Earls and Dukes of Suffolk, were one of the most powerful families in the country. Wingfield Castle (not open to the public), their home, and in reality a fortified house, was built by the 2nd Earl, the license to crenellate being granted in 1384. The original three-storey Gatehouse with its polygonal turrets has survived but the part timber-framed house behind is Tudor. Nonetheless it stands proud and isolated against the sprawling village green.

## Food & Accommodation

**The Fox & Goose** *(01379 586247), Fressingfield, near Wingfield.* A long established restaurant with a truly convivial country pub feel, and one which formerly housed a Guildhall; hence the fine timbers which are still evident. The menu is both international and modern eclectic so don't be surprised to see the likes of fish and chips, caviar, crispy Peking Duck and stewed rabbit on offer at the same time but all of it is excellent.

St. Andrew's Church, nearer the village proper, was built in 1362 as the collegiate church of Sir John de Wingfield's College next door. It houses a number of monuments to the de la Pole family. *Wingfield College (01379 384505)*, a superb timbered Hall, was until 1534 a college for priests. Hidden behind a Georgian facade for over two centuries, it was restored during the 1980's by Ian Chance. It is now host to a regular programme of concerts and recitals - Wingfield Arts and Music - as also a collection of prints, textiles and a working press. *Open variously Easter to September.*

*Wingfield College*

# Laxfield

A little to the south, Laxfield is perhaps best known as the birthplace of Cromwell's henchman William Dowsing (1596-1679), the destroyer of vast quantities of church ornament and decoration. In 1644 alone, he purged over 150 Suffolk churches of their popish relics - brasses, paintings and stained glass. He does appear to have found some clemency though for his own parish, All Saints still retaining its fine screen and font.

*The East of England Birds of Prey Conservation Centre* (01986 798844) can be found at St. Jacob's Hall in the village, its aim being to provide a true reflection of the role birds of prey play in their own natural environment. You can either wander around the avaries, take a stroll through the woodland site, or catch one of three daily flying displays. Species you are likely to encounter include the snowy owl, the bateleur eagle, and the ferruginous buzzard. *Open daily. Admission charge.*

## Food & Accommodation

**The King's Head** *(01986 798395), Laxfield.* Known locally as the Low House, this thatched Tudor pub has changed little since Victorian times. There is no bar and instead you are served straight from casks in the back room. Simply furnished with high backed settles and pews and warmed by open fires it is at once charming and cosy.

# Hoxne

Situated along the banks of the River Waveney just east of Eye and Diss, Hoxne (pronounced Hoxon) has an attractive village centre with some timber-framed and thatched properties. Note also Mulberry Cottage built in typical 19th Century Suffolk style - barn shaped and with tall chimneys. In the Church of St. Peter & St. Paul are a number of medieval wall paintings including those of the Seven Deadly Sins and the Seven Works of Mercy.

The village is however best known for both its affiliations to St. Edmund and for the incredible hoard of Roman treasure unearthed in a field close to the village in 1992. The find included around 15,000 gold and silver coins together with a wealth of other precious objects.

Abbey Farm just to the south of the village is reputedly the site of King Edmund's death in 869/870 AD (see the Bury St. Edmunds Chapter for further details). Legend tells that he was betrayed by a couple as they crossed Goldbrook Bridge on their way to be married. Edmund was subsequently caught by the Danes and slain by a volley of arrows. A Benedictine Priory on the site of the current Abbey Farmhouse was later founded to commemorate the King by that time canonised as St. Edmund.

If time permits visit *Goldbrook Plants* (01379 668770), *Hoxne,* a specialist nursery known for their large collection of foliage shrubs and hardy plants especially Hostas and Hemerocallis. They also hold the National Collection of Astrantia and Water Iris. *Open Wednesday to Sunday.*

## Food & Accommodation

**The Swan** *(01379 668275)*, Hoxne. A Grade II listed former coaching inn where its 15th Century interior is still obvious - oak beams and floors and large inglenooks. Two solid oak counters form the front bar; there is also a back bar with a snug. Good, reasonably priced food and good Suffolk real ales.

# Eye

The name Eye is derived from the Saxon *Aye* meaning island and the town originally surrounded by water. At one time the small River Dove would even have been navigable through a network of other rivers as far as Cromer on the Norfolk coast but today seems content to find its confluence with the River Waveney. A thriving market town in the mid 1800's, important for its lace, corsetry and shoemaking industries as also for its flaxworks and breweries, decline followed swiftly and by the mid 19th Century, the main railway station having been moved to Diss, Eye became little more than the quiet but serene backwater it is today.

Reminding us of the town's former prosperity are the scanty remains of the Malets Norman Castle (the family also established a Benedictine Priory here), the 16th Century timber-framed Guildhall near the Church with its upper oriels and carved sills, and the majestic Church of St. Peter and St. Paul. You cannot miss the extraordinary 101 feet high flushwork flint tower of the latter with its frieze and shields at the base, nor indeed the two-storeyed porch against which rests a 'dole' table once used for distributing bread to the parishes poor each Saturday. Note also the striking rood screen with its triple cornice, dating from 1480; this was restored in 1925 but the painted figures are original. A wander around Eye will also reveal several fine serpentine, crinkle-crankle walls, a method of building which is peculiar to Suffolk.

**Sir Frederick Ashton** (1904 -), the English dancer and choreographer has spent many of his later years at Chandos Lodge, Eye. Variously choreographer to Sadlers Wells Ballet and Director of the Royal Ballet, Ashton is responsible for many superb creations not least *Cinderella*(1948) and *A Month in the Country* (1976). Extending this genius to his own garden, Ashton created something of a geometric ballet, shaping his box and yew hedges into the likes of balls, pyramids and skittles.

A few miles south-east of Eye is the moated and Elizabethan farmhouse of *Tannington Hall* *(01728 628226)*. Here, you can take a horse drawn carriage drive from their own stables and which includes lunch or supper at the Hall or indeed at the King's Head in Laxfield; the owners collection of horse drawn vehicles is also on show. And at Stradbroke, a few miles east you can find potter **Robin Welch** *(01379 384416)*. Known for his coiled and thrown stoneware, the unusual shapes enhanced by subtle and repeated glazing, Welch's work is included in major museum collections throughout the world. *You must phone first to check if a visit is convenient.*

# Food & Accommodation

**The Oaksmere** *(01379 870326), Brome, Near Eye.* A straight tree-lined drive leads to this comfortable and friendly hotel which belongs to the Waveney Inns Group. Partly 16th Century and partly half-timbered, the building sits amidst a splendid box and yew topiary garden. Antiques enhance the interior much of it given over to business use though not so the conservatory, elements of which are 18th Century, and which retains its antique vine and a super tiled floor, nor the low-ceilinged Tudor bar. The bedrooms blend together a sympathetic mix of antiques - some have four posters - and modern fixtures and fittings.

**The Black Horse Inn & Stables Restaurant** *(01379 678523), The Street, Thorndon.* Innovative, good quality food is the key to this establishments success. The restaurant is a converted stable and the seating arrangements make use of the original stalls. The inn itself is a 16th Century freehouse and in the timbered bar area is a 42 feet deep well, thankfully covered by reinforced glass. It is a warm and convivial place and occasionally you may even find yourself entertained by a local troupe of Morris dancers.

**The Four Horseshoes** *(01379 678168), Wickham Road, Thornham Magna.* Thought to be 12th Century in origin with mud and daub walls, this thatched and low beamed pub is a busy and lively place. Good value food and good ales. Accommodation is also available.

**The Old Guildhall** *(01379 783361), Mill Street, Gislingham, near Eye.* This 15th Century thatched and pink-washed Guildhall was once the centre of local government but is now a small hotel offering all the comforts of the 20th Century. A traditional atmosphere pervades helped by low beamed ceilings, open-timbered partitions, open fires and appropriately chosen furnishings. The restaurant is also geared towards traditional English fare but all of it to a steady standard.

The tiny Church of St. Mary's at nearby *Thornham Parva* is a must for not only is it one of few thatched churches to survive but it is especially noted for its retable or altarpiece. It depicts nine brightly painted panels, eight saints including St. Edmund and the Crucifixion. Thought to have been the work of a royal workshop, it dates from the early 14th Century but was only re-discovered in the stables of Thornham Hall in 1927. It is rightly considered one of the greatest treasures to be held by a parish church.

At nearby *Thornham Magna* is a 2,500 acre estate of farmland, wetland and ancient woodland, worked by the *Thornham Field Centre (01379 838153)*. There are some fine walks to be enjoyed around here and unusually the *access for disabled visitors is good.*

# Diss

Just inside the Norfolk border now and to Diss where the older part of town can be found around Diss Market Place and Mere, the latter a six-acre lake and a haven for wildfowl; the fishing here is reputedly good. The name Diss is thought to derive from the Anglo-Saxon *dice*, meaning standing water. Many period buildings, part-timbered and with jettied upper-storeys, can be found in or near the Market Place. Perhaps the most interesting is the half-timbered Dolphin Inn with its overhangs. A number of fine Georgian buildings are also evident as is the Corn Exchange of 1854 and the Maltings built for Lacon's Brewery in 1788. The early 14th Century tower of St. Mary's Church is sur-mounted by a lantern and arches on either side. John Skelton, poet laureate dur-ing Henry VIII's reign, was the rector here; during one difficult period during his career, he was forced to take refuge from his enemies in Westminster Abbey.

Market Day at Diss is on Friday, and early closing Tuesday. *Auctions*, managed by *Thos. Gaze & Son (01379 650306)* are also held on Fridays. On Park Road, on the A1066, near Diss town centre, you can find the Water Garden and Aquarium Centre of *Waveney Fish Farm (01379 642697)*. Hardy water lilies, floating and aquatic plants together with moisture loving shrubs and alpines are their speciality. *Open daily.*

A few miles south-east of Diss is *Billingford* tower *Cornmill*. *Open daily* and keys are available from the Horseshoes Pub. If you do visit the Mill, also take a look at the interesting, early 14th Century wall paintings high on the south wall of St. Leonard's Church. Good views of the Waveney Valley can be had from

*Thelnetham Windmill*

the churchyard. Just able to count itself as part of Suffolk **Thelnetham Windmill**, west of Diss, is one of only four tower mills still to be found in the county. Built in 1819-20 of red brick but tarred to prevent the rain from getting in it is a four-storey structure with conical cap and powered by four huge sails. Restored by a group of enthusiasts, It is usually *open at weekends* and still grinds corn, wind permitting. Stone ground flour and other grain products can be bought on site.

Just south of here is **Wattisfield** which cannot be separated from its associations with pottery manufacture, from the Iron Age through Roman occupation until the present day. Particularly in Roman times, this part of Suffolk was dotted about with groups of kilns, approximately 25 of them being found on just one belt at Foxledge Common, and another unearthed at the village itself and now preserved in **Henry Watson's Potteries Ltd**, *(01359 251239)*. Watson's originally established during the 1800's have continued this tradition and are specialists in kitchenware, known for their 'Suffolk Collection' of terracotta storage jars. Their shop in the village is *open Monday to Saturday.*

West of Diss sees us in **Bressingham** (Norfolk), known principally for its large garden and nursery, **Blooms of Bressingham** *(01379 688133)*. Begun by horticulturalist Alan Bloom, he and his family have created an informal, bedded collection of over 5,000 species of hardy perennials, heathers and conifers. *The nursery, open daily,* adjoins the garden, and Blooms have achieved high regard as growers and suppliers to the retail trade.

In addition, Blooms also own and operate the **Bressingham Steam Museum** *(01379 687386)* within their own grounds. More than 50 engines and roundabouts are on display in the Exhibition Hall, including a model of the famous *Pacific Type 4-6-2*. A narrow-gauge, steam hauled train runs through the grounds enabling visitors easy access to these enviable gardens. *Open daily, April to September and with reduced opening times during October. Admission charge.*

**Redgrave** village marks Suffolk's northern most boundary and is the point where the Rivers Waveney and Little Ouse meet. **Redgrave and Lopham Fen**, our purpose here, is primarily comprised of a large sedge and reed bed around which runs a boardwalk.

Finally, further west to **Garboldisham**, where many of the houses are built from clay lump - large blocks of unfired clay, laid on top of each other. It is reputed to last for centuries, provided it is kept very dry (pretty difficult with this country's climate). Additionally, there are several unopened tumuli near the village, and an earthwork, known as the Devil's Dyke, which runs for approximately two miles on the west side of the parish; it is thought to have been built for defensive purposes by one or other of our distant ancestors.

# *Food & Accommodation*

**Salisbury House** *(01379 644738), Victoria Road, Diss,* is a privately owned restaurant with limited but homely bedroom accommodation. It was originally built as a store for the nearby windmill, and only its facade is Victorian. The menu at this popular venue changes regularly to take advantage of seasonal produce, and additionally an extensive range of wines is offered.

**The Old Rectory** *(01379 677575), Gissing, near Diss,* is a private home offering B & B styled accommodation. The Old Rectory is a spacious and well-furnished Victorian building standing in three acres of garden and woodland. Personal touches in the bedrooms and bathrooms are very welcoming. Dinner is usually available on Friday and Saturday, and only by prior arrangement.

**Strenneth Farmhouse** *(01379 688182), Fersfield, near Diss.* An old brick built farmhouse offering B & B accommodation in a remote but peaceful setting (do not be put off by the motley collection of farm buildings around it). Un-even floors, beams and low ceilings abound. The bedrooms are well furnished, and the good no-choice dinners are optional.

**Scole Inn** *(01379 740481), Scole, near Diss.* Although Scole itself is not the nicest of places, the Inn itself is well worth a visit. Originally built for a wealthy wool merchant in 1655, its Dutch gabled front is most dignified. A Grade I listed building, it still boasts weathered timbers, leaded windows and beamed fireplaces. In his hurry to escape the law, highwayman John Belcher would regularly ride his horse up the huge oak staircase here. In some of the bedrooms in the main building, antique furniture - tester and half-tester beds - is very much in evidence. If you are staying, try to avoid those bedrooms in the converted Georgian stables as they are smaller and lacking in character when compared to the rest. Choose from a good range of bar food or the separate restaurant.

**Garden House** *(01379 687405), Thetford Road, Bressingham, near Diss.* Dating from the 16th Century, this rambling old pub oozes with charm, not least because of its thatched roof and multitude of timbers. Good food and traditional ales complete the picture.

# High Suffolk

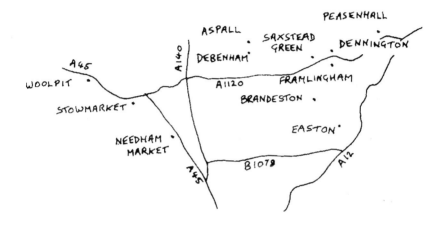

High Suffolk or mid Suffolk is that area of the county traditionally considered its agricultural heartland. Such prowess is not to be disputed, high crop yields being little more than confirmation of the fertility of these prairie-like open fields which so dominate the landscape hereabouts. We begin our tour of this area in the market town of Stowmarket before moving slightly north to Woolpit, known for its former brick manufacturing industry. We then take an easterly course through the rest of this centrality generally following the line of the A1120 through Earl Stonham, Earl Soham, Saxtead Green, just south to Framlingham and then back again to our route via Peasenhall.

## Stowmarket

Whilst the busy market town of Stowmarket was once known for its successful woollen industry, today its main manufacturing base is comprised of chemicals and agricultural implements. Again, where hops were once grown in the valley, the emphasis now has shifted to barley, an equally important ingredient for the brewing industry. That Stowmarket remained a successful commercial centre through the 18th and 19th Centuries is attributable in great part to the canalisation of the River Gipping (1793) facilitating the movement of goods direct to Ipswich and, thereafter, via the railway which arrived in 1849.

The main purpose of our visit though is *The Museum of East Anglian Life (01449 612229), Abbot's Hall,* which covers the agricultural, social and industrial history of the region. Most of the exhibits are housed in a collection of buildings ranging from a 14th Century farmhouse, 18th Century timber-framed smithy to an 18th Century watermill and 19th Century drainage mill. The oldest of all though is Abbot's Hall Barn with its 13th Century origins. It is a superb site housing an incredible array of items, anything from a Thetford built Burrell steam engine to the perhaps more manageable Suffolk Punch Horse. *Open daily, Easter to October. Admission charge.*

A museum of a different kind can be found at nearby *Cotton,* namely *The Mechanical Music Museum (01449 781354).* Here an interesting collection of mechanical music exhibits including street pianos, pianolas, musical boxes, polyphones, fairground organs, reed and barrel organs and even a Wurlitzer and a musical chair can be seen. Occasional concerts are also held in a building designed along the lines of a 1930's cinema. *Open Sundays, June to September. Admission charge.*

Also of a musical bent is the barrel organ to be found in King Charles the Martyr Church, *Shelland,* three miles west of Stowmarket. Made in 1810 and comprised of three barrels each with 12 tunes - and which somehow provides a total of 250 hymns to choose from - the organ is still used for regular services. Other unusual features include box pews, a triple decker pulpit and wig stand.

*Combs Wood,* just south-east of the town is a particular beauty spot in spring when wood anemone and oxlip (a strong feature of mid Suffolk flora) seem to

**Windpump at the Museum of East Anglian Life, Stowmarket**

carpet the ground. Managed by the Suffolk Wildlife Trust, the wood is principally known for its rare hawfinch which breeds here.

The village of *Combs* also has an interesting history not least because of the Tannery begun by the Irish Denny family in 1711, and although it later changed hands the operation continued until as late as 1900. During the Crimean War, leather was sent to Russia to equip, ironically enough, both armies in boots and another export, this time to Egypt, were the elephant hides known as 'gin' leather. This was also the first operation to use the new method of bark for tanning. Finally to St. Mary's Church to see some fine medieval glass which survived an 1871 explosion at the Tannery. Principal amongst these are those windows which depict the life of St. Margaret, the Seven Works of Mercy, and the Tree of Jesse.

An important market town in the Middle Ages nearby *Haughley* today is an attractive village with scanty evidence of a motte and bailey castle; this timber castle is no longer but the village pond once formed part of the moat surrounding it. Today the village is home to New Bells Farm, the pioneering research centre belonging to the Soil Association.

There must indeed be something in the soil here for at *Haughley Park* (01359 240205) we have the chance to enjoy over 150 acres of park and woodland, parts of which are carpeted with bluebell and lily of the valley. Nearer the Jacobean mansion they surround, are some unexpectedly 'secret' gardens edged by clipped hedge or brick and flint walls and behind which hide immaculate flower beds, shrubs and climbers; each independent area enjoying its own peculiar character. There is also a kitchen garden and some especially fine trees to look out for: an oak with a girth of 30 feet and said to be over 1,000 years old as well as a magnolia 40 feet wide. *The House and Gardens are open on Tuesdays, May to September. Admission charge.*

## Food & Accommodation

**The Brewers Arms** (01449 736377), Rattlesdon, near Stowmarket. A welcoming atmosphere can be found in this 16th Century pub tucked away in a quiet hamlet. Refurbished in recent years, much care has gone into its decoration, and to be expected the ales are well kept and the excellent menu changed daily.

**Cherry Tree Farm** (01449 766376), Mendlesham Green, Near Stowmarket. A quiet, rural setting awaits guests to this B & B establishment. The building itself is 15th Century in origin and its structure timber-framed. Exposed beams and an inglenook fireplace make the dining room a cosy place and the bedrooms are well furnished with occasional antiques.

**The Trowel & Hammer** (01449 781234), Mill Road, Cotton, near Stowmarket. A steady and pretty pub with a relaxing atmosphere. Exposed beams, an open fire and wood burning stove make it all the more comfortable. Generous food - English and an extensive choice of Greek dishes - and good Suffolk ale.

# *Woolpit*

Now to Woolpit which is supposed to derive its name from the wolves which once scavaged the lands about here and indeed the last wolf in England is said to have been killed in a pit close to the village. What pits remain today, however, are of the vast brick quarries from which the Woolpit brick was sourced during the 17th Century through to the mid 20th Century. A grey, whitish-brown in colour and composed of gault clay these bricks found there way into a considerable amount of 19th Century west Suffolk and Cambridgeshire architecture. They were also employed in the building of America's Presidential home, The White House.

The village itself is mainly Georgian with some timber-framed and plastered buildings, and with a covered waterpump in its square commemorating Queen Victoria's Diamond Jubilee. St. Mary's Church with its spectacular Victorian spire and a magnificent south porch stands as a proud backdrop. Although its whereabouts are unknown, many medieval documents refer to the Chapel of Our Lady of Woolpit, and water analysed within the reputed vicinity is said to be of an unusual mineral composition. In any case, pilgrims on their way to Walsingham are recorded as using Woolpit as a stopping place on their journey northwards.

Legend in these parts tells of two green children, a boy and a girl, who came up through a hole in a field at harvest time having been attracted by the sound of Woolpit's church bells. Taken to the home of a wealthy local man, Sir Richard de Calne, they would in the first instance only eat greens. Bit by bit, this was supplemented by meat and bread with the net effect that their general green hue was lost. Shortly afterwards, the boy died but the girl was baptised, married and had children. She later told how she originated from St. Martin's Land, a country of perpetual twilight to be found beyond a great river, and that the two of them had followed the ringing bells only to lose their way home!

*Woolpit Bygones Museum* (01359 240822), *The Institute, Woolpit* houses a special exhibition documenting the 400 hundred year old history of the Woolpit brick-making industry, and at a nearby farm the Museum's *Farming in a Suffolk Village* section can also be found. **Open weekends, Easter to September.**

## *Food & Accommodation*

**The Gardeners Arms** (01359 270460), *Church Road, Tostock, near Woolpit.* Found on the edge of the green, The Gardeners Arms has a history dating back over 600 years. The comfortable lounge bar has a magnificent fireplace which stretches almost across the entire length of the wall as also low beams. The public bar makes use of church pews and a tiled stone floor. Very well kept ales and good home made food make it a popular venue. The pub also has its own quoits team, so you may well catch them at play in the garden area.

# Needham Market

The River Gipping which rises a little beyond Stowmarket runs just to the east of Needham Market and the attractive Gipping Valley Pathway now marks its eastern banks. The lake off the River is a conservation area yet also finds a variety of other uses from fishing to windsurfing. Walking south along the River bank you will pass a handful of interesting buildings - Bosmere Hall, the timber-framed Pipps Ford (see below) and Baylham Mill. Back in the town centre a number of Tudor buildings can be found, and from here we go to St. John the Baptist's Church to see a spectacular hammerbeam roof complete with angels, their wings spread out in glorious adoration. As Pevsner says, '... *the eye scarcely believes what it sees.*' (*Suffolk* in the Buildings of England series, 2nd Ed. 1971).

**Joseph Priestley** (1773-1804) was the minister for the Congregational Church in 1757. Also a noted pioneer in the chemistry of gases he wrote his *History of Electricity* in 1767 and was one of the principal discoverer's of oxygen. Often branded an atheist, and his later Birmingham home destroyed by the mob for his his contentious reply to Burke's *Reflections on the French Revolution*, he finally moved to America in 1794 where he was at last well received.

Often disregarded in favour of the better known Orwell, Deben and Stour, the beauty of the River Gipping is unmistakable. A view shared by many, it is perhaps best recorded in an extract of verse by the poet Elizabeth Cobbold (1767-1824):

> *'... What tho' thy neighbour Orwell boast*
> *His variegated length of coast,*
> *His busy trade and shipping;*
> *Tell him that happiness may 'stray*
> *Where pomp could never find the way,*
> *And glide thro' vales with Gipping.*
>
> *No envious sande thy course perplex,*
> *No howling storms thy waters vex,*
> *Their shores of verdure stripping;*
> *They peaceful streams translucent glide.*
> *While Flow'rets bend on either side*
> *To view themselves in Gipping.'*

At nearby **Creeting St. Mary** ice cream lovers will find a real treat in store at **Aldar Carr Farm Shop** *(01449 720820), Aldar Carr Farm.* Here you can chose from over 12 flavours of home-made ice cream much of it flavoured by soft fruit grown on the farm itself. Tayberry is simply delicious but more unusual varieties can also be tried including spicy apple, gooseberry and elderflower, and in the festive season there is even a Christmas pudding flavour. Home-made jams are also available.

Alternatively, why not try **James White Apple Juice & Cider Co.** *(01473 890111)*, *The Farm Shop, Helmingham Road, Ashbocking,* who produce a range of bottled fresh English apple juices from the dry and crisp Bramley to the flowery sweet Russet. English pear and grape juices, cider vinegar and a range of ciders made from a mix of cooking and eating apples are also available.

Food lovers should also try **Stonham Hedgerow Products** *(01449 760482)*, *Hemingstone Fruitique, Main Road, Hemingstone,* where an incredible range of home-made jams, jellies, marmalades and chutneys can be bought including a powerful Suffolk Chutney made from a mix of apple, treacle, mustard and curry powder.

## Food & Accommodation

**Pipps Ford** *(01449 760208), Needham Market.* An attractive part-timbered Tudor farmhouse in a pretty and rural setting and offering warm and friendly accommodation. Beamed ceilings, inglenooks and uneven floors make it a characterful place to stay. The food is good quality and unless you state otherwise the assumption is that you will dine here. Unusually, **the hotel is well geared up for disabled visitors with four groundfloor bedrooms and one especially equipped.** Wheelchair access to the hotel (one step)

**Mr. Underhill's** *(01449 711206), Stonham, near Needham Market.* If you are prepared to help the owners agree your menu in advance then you will enjoy some excellent food here. The only subsequent choice you can make is from a selection of desserts. Don't be put off by this slightly odd way of doing things as it does work well and the end result is very stylish. There is also an excellent choice of wines.

Beginning our journey eastwards, basically along the line of the A1120, a couple of interesting churches should first be mentioned. First to St. Mary's at *Earl Stonham* with its splendid chestnut hammerbeam roof. Of 15th Century origin, its carvings depict angels, apostles and saints alternating with carved pendant bosses. Note also the remains of some ancient wall paintings, amongst them the Martyrdom of St. Thomas a Becket and the Adoration of the Maji, and also look for the triple hourglass.

Next to All Saints *Crowfield* where the Church stands just a mile outside the village. It is basically a 14th Century flint and wood building with a 15th Century panelled porch and chancel, the only such chancel in Suffolk. The poppyhead carvings on the bench pews, with matching work in the choir stalls, are especially interesting, depicting as they do a wide range of fruit and foliage - from apples to hops to strawberries, beech and maple leaves.

At *Helmingham Hall* *(01473 890363)*, just to the south west of the main road, we find the home of Lord & Lady Tollemache, of Tolly Ales Brewery fame, begun in 1886. The Tollemache's are, however, one of those few ancient families that have lived in Suffolk continuously since the Middle Ages. The Hall, not open

*All Saints Church, Crowfield*

to the public, is a moated Elizabethan mansion but it provides a perfect back-drop for the gardens which are accessible. The latter are renowned for their herbaceous borders, old fashioned roses, an Elizabethan kitchen garden, and the more recent knot and herb garden. *Open Sunday afternoons from the end of April to the beginning of September. Admission charge.* The facilities also include a gift shop, farm shop and afternoon teas in the Old Coach House.

# Debenham

Debenham, just north of our route, is an unspoilt village close to the banks of the River Deben. The alkaline soils around here produce some of the world's largest yields of wheat and barley. And thanks to a farm labourer who planted seeds from an unusually large ear of barley he had noticed one day in 1820, the Chevallier strain was born (Chevallier the landlord though and not the labourer). Only in fairly recent years has this strain been superseded by varieties which are genetically engineered.

Another enterprise was begun in 1650 by cordwainer Timothy Abbot. The business was obviously successful for at the turn of the following century his descendent's purchased the local grocery shop which still thrives in the village today. Another thriving enterprise is *Carters Ceramic Designs (01728 860475), Low Road, Debenham,* where Tony Carter produces his highly distinctive and collectible tea-pots. *The pottery and shop is open throughout the week, excluding Sundays.*

Practical Debenham businessmen have not it seems been in short supply for another former resident was responsible for the chain of High Street stores

87

which bear the village's name. Talking of shops, Angus McBean (1904-1990), photographer of the rich and famous and credited with 'finding' Audrey Hepburn, once lived above an antique shop in the village. Although many of his surreal like images can be seen in the National Portrait Gallery, London, the majority have found their way into Harvard University's collection.

Debenham has clearly been a prosperous place through the ages, witness for example the 33 dwellings destroyed by fire in 1744. As for St. Mary's Church, it has retained two of its Anglo-Saxon windows, its massive rood beam, and is renowned for its fine bells originally cast in 1761 and re-hung on ball bearings in 1932. Some incredible changes have been rung on these bells and perhaps most extravagantly in 1890 when two changes - one of 5040 and the other of 5056 - were rung in little more than three hours.

> **Richard Hakluyt** (?1552-1616), the geographer and rector, once lived in the nearby hamlet of Wetheringsett where he is said to have written probably his most important work *Principal Navigations, Voyages and Discoveries of the English Nation* (1589). Other important works by Hakluyt include *Divers Voyages Touching the Discovery of America* (1582) and his introduction of globes into English schools. In 1602 he was made a prebendary of Westminster and 14 years later he was buried in Westminster Abbey.

Just south-east of Debenham is Crowes Hall, once a fine moated mansion built in the early 1500's but all that remains today is part of the Gatehouse and a significant part of the North Wing. Nonetheless it is typical of the many moated properties to be found in Suffolk and especially in this part of the county. A number of factors account for their frequency and perhaps most obviously, with the land so flat, they provided an invaluable defence against unwelcome intruders and invaders. They also acted as stew ponds, carp and other fish being bred specifically for the owner's dinner table. Additionally, these moats were an essential ingredient for good land drainage. A homestead built on an island surrounded by a moat ensured the site was well drained; such solid groundworks were pre-requisite given the flatness of the prevailing countryside.

*Aspall*, a little to the north of Debenham, is something of a straggling lost village in remote countryside. The Jacobean Hall with its Queen Anne front chequered with red bricks and dark blue headers is a typically moated edifice complete with the stew ponds we have just outlined, as also a pigeon loft. It is still owned by the Chevallier family known not only for the strain of barley they cultivated but also for their introduction of cider to this part of the county. As French Huguenot refugees, they left their Normandy home for Suffolk bringing their cider mill with them. The mill, thought to date from the mid 1000's can still be seen - a simple granite trough round which rolls a huge stone wheel - although it is understandably no longer used. Cider is still made by *Aspall Cider* (01728 860510), *Cyder House* where the press room can also be visited. *Open daily Monday to Friday.*

**Cider** has been produced in Suffolk for well over 900 years and although it was once a much more common refreshment than currently, increased consumption has nevertheless been a feature of the 1990's. The introduction of beer in the 18th Century contributed to much early decline but then the 19th and 20th Centuries saw increased local farm production destined for the labourers working the hay and harvest fields. This practice died out after the two World Wars, but more recently our penchant for the unusual and the locally made has seen something of a cider revival.

## The Deben Valley

The valleys of the Deben are so lush and beautiful that it is worth spending a couple of leisurely afternoons enjoying the peace and tranquillity they afford. To this end the two walks which follow also take in some extraordinarily attractive villages, further endowed by good pubs, and what better way to extend any visit than this!

## Walk 12: Brandeston and Cretingham

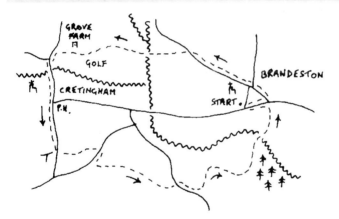

### Directions:

1. From your park near Brandeston Church, walk along the road heading east towards Kettleburgh. Take the second lane on your left (not the one near the Church) and walk along this lane towards Earl Soham. Just after a track on you right leading to West Hill Farm, look for a stile and path on your left which skirts the northern fringe of a small road. 2. Continue along the path as it leads through another wood and out onto a golf course. Bear left towards the Clubhouse and keep the office on your right to walk through the car park to a track leading to Grove Farm House. 3. Once at the road, keep left and then left again at the next junction to go through Cretingham. Go past the Church on your right to a junction, and here go straight across. 4. Take the footpath on the left near a telephone box and walk across fields to get to another lane. Turn right here and after a short distance look for a path on your left leading across a field. 5. Continue across the fields to a farmhouse where you follow the track round to your left.

89

At the next lane go right and after a short while take a path on your left. At the second field, go sharp right after crossing a stile and onto a small wood. Keep left here to follow the path along the woods western fringe, over the River Deben and back to Brandeston. 6. Turn left at the road to return to the Church.

**Start: Brandeston Church**
**Approx. Distance: 5.5 Miles**
**Approx. Time: 2.5 Hours**
**Map: Landranger 156**

Following the Deben south sees us to *Easton* and although Easton Hall is no longer, the grounds are still surrounded by the longest ribbon wall in the county and that using the crinkle-crankle technique. Although small and spread out it is a picture book village with three fairy tale like circular thatched cottages each with a central chimney, half-moon windows, and back wing and which would once have been estate properties belonging to the Dukes of Hamilton. Other thatched properties, many of them more opulent, are also obvious as is the octagonal dovecote now forming part of another private home.

A visit to *Easton Farm Park (01728 746475), Easton,* will appeal to those of an agricultural persuasion. Although it is a working farm many old crafts such as traditional threshing are still practiced here. There is also a blacksmiths, an historical collection of machinery, and an octagonal Victorian dairy. *Open Easter to September. Admission charge.* Alternatively, a short distance away is *Letheringham Watermill* with its gardens and wet meadows. *Open variously between April and September.*

## Food & Accommodation

**The Queen's Head** *(01728 685307), Brandeston.* A spacious but cosy 400 year old pub which is well known throughout the area and one which has won a number of awards. Choose from well kept ale, including Adnams on handpump, good quality home-made food and good value bedroom accommodation.

**The White Horse** *(01728 746456), Easton.* Recently renovated and refurbished, this unspoilt 16th Century establishment has more the look of an idyllic country cottage than an inn but you won't be disappointed. In winter, warm yourselves by the open fires with good ales and food

*Easton*

# *Walk 13: Easton Park*

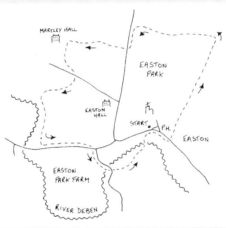

## Directions:

*1.* From your park near Easton Church, head south-west through the village for a short distance, going left up a track near Lavender Cottage. Follow the wall on your left to the edge of Euston Park where it joins Maids Wood and continue round to the left of the Park. *2.* Follow the path as it continues to skirt the Park and so to a lane. Go left at the lane to pass Martley Hall also on your left. A short distance beyond this, go right into a field, round its edge and as it skirts a belt of trees. *3.* Midway along that group of trees, take a path on your left leading down to the lane. Go left at the lane and after approx. 80 yards go right into a field. Follow the path round to the right to a stream, and then left as it runs close to the River Deben. *4.* At the lane, go left to walk through the southern part of the village. At a grassy triangle, go right, and in a little while left to cross the River Deben. (To see Letheringham Watermill, go right once over the River and retrace your steps.) Turn left once over the bridge onto a track, and then left on a path over footbridges back over the River Deben and so to the road. Turn right to return to the Church.

**Start: Easton Church Approx. Distance: 3.5 Miles**
**Approx. Time: 1.5 Hours Map: Landranger 156**

# Earl Soham

Retracing our steps back to the A1120 takes us to Earl Soham, once the property of the Earls of Norfolk, and somewhat unusual in that it has three village greens; just beyond one is Cobbolds Row, a terrace of almshouses named after a local brewer, ancient cottages and the 'Black Chapel', the original Baptist Chapel, snuggle around Little Green, and on the main green is the village sign depicting a falconer; falconry once being the local sport. Most houses date from from the 16th and 17th Centuries, and many are thatched but a Roman villa is known to have stood where the moated manor of Earl Soham Lodge can now be found. The Romans were not the first here for a pre-Saxon site, in fields behind Church Farm, has been identified.

William Goodwin, a surgeon and farmer, who lived at Street Farm during the 18th Century has left us an interesting account of smuggling during his time in the area (his Diary can be examined at the Suffolk Record Office). He tells of bands of smugglers passing through the village on their way back from Dunwich laden with contraband spirits and which would often have been hidden in the pulpits of local churches until the excise men were well out of the way. Quite a sight it must have been from the beach, if you could get there, for Goodwin goes on to describe 100-300 horses and 40-100 wagons at any one time being loaded with bounty.

## Food & Accommodation

**The Victoria** *(01728 685758), Earl Soham.* A friendly pub which offers some very good beers brewed on the premises (Earl Soham Brewery), including a bitter named after Victoria and another called Albert. The tiled and boarded floors, stripped panelling, well-chosen furnishings, open fires and pictures of Queen Victoria all go into making for a relaxing stay. Note weekends can get very busy.

Finally, before our entry into Framlingham, our route is graced with the finest *Post Mill* in the county at *Saxtead Green*. There has been a Mill on this site since 1287 but the earliest reference to the current one is 1706, and it was still in commercial use for grinding corn and animal feedstuffs until 1947. It is an impressive three-storey roundhouse structure complete with hooded porch, sails and fan-tail. Managed by English Heritage *(01728 685789)* you can explore the various floors via wooden stairs. *Open daily, excluding Sundays, April to the end of September. Admission charge.*

# Framlingham

The best approach into Framlingham is probably along the B1116 which affords a spectacular view of *Framlingham Castle*. This was one of the first fortresses in England to be built with a curtain wall rather than with a predominant keep, and is a design which returning Crusaders copied from the 'infidel' Saracens. Earlier examples of this design include Windsor and Dover Castles, some of the strongest defensive structures in Europe.

**Saxtead Mill**

From Norman times through to the mid 16th Century, Framlingham Castle was the seat of three hugely powerful families - the Bigod's, Mowbray's and Howard's, and the latter were also the Duke's of Norfolk. Today, although the curtain wall and 13 towers, some with elaborately decorated chimneys, remain and are very impressive, little else has survived save a hollow courtyard, and elements of the great hall which later formed part of the poorhouse founded by Sir Robert Hitcham. Prior to its use as a poorhouse it also saw service during Elizabeth I's reign as a prison. Managed by English Heritage *(01728 724189)*, and open *daily throughout the year,* you can walk along the full length of the curtain wall which affords some excellent views over the town and the reed-fringed mere below. *Admission charge.*

**Framlingham Castle**

A vast quantity of oaks grew in the deer park which surrounded the Castle and the diarist **John Evelyn** (1620-1706) in *Sylva, or a Discourse of Forest Tress* (1664), tells us that these were famous for being the tallest oaks in the country. Many of them would have found their way into boat keels, and just one tree is recorded as having been sufficient for four of the *Royal Sovereign's* beams, each of them 44 feet long.

St. Michael's Church built through the mid 1600's to mid 1700's is both stately and large. Here your will find one of the best series of Renaissance monuments in the country and mainly commemorating various members of the Howard family. Note in particular those to Henry VIII's son, Henry Fitzroy, Duke of Richmond (d.1536) and his wife Mary Howard (d. 1557), and that of Thomas Howard, the 3rd Duke who died in 1554 but not before he won the Battle of Flodden for the Crown. A particularly magnificent tomb (1614) of painted alabaster complete with effigies recalls the fate of another Howard, Henry Earl of Surrey, whose fate under Henry VIII was rather less illustrious; he was beheaded in 1547 on a trumped up charge of treason. The Church also retains an unusual 18th Century allegorical painting as it does its fine reredos.

The town itself is charming, the River Ore flowing through the marshes behind it. Of further architectural interest mention should be made of the 1654 single-storeyed Hitcham Almshouses, the slightly later Ancient House with its wooden cross-windows and pargeting, and Mills Almshouses, a majestic range of blue and red chequered brick built in 1703. Mills House itself is timber-framed and 16th Century and at the front is Thomas Mills' small mausoleum.

One interesting retail operation worth a visit is *Bed Bazaar (01728 723756), The Old Station, Framlingham*, and known for their incredible selection of genuine antique brass and iron beds. Alternatively, try potter **Christel Spriet** *(01728 724333), The Hermitage, 33 College Road*, known for her sculptural pots. Please note you must *phone first to check to see if it is convenient.*

## Food & Accommodation

**The Crown** *(01728 723521), Market Hill, Framlingham* belongs to the Forte Heritage Group and is a friendly, bustling black and white inn of Tudor origin. Much 16th Century period charm has been retained - including the courtyard - and it overlooks the triangular Market Place. It takes little to imagine its heady days as a staging inn with the clattered arrivals and departures of horse drawn coaches. The decor is typically Forte in style and very comfortable for that and of the bedroom accommodation try the one with a panelled four-poster.

**The White Horse** *(01728 638280), Badingham, near Framlingham.* A typically handsome 15th Century Suffolk establishment where the two bars display an interesting collection of rural artefacts and have the benefit of large inglenooks. Food is a strong feature with vegetarian options something of a house speciality. Good ales include a draught mild.

Places to visit nearby include the ***390th Bomb Group Memorial Air Museum** (01449 781561), Parham Airfield*, near Framlingham which acts as a memorial to the US 8th Army Air Force stationed here between 1943 to 1945. The exhibits include engines, components of crashed aircraft, and reconstructions of a radio hut and wartime office. *Open Sundays, March to October and also Bank Holiday Mondays. Admission free.*

If this is not to your liking, try the ***Boundary Gallery** (01728 723862)* in *Cransford* which exhibits the work of quality Suffolk artists. *Open variously throughout the week.* Of a different flavour is ***Shawsgate Vineyard** (01728 724060), Badingham Road, Framlingham.* A variety of vines are grown on this 20 plus acre estate including Reichsteiner and Chardonnay. *Guided tours and tastings are available (phone first to check availability)* and there is a shop selling not only the estates wines but a number of related products as well.

Go to ***Bruisyard Vineyard** (01728 638281), Church Road, Bruisyard* to visit another local vineyard which is part of a larger agricultural enterprise. Average production from the Muller Thurgau vines here is about 2,000 cases per year, and the wines are mainly of a fruity medium dry taste. The various production processes, from pressing through to fermentation and bottling, can be seen on regular *tours run between Easter and the end of November; these are only by appointment though*. Wine is, however, sold from the winery shop. Additionally you can wander around the herb and water gardens.

Perched on the A1120 just outside Framlingham is ***Dennington***, now little more than a pleasant cluster of houses by a village green. It was once the site of huge cattle and horse fairs and the parish then much larger and probably rather more prosperous.

*Parclose Screen in St. Mary's Church, Dennington*

*Lord & Lady Bardolph's Monument, St.*
*Mary's Church, Dennington*

Evidence of such former prosperity is only a stones throw away, marked by one of the most lavish and rich church interiors you will encounter for a long time. St. Mary's is thought to have been built on the site of a Druidic Temple and much of it is 14th Century. To the interior though to enjoy some exceptional wood carvings from the bench ends to the 17th Century three-decker pulpit, the extremely rare 16th Century pry canopy suspended over the altar and probably made in 1500 from one piece of wood, and the parclose screens, in the south and north chapels which are much like rood screens albeit of a richly decorated and unusual kind. Of the benches look out for the pelican and a mermaid, and not forgetting the most extraordinary of them all which depicts a sciapode - a strange creature resting under the shade of his huge foot - and thought to be the only such rendition in England. The mid 15th Century alabaster monument in the south chapel to Lord and Lady Bardolph is complete with their recumbent effigies and provides yet another extravagant feature to this most splendid of churches.

# *Walk 14: In and Around Framlingham*

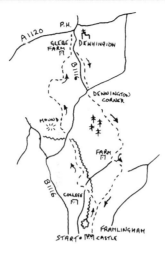

## *Directions:*

1. From your park at the Castle, walk towards the Castle itself. Go through the turnstile on your left, just before the drawbridge. Cross a small bridge to walk left along a path around the former moat. Continue straight ahead over a second bridge and use the YWM sign around Framlingham College playing field. 2. At the lane, go left and after a short distance turn right onto a footpath just past the farm. Go through a hedge to a track leading between some farm buildings. Go left to cross a field keeping the stream on your right. Continue straight ahead, ignoring the path to your right, to the B1116. 3. Go left at the road, and within a few yards go right (signed YWM) on a path leading round a field, and keeping right of a mound. Scramble through a gap in the hedge and over a turf bridge to the field. 4. Keeping a small wood on your right, continue straight ahead to a track close to more farm buildings. Follow the track round to the right and then take the left hand footpath towards the moated Glebe Farm. Once at the B1116 again, go left towards Dennington Church. 5. Once you have explored the Church at Dennington, retrace your steps back to the B1116 to Dennington Corner (approx. one mile). Where the road bends sharp right, go straight ahead instead onto a footpath. Go through two fields aiming for the north-east corner of Lodge Wood. Walk along the edge of the wood, keeping it on your right, and beyond the wood to a lane. 6. At the lane, go right, and after a short distance take the left hand farm track. At the top of the small incline go right on a path leading back to Framlingham. Cross a bridge from where you have a choice of paths which will shortly return you to your start near the Castle.

**Start: Framlingham Castle**
**Approx. Distance: 5 Miles:**
**Approx. Time: 2.5 Hours**
**Map: Landranger 156.**

# *Peasenhall*

Our last port of call in this central part of the county is Peasenhall. Although Peasenhall and Sibton are two separate parishes, there is little distance between the end of one and the beginning of the other and collectively they function as one village. After the Conquest, William granted the manor of Peasenhall to the influential Bigod family and that of Sibton to Sir William Malet. And it was to Sibton that just under a hundred years later the Cistercians arrived to build their Abbey of the Blessed Virgin Mary; today, only the most modest of ruins have survived.

## *Food & Accommodation*

**The New Inn** *(01628 825925), Peasenhall* actually provides three self-catering cottages in a 15th Century building, renovated to a high standard and managed by The Landmark Trust. The centre of this beautiful range of buildings was once a medieval woolhall, and the house served as an inn until 1478. (**Sleeps 5/4/4.**)

Peasenhall is the more interesting of the two places, probably because it enjoyed later wealth in the form of the famous James Smyth & Sons agricultural drill works, a piece of equipment which was exported the world over. The works only ceased to trade in 1967 and new enterprises have found their home on its site. Of less well repute is Stuart House, the scene of Rose Harsent's murder in the last century, and one which to this day remains unsolved but documented in many books and recently one of the subjects of the television series *Strange But True*. Look for the little attic window in which Rose would light her candle by way of a message to her lover.

If you are looking to stock up on a few grocery items then go to *Emmett's Stores (01728 660250)* on the *High Street* where they specialise in cured bacon and ham. Try their own recipe sausages or their sweet-pickle Suffolk ham tinged with their own secret mix of beer and black treacle.

*The New Inn, Peasenhall*

# The Wool Towns and Villages

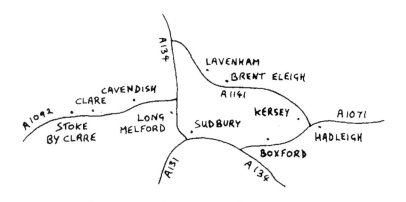

Suffolk's wool towns and villages are nothing short of remarkable, not least for the extraordinary amount of medieval architecture they reveal. All though enjoy their own distinctive character and flavour and are best explored over a period of several days. For our purposes, the journey commences in Hadleigh and from we here we take a north-westerly route towards Lavenham. Then to Long Melford following the course of the River Stour through Cavendish and Clare before dropping back to Sudbury, the largest and most commercially geared of all the towns in this part of Suffolk.

## Hadleigh

Hadleigh, meaning *head-place* has enjoyed a rich and colourful history, one which reached its height of prosperity in the 14th and 15th Centuries and one heavily dependent on the wool industry of those times. Hadleigh's importance then can be attributed to its position on the River Brett which gave easy access to the water needed to first wash the wool and then full the cloth, and which also enabled its onward transportation.

*Hadleigh's Guildhall*

A number of buildings add testament to this former wealth not least the red-brick Deanery Tower built in 1495 by Archdeacon Pykenham and which is a thoroughly splendid building with polygonal turrets. It was once the entrance to Pykenham's ecclesiastical palace which has since been demolished. To the right of the Tower is the Deanery, built in 1831, in mock-Tudor style and enlarged just a decade later. Also within the grounds is St. Mary's Church with its own imposing tower and lead spire, no less than 135 feet high and which holds the Angelus Bell, one of the oldest in England. Also of note is the 14th Century octagonal font and an imposing east window in Perpendicular style.

Now to the Guildhall, opposite the Church, and a 15th Century timber framed building consisting of two parts. The centre has three-storeys and two over-hangs. To the left of this is the Long Room, essentially the original Guildhall (on the first floor) with almshouses below. Other buildings to take stock of include the Georgian Corn Exchange (1813) with its Tuscan columns, the slightly earlier timber-framed Pykenham Almshouses (1807) and Overall House so named after Bishop John Overall who translated the Authorised Version of the Bible for James I. The High Street seems to stretch on for an eternity though not so obviously as at Long Melford, and many colourful coats of arms set in relief can be seen on the various buildings.

Marked by a large obelisk on Aldham Common is the spot where the one-time rector of Hadleigh, *Rowland Taylor,* was burnt at the stake for refusing to allow Mass to be celebrated in St. Mary's. The year of his execution,1555. This was just one of the countless persecutions under the Catholic Queen Mary Tudor and many other heretics - Protestants and Non-Conformists alike - were dealt with in similar fashion. Ironically, it was at a rectory in the town, in 1833, that the Oxford Movement - with its campaign to restore High Church ideals to the Church of England - first began. Taylor would no doubt have found this equally unpalatable.

## Food & Accommodation

**Hintlesham Hall** *(01473 652268)*, Hintlesham, near Hadleigh. A plush aristocratic like country house hotel - one of Suffolk's finest - set in 200 acres of parkland and gardens. Although it dates from the 15th Century, this is hidden behind an impressive Georgian facade. The interior is gracious Georgian charm with furnishings to suit. All in all a top rate establishment with prices to match but a great place to treat yourself to.

Just north-west of the town is **Groton Wood**, a mix of modern coppiced and ancient woodland managed by the Suffolk Wildlife Trust. Here you will find the best stand of small-leaved limes in the county plus a wealth of woodland plants - bluebell, primrose, violet, orchid and woodruff. Additionally, over 70 species of bird have been recorded here. *Open all year.*

To the east of the town is **Wolves Wood**, an RSPB Reserve of mixed woodland, and where the range of birds to be seen is excellent, from greater and lesser spotted woodpecker to kestrel, tawny-owl and nightingales. *The nature trail is open all year* but is perhaps best visited during spring and early summer when the plantlife is also at its best - yellow archangel, primrose, violet, bluebell and orchid.

For those with different inclinations, **East Anglia Shooting** *(01473 822922)*, in conjunction with the East Anglia Tourist Board, arrange guns on pheasant and partridge shoots at a number of estates in the region; both individuals and groups are catered for.

**Hintlesham Hall**

## *Walk 15: Hadleigh and Kersey*

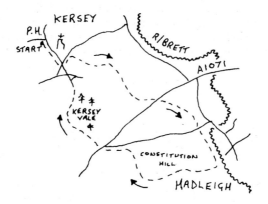

### *Directions:*

1. From your park on the main street running through Kersey, head towards the Church. Just beyond the Church go left along a road (signed Hadleigh/Bildeston). Within a short distance take the footpath on your right leading across a field. 2. Continue along the edge of further fields until you come to a track where you turn left. After approx. 10 yards go right along a path with the A1071 visible in front of you. Ignore a path to your right, and where the paths fork a little further on keep left dropping down to the main road through a gap in the hedge and to some gates. 3. Cross over the gate opposite you, and bear diagonally left over the field to a path running between hedges. At a road, go right as far as the cemetery and cut across the sports field near this to the River Brett. 4. Go right into the track here and then into the reserve using a gate on your left. Continue along here for about half a mile. 5. Go right up a hill (Constitution Hill) and past the entrance to Broom Hill Reserve. Ignore a path on your right, and instead continue up the hill and onto a track where you turn right aiming for a farm in front of you. 6. At the minor road, go left and at the A1071 again go left and after approx. 45 yards take a footpath on your right (signed Kersey Vale). This path works its way down into Kersey Vale, over a stream, and then right onto a track. Follow the track round to the left and back into Kersey village.

**Start: Kersey High Street**
**Approx. Distance: 5 Miles**
**Approx. Time: 2.5 Hours  (Allow longer though if you intend
to explore Hadleigh's rich offerings)**
**Map: Landranger 155**

Our route to Lavenham takes us through some delightful villages not least the very picturesque *Kersey.* Here the streets lead down to a shallow ford; and rise back up to the Saxon Church. The name Kersey is thought to derive from *Car's Eye*, meaning a stream which runs into a brook. Most of the cottages are colour-washed and timber-framed and the scene is quintessentially Suffolk. Kersey is also thought to be the original home of a coarse ribbed cloth for which Suffolk weavers were famous during the latter part of the Middle Ages. Although there is no proof of this, cloth was certainly made here and even Shakespeare records the same in *Love's Labours Lost* where Berowne says:

> *'Hence forth my wooing mind shall be exprest*
> *In russet years and honest Kersie noes, ...'*

Close to Kersey, **Lindsay** became known for its own woolsey cloth, the wool washed in the village stream before its subsequent spinning and weaving. We are really here though to visit **St. James Chapel**, a tiny 13th Century building with a thatched roof and lancet windows, and which was once probably attached to Lindsay Castle of which only a few insignificant earthworks remain. After dissolution, the Chapel is thought to have found use as a barn until its restoration in 1930. Today it is cared for by English Heritage and *is open all year, free of charge.*

To the north is **Chelsworth**, an unspoilt village replete with colour-washed thatched cottages, an elegant Tudor Grange, and a double-humped bridge over the River Brett dating from 1754. To the west of the village is Cobbold's Mill, once the home of the founder of the Nonesuch Press, Sir Francis Meywell.

Still further north is **Bildeston** once also famous for its cloth, especially blankets, but today is a quiet if pretty village. Note the terraces of old weavers cottages, many of which would have had interconnecting attics which served as long, if rather dark, workshops. The brick built Clock Tower (1864) in the village square

*Quaint cottages perched on Kersey Hill*

is described by Pevsner as *'hideous'*, and whether or not one agrees it serves to remind us of how different the times must have been for those poor souls relegated to the workhouse from where this piece came. Other structures of note are Garrod's Farmhouse, with its 15th and 16th Century timbers - from the small carved porch to the two tiny carved mullioned windows - and the timbered pub of which more details are given below.

## Food & Accommodation

**The Bell Inn** *(01473 823229), The Street, Kersey, near Hadleigh.* A well known inn with over 700 years of history behind it and offering well above average food and an excellent range of ales. Exposed timbers, low beams, open fires and country furnishings make for a cosy stay. Accommodation is also available.

**The Crown Inn** *(01449 740510), 104 High Street, Bildeston, near Lavenham.* A former 15th Century merchant's home and later a coaching inn, The Crown was once known as the most haunted pub in the country. Recently restored, the superb interior has been well retained, not least the huge inglenooks. Good beer, good food and well-furnished bedroom accommodation.

**The Peacock Inn** *(01449 740758), The Street, Chelsworth, near Lavenham.* An elegant well-restored 14th Century inn with a large beamed bar split into smaller areas by a semi-open timbered partition. Note also the exposed Tudor brickwork in the lounge area. Well kept ales, a good selection of wines and an excellent range of food are our purpose though. Accommodation is also available.

**Red House Farm** *(01787 210245), Kersey, near Hadleigh.* Surrounded by open countryside between the villages of Kersey and Boxford, this mid 1800's farmhouse is as good a spot as anywhere for B & B. The bedrooms are well furnished and guests make use of a separate breakfast room and a dining room where evening meals can be had by prior arrangement. The swimming pool can also be used by guests.

Just outside Lavenham, **Brent Eleigh** is typical of the villages in this part of the county. Our main purpose here is St. Mary's Church where we find medieval murals of great importance and not re-discovered until 1860. These paintings are thought to date from as early as 1290 though some people prefer the later date of 1400.

The most central of them, designed as an altarpiece, depicts the Crucifixion with the Virgin Mary and St. John, and is painted in red, earthy colours against a pale green background. To the left of this, on the north wall, is a painting of two kneeling angels; this would originally have been bright turquoise but the colouring is now rather darkened. Probably the most important of the three murals, however, is that on the south wall, i.e. to the right of the central image,

**Detail of Brent Eleigh Church's Wall Paintings**

but unfortunately this is also the most fragmentary. It is thought to represent the Harrowing of Hell with Christ pulling Adam and his companions out of Hell (it has to be admitted that this is fairly difficult to establish) and a tonsured priest who would appear to be the picture's donor (this is the most evident aspect). Other items of interest in St. Mary's include the 17th Century box pews and a Baroque monument to Edward Colman.

Other places to visit nearby include ***Corn Craft*** *(01449 740456), Bridge Farm, Monks Eleigh, near Lavenham,* makers of traditional corn dollies and dried flower products. The flowers are grown and dried on their own 70 acre site. ***Open daily and demonstrations of the skills involved are by appointment only.***

## Lavenham

The most picturesque of all Suffolk's villages has to be Lavenham, after all it is one of the most important places in the country for architecture preserved from the Middle Ages. Pretty well every street is lined with timber-framed houses many with their original windows still in tact. It is truly a sight to be seen.

Lavenham's prosperity was at is height around 1500 when it was the 14th richest town in the country and when nearly very house would have operated their own looms, and much of their product exported to Spain and Holland. The town was initially known for its blue cloth and later for its fine yarn, damask and flannel. As the weaving industry declined these were replaced with slightly coarser fabrics, namely the twill woven serge and shalloon and until even these were finally superseded by coconut matting, crinoline and horsehair mattresses. The last weaving mill closing in 1930. A number of factors contributed to the decline of Lavenham's industry not least the development of water power for fulling cloth and so the rise of larger scale operations in the north of England where abundant hill streams freely generated this power source. The invention of power looms and spinning jennies knocked East Anglia's industry further back and then the arrival of coal generated power truly saw the North supreme. At least though Lavenham was spared the ravages and spoils of the Industrial Revolution allowing us opportunity to walk down a beautiful memory lane.

The Church of St. Peter & St. Paul, with its 141 feet high tower, was built between 1444 and 1525 at the height of the town's prosperity, and heavily financed by wealthy wool merchants. Especially noteworthy is the elaborate stone carving and fan vaulting of the south porch, a gift from John de Vere, the Earl of Oxford, and to whom the Brauch Chapel is dedicated. The Spring Chantry commemorates another family of benefactors, namely Thomas Spring and his wife, and this adorned with a splendid intricately carved parclose screen.

Dominating the Market Place, the 16th Century, half-timbered **Guildhall** *(01787 247646)* was just one of four guilds in the village and this built by the Guild of Corpus Christi in 1529 soon after their initial formation, and whose aims were rather more religious than commercial. With carved corner posts - one of which celebrates the 15th Earl of Oxford, also John de Vere, and seen holding a distaff and the Guild's Charter granted by him - the entrance porch is quite superb. The original oriel windows also remain intact. Once the Guild, along with all the others, had been suppressed it found use first as a prison, then as a school store. Now managed by the National Trust and ***open daily from the end of March through to early October,*** it houses a fine exhibition documenting the 700 years of the medieval woollen cloth industry. ***Admission charge.*** There is also a shop and tea room here.

*The Guild of Corpus Christi, Lavenham*

The **de Vere** family originated from Zeeland but first came to Britain with William The Conqueror (1066). Their main holding was Hedingham Castle, just over the Essex border, but in the 17th Century the 17th Earl (1550-1604) sold his inheritance. This Earl was to become one of the best of Elizabeth I's court poets and many people are of the opinion that he is the true author of Shakespeare's plays. Most recently, a fairly convincing case for the same was made in Andrew Field's work of historical imagination *The Lost Chronicles of Edward de Vere (*1990).

Opposite the Guildhall is the Market Cross, built in 1502. One can only imagine today what a hive of activity the Market Place must have been, but to help us in doing so we need only conjure up Elizabeth I's visit in 1578 when she was accompanied by an escort of no less than 500 squires, all rigged out in black and white silks, and supported by a veritable 1,500 strong army of servants and all on horseback. Furthermore, until 1842, on November 5th, Guy Fawkes Night, the market was home to a bull baiting spectacle, Lavenham the last place in the British Isles to hold such an event.

Also connected with the cloth industry is **The Priory** *(01787 247417), Water Street.* Originally owned by the Benedictines, it subsequently became the home of a wealthy wool merchant. It was restored by the Casey family at the end of the 1970's and is now open to the public. It is quite a complex timber structure, made up of five separate frames with the original medieval hall in the centre. Elizabethan wall paintings were discovered during the building's restoration and other items on display include paintings, drawings and the stained glass by the Hungarian Ervin Bossany (1881-1975), perhaps best known for his windows in Canterbury Cathedral. Additionally, there is a uniquely designed herb garden where over a hundred varieties are grown. **Open Easter and May to September. Admission charge.**

**The Church of St. Peter & St. Paul, Lavenham**

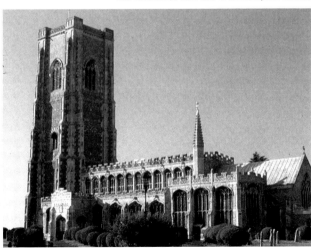

Although **the origins of the cloth industry** are nigh impossible to find let alone document, it is nevertheless known that during the 15th Century a number of different types of cloth were made in Suffolk. The three most important types were narrow cloths, broadcloths and 'streytes'. Statute required that an East Anglian broadcloth be 28 yards 28 inches long, 5 feet 3 inches wide and weigh 38llbs. A 'streyte' was stipulated as being half the length, half the width and half the weight of the broadcloth. Lavenham and Clare were especially known for their broadcloths as was Glemsford but Hadleigh seems to have been best for narrow cloths, but this represents only the most basic of divisions between the various specialities of the different towns and villages. Other types of cloth included the light 'handywarps,' 'kerseys' and 'undyed whites' or 'Coxsallwhites

Also on Water Street is the 15th Century de Vere House, dismantled by vandals but now re-erected by preservationists. In Shilling Street, note Shilling Grange, once the home of Jane and Ann Taylor known for their childrens nursery rhymes. One of theirs which we will all recall is *Twinkle, Twinkle, Little Star.* Next, to **Little Hall**, headquarters of the Suffolk Preservation Society founded in 1929. Also on the Market Place, Little Hall is another extraordinarily fine half-timbered building of the 14th and 15th Centuries, sympathetically colour washed in a yellow-apricot hue The most splendid part of the Hall is its central hall complete with open roof-trusses. *Open weekends, April to October. Admission charge.*

## *Food & Accommodation*

**The Angel Hotel** *(01787 247388), Market Place, Lavenham,* is a friendly and informal inn first granted a license way back in 1420. Impressive inglenooks, beams, exposed brickwork, and a Tudor fireplace set the scene. Good food and beer. Accommodation, all en-suite, is typically characterful of such an old inn and guests also have use of a residents lounge with its impressive 16th Century ceiling.

**The Great House** *(01787 247431), Market Place, Lavenham.* Behind this restaurant's Georgian facade is a structure which dates from the 1400's. The cosy restaurant is in a part of the building which oozes with charm: an open fire, low ceiling and carved beams. The menu is classical French with a few modern nuances, and generally very well priced. On balmy summers evenings you can even enjoy your meal on a lovely enclosed terrace. Characterful accommodation is also available.

**The Swan** *(01787 247477), High Street, Lavenham.* This is a Forte Group flagship hotel and no wonder for it is a super place to stay, occupying almost an entire street of half-timbered frontages. Modern day comforts have not obscured some very charming features, namely low ceilings, uneven floors and narrow passageways. The restaurant is a grand place with its high timbered roof, minstrel's gallery and food to match. The only draw back is that it gets extremely busy especially during the summer months. If you are able to stay, take a suite as the extra space and interest created by another room is a real plus.

*Little Hall, Lavenham*

# Walk 16: Lavenham and Brent Eleigh

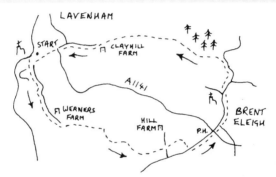

## Directions:

1. From the car park near Lavenham's Church, go right into Church Street and right again into Bear's Lane. Ignore a footpath on your right, instead continuing along the lane to Weaners Farm. Just before the second farm, go left on a path which skirts the buildings to a pond. Go left here into a track along the edge of a field. 2. Continue straight ahead at a junction of paths, and then right at the end of a long field. At the next meeting of ways, again continue straight ahead on a path along the edge of a field. Turn right and immediate left at the drive to Hill Farm and round another field. 3. Once at Cock Lane, go left, uphill and then down into Brent Eleigh. 4. At the A1141 go straight over and up Hall Road to the Church. Continue past the Church and where the road forks, go left. 5. Just as the road bends sharply right look for a track on your left. This is Clay Lane and will take you past the southern fringe of Spragg's Wood to Clayhill Farm. 6. Use the metalled road here to take you back into Lavenham. At the road, go left for approx. 20 yards and then look for a footpath on your right which leads back into Bear's Lane. Turn right at the lane to find the Church.

**Start: Lavenham Church  Approx. Distance: 5 Miles**
**Approx. Time: 2 Hours  Map: Landranger 155**

# Long Melford

Considered the country's best preserved linear village, Long Melford's High Street, once a Roman highway, is over a mile long, its succession of attractive frontages today housing a great many reputable antique shops, tea rooms and pubs. Inevitably, the village's name is derived from its vast length but also from a watermill (mill ford) demolished in the 1950's There are quite a sizeable amount of 18th and early 19th Century buildings in the village, attributable in great part to the fact that the Stour was once navigable; as a river port, Long Melford did not suffer the same decline in the cloth industry as did neighbouring Lavenham but instead enjoyed much Georgian and Victorian prosperity. First to the north end where the finest of the buildings can be found around a large triangular green - once the site of a large horse market - and which runs down to the River Stour. Holy Trinity Church dominates the scene.

Built during the 15th Century, the Church is an imposing, late Perpendicular structure, its nave and chancel over 150 feet long, and which still holds its original and important collection of Flemish glass in the north aisle depicting a series of dignatories from mayors to judges, priors and priests. Beyond the windows, in the north wall, is a fine mid 14th Century alabaster relief depicting the Adoration of the Maji. The Church monuments are equally of note not least the brasses to the Clopton family who financed much of the Church's building. In the east window of the Clopton Chantry, look for the tiny Lily Crucifix which has something of a mystical air about it. Then to the Lady Chapel, a separate building dating from 1496 and which is approached from the body of the Church via the south-east door. This is unique in that it has an indoor cloister built around it though for many centuries it found use as the local school.

In front of the Church, also on the green, stands the brick built almshouses of the Hospital of the Holy and Undivided Trinity. Founded by William Cordell in 1573 for 12 poormen, it was altered and improved in Victorian times but still cares for 12 occupants although not all of these are villagers as was intended.

Also at this end of the village is the Elizabethan *Melford Hall* (01787 880286), open to the public and managed by the National Trust. The Hall was originally built for William Cordell, the same as founded the Hospital, in 1578. Cordell was an astute and wealthy lawyer who later became Solicitor-General, then Master of the Rolls under the Tudors. The property was eventually bought by Sir Harry Parker, 6th Baronet, in 1786, and descendent's of his continue to occupy part of the Hall. Amongst the Hall's more important contents is the stained glass portrait of Elizabeth I in the East Gallery, a superb collection of Chinese porcelain seized from a Spanish galleon in 1762, a good collection of paintings and sea charts, the Regency Library and the original Tudor panelling in the Banqueting Hall. Upstairs are two rooms celebrating the work of Beatrix Potter who was once a regular visitor to the Hall.

The grounds are equally grand and include a number of rare trees, fine topiary

*Long Melford's Holy Trinity Church*

and an unusual Tudor pavilion. ***Open variously, May to October. Admission charge.***

A few miles north of Long Melford is **Giffords Hall Vineyard** *(01284 830464)*, *Giffords Hall, Hartest,* part of a small agricultural enterprise which produces a variety of wines using Madeleine Angevine, Reichensteiner and Pinot Noir vines. Set amidst rolling countryside, although the vineyards holdings are flat, it is as good a place as any in Suffolk for sampling the local wines. ***Winery tours and tastings are available from Easter through to October. Admission charge.***

## Food & Accommodation

**Black Lion & Countrymen Restaurant** *(01787 312356), The Green, Long Melford.* Situated on the green and once an old coaching inn, this family run hotel is probably best known for its restaurant which is well frequented by locals. It is a comfortable and spacious hotel with a tasteful, rustic interior which makes good use of antiques and appropriate furnishings.

**The Bull** *(01787 378494), Hall Street, Long Melford.* Part of the Forte Heritage Group, The Bull today is a fine example of Elizabethan architecture, although it was originally built for a wealthy wool merchant in the earlier 1450's. By 1580 it had become an inn with much trade as a Posting House being situated midway along the London to Norwich route. Oak beams, Elizabethan hearths and fireplaces abound and there is even an old weavers gallery overlooking the courtyard. As you can expect from Forte, all modern facilities are tastefully combined into this ancient inn.

**Scutchers Bistro** *(01787 310200), Westgate Street, Long Melford.* This is a good solid bistro-styled restaurant where much of the emphasis is Mediterranean but with an occasional English edge. Nonetheless, the range of food on offer is wide and the choice of wines is unusually good.

111

**Cavendish Village Green**

We now begin our westerly route through Glemsford and Cavendish to arrive in the small market town of Clare. *Glemsford* is not the most attractive of spots from a tourist's point of view but there are elements of interest, not least a fair proportion of half-timbered buildings, including the late 15th Century Peverells on Tye Green, built for George Cavendish (?1500-1562). Cavendish was Wolsey's gentleman usher from 1527 until the latter's death a few years later, and although Cavendish wrote a *Life of Cardinal Wolsey* in 1554, it did not find its way into publication until 1641.

The cloth industry seems always to have been important to Glemsford; in the Middle Ages they produced their own weave called 'Gleynforths' and in more recent times the production of flax and silk thread have predominated. The flax factory is now an operation of an altogether different kind, but the silk mill stands on the site of an ancient watermill. Silk thread has been produced here since 1824 and is then taken to Sudbury to be woven; both the Queen's coronation robe and Princess Diana's wedding dress used thread originally produced at Glemsford.

The weaving of coconut fibres into matting and the processing of horse hair were also important 19th Century industries in the village and accounted for no less than ten factories. Today the company of Arnold & Gough process and curl the horse hair which goes into the making of judges' wigs. They also prepare the military sporrams and regimental cockades on bearskins and busbys.

Next, to *Cavendish* which enjoys probably the most attractive village green in Suffolk , dominated as it is by St. Mary's Church and a pretty array of cottages, some of them pink-washed. Of St. Mary's more notable features mention should be made of the Roman bricks in the south aisle, the Flemish tiles in the north, and the tower's ringing chamber which was once occupied, as is evidenced by the fireplace.

*Little Hall, Lavenham*

*Southwold Lighthouse (previous page)*

*The Guild of Corpus Christi, Lavenham*

*The Guildhall, Hadleigh*

*The Shire Hall, Woodbridge*

*The Moot Hall, Aldeburgh*

*The Butter Cross, Bungay*

*The smallest Pub in England*

*Brandon's appropriately named central Pub*

*Colourful Village Signs*

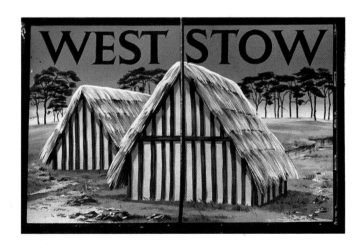

*St. Michael's Church, Beccles*

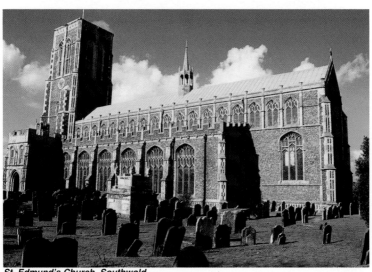
*St. Edmund's Church, Southwold*

*John Piper's Stained Glass Window in the
Church of St. Peter & St. Paul, Aldeburgh*

*St. Edmund's hammerbeam roof, Southwold*

*Holy Trinity's tie-beam roof, Blythburgh*

*Detail of the hammerbeam roof,*
*St. Edmund's, Southwold*

*Rare Jack-o'-the-Clocks at Southwold's St. Edmund (left) and Blythburgh's Holy Trinity (right)*

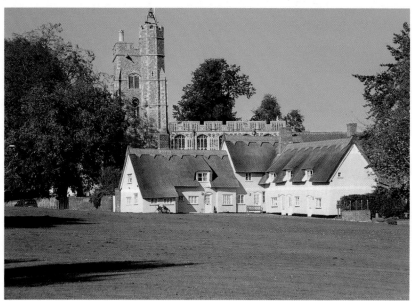

*Cavendish Village Green*

*Saxtead Post Mill*

*The crumbling cliff line at Covehithe*

*Dunwich Beach*

*Woodbridge's Tide Mill*

Sir John Cavendish financed the building of the chancel but his own fate was not so securely assured; he was executed in 1381 by rebels of the Peasants' Revolt because his son had killed Wat Tyler, their leader, and this despite the fact that Tyler had been accorded an amnesty by Richard II. Quite who the villagers of the time sympathised with is not clear but today the village sign depicts Wat Tyler.

Several notable buildings can be found in the village, not least the Old Grammar School and Old Workhouse both now private homes. Additionally, there are the almshouses on the village green known as Hyde Park Cottages, Pocky Hall once used as an isolation hospital presumably for victims of smallpox, and the Old Rectory which is a 16th Century, two-storey, timber-framed structure with over-sailing upper floor.

Do not, however, satisfy yourselves with just a quick wander around the village for their are two places which deserve rather more attention. First, is **Cavendish Manor Vineyard** *(01787 280221), Nether Hall,* just a short distance from the Church. The first vines were planted here in 1972 and today the estate is flourishing. ***Tours of the vineyard and wine tastings can be enjoyed alongside*** a visit to **The Museum** contained within the Hall and which includes an art gallery hung with paintings from the 17th through the 19th Centuries, and a 16th Century barn housing old agricultural implements. ***Open daily. Admission charge.***

Our second port of call is the **Sue Ryder Home,** headquarters of that Foundation, and originally begun in 1953 by Sue Ryder herself for victims of Nazi persecution, and now dedicated to the relief of suffering anywhere; there are now about 50 such homes dotted around the world all dedicated to helping the sick, handicapped and survivors of concentration camps. In the grounds is a *Museum (01787 280252)* illustrating the work of the Foundation over the years and from its early beginnings as just a chain of second-hand charity shops. ***Open daily. Admission charge.*** There is also a tea room here.

Sue Ryder's husband, **Leonard Cheshire,** also deserves special mention here for his Cheshire Foundation now runs well over 250 homes for the handicapped. An ex-RAF pilot, Cheshire began an unusual industry in 1990 which involved the manufacture of ball point pens using rockets scrapped by the former Soviet Union. Over 100 million pens have been produced, all of them numbered so as to remind us of the magnitude of war victims in just our own 20th Century; each pen representing just a single victim. The profits from this operation have helped to finance an international disaster fund for those caught up in the violence of politics and religion alike.

## *Walk 17: Cavendish and Clare*

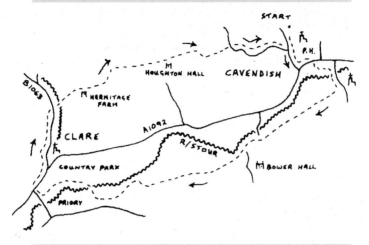

### *Directions:*

1. From your park on Cavendish's village green, head further into the village until you come to a pub, The Bull. Opposite this is a path along the drive into the Sue Ryder Home grounds. Continue along the drive towards a stream and instead of crossing this go along the left bank to a fence. Cross over the next bridge, then a stile and so until you reach a minor road. 2. Go right into Pentlow Road, and over the old railway bridge and along the road to Pentlow Church. Where the road forks here, look for a bridleway (signed) on your right. 3. Within a short distance you will cross over to the other side of the ditch to follow the track. Keep along this track, through a small copse of trees and on to Bower Hall. 4. Continue straight ahead here along a road and when that bends to the left, take the track on your right instead (following a blue arrow). Follow this track, avoiding the river on your right, for about one mile, and ignoring a path joining from your left. 5. Follow the path sharp right as it goes downhill, and then left into a road. 6. Once you join another road, go right and then look for a path on your right which leads down to the river. 7. Once over the bridge, head across the meadow to a kissing gate, close to an old mill. 8. Continue along the road to cross another railway bridge and then bear left into Bailey Lane, and then head left along the path which leads into Clare Country Park. Continue along the disused railway track (the remains of Clare Priory on your left) until you reach a road. 9. Go right here and once at the A1092, go right heading into the centre of the town which is well worth exploring. 10. Take the first road to your left, the B1063, which will lead you both to the Museum and the Church. Continue along the B1063 until you come to a new housing development on your right called Hermitage Meadows. Go through here and to a track leading to Hermitage Farm and then right following the yellow path signs. 11. Go through a gap in the hedge, turn left and follow the path uphill, through a line of trees and then left along the edge of a field. Turn right to reach a high point and then head for a farmyard (Houghton Hall) following the track downhill. Once at the bottom, go

right. 12. Within a short distance you turn left across a bridge and stile, over a bridged ditch and once again up hill. 13. Once at the lane, go right and follow it until you reach a junction where you go right again to get back to the village green.

**Start: Cavendish Village Green**
**Approx. Distance: 7.5 Miles**
**Approx. Time: 3 Hours (Allow longer to explore Clare)**
**Map: Landranger: 155**

# Clare

Clare is an attractive but small town which was once much more important. The Norman Castle built soon after the Conquest, in 1090, by Richard Fitzgilbert saw the centre of the then village shift eastwards from what was an essentially Romano-British camp, established as early as 300 AD and called *Ebury*. It was the Norman structure though which was to become an important military stronghold, especially during the Middle Ages, commanding as it did passage along the Icknield Way. Today, only part of the Castle keep still stands.

The Castle seems to have seen something of a chequered history from what were the heady heights during Gilbert the 7th Earl of Clare's days - he being one of the most important men in the country during King John's reign. But the de Clare we hear of most frequently is his granddaughter, Elizabeth, who on her mother's side was also Edward I's granddaughter. Although she was married on three occasions, none lasted long and she was widowed for good at the tender age of 28!

She settled in Clare reputedly living in great style, but to her credit she did found Clare College, Cambridge. The Earldom of Clare however became extinct after Gilbert was killed on the battlefields of Bannockburn in 1314, and by the end of the 1300's the Castle had passed to the Crown. No longer used as a residence, it quickly fell into ruin, its timbers and masonry employed in other buildings around the town.

In 1863, the Great Eastern Railway constructed one of its stations and lines through the former bailey. This too was fated, closing a hundred years later; one of the many victims of Dr. Beechings cuts. Today, it acts as an Information Centre for the 25 acre Country Park which uses the lands once belonging to the de Clare's.

Another important structure, this time of a religious bent was the first Augustinian Priory to be built in England, founded by Robert de Clare in 1248. Only two of the original buildings have survived - the old infirmary and the Church, the latter reconsecrated for Augustinian worship in 1953.

Do visit the Church of St. Peter & St. Paul, its tower dominating the centre of the town. Mainly a 15th Century building, it contains some excellent Jacobean stalls, in the east window a piece of Tudor heraldic glass, a 400 year old brass

*The heavily pargeted Ancient House, Clare*

eagle lectern said to have been given by Elizabeth I, and unusually Roman bricks have even been employed among its flint walls.

Standing literally opposite the Church is the *Ancient House Museum* which displays an excellent example of the Suffolk art of pargeting; a method by which moulded and decorated plaster is applied to the timber framed structure. The house itself dates from 1473 but the intricate floral pargeting will be of a rather later date impossible to document precisely but thought to be mid 16th Century. The Museum contains mainly 19th and early 20th Century exhibits though there are some prehistoric bits and pieces. *Open occasionally, May to September. Admission charge.*

Our last port of call is the *Nethergate Brewery* (01787 277244) also on the *High Street*. Only barrelled ales are brewed by this small traditional operation and they have a reputation for producing prize-winning quality. Conducted *tours and tastings are by appointment only,* for which a small *admission charge* is made.

## Food & Accommodation

**The Bell Hotel** *(01787 277741), Market Hill, Clare.* Dating from the late 1500's, this is a most congenial white-faced, half-timbered, old inn. Variously an alehouse, renowned Posting House, and candle making operation - tinkers from all over the region purchased the latter for resale - today it has been carefully modernised. Exposed beams and open fireplaces have been retained, and the bedroom accommodation is equally characterful where many of the rooms enjoy half-testers or four-poster beds, The food is of a good standard whether in the restaurant or the wine bar and the choice of wines very extensive.

**The Plough Inn** *(01440 786789), Hundon, Near Clare.* A traditional pub which commands good views over the surrounding countryside. The atmosphere is also traditional, the food good home cooking and the ales mainly Suffolk brewed. Accommodation, all en-suite, is also available.

*Stoke-by-Clare* is a pretty dormitory village dominated by its Church, St. John the Baptist. To the Church again we go with its beautifully small 1498 pulpit, a 1550 wall painting and a piece of 15th Century stained glass depicting a post mill.

A Benedictine Priory was transferred here from Clare in 1124, later becoming a college for secular priests - Grenville College. Little today remains of the Priory but at one time during the 18th Century it was home to the most miserly eccentric MP, John Elwes. Story has it that his wealthy mother starved herself to death not wanting to part with her money, and John himself was averse to cleaning his boots for fear it would wear them out! After injuring both his legs in an accident, he paid a doctor to heal one preferring to save money by following the doctor's practice himself on the other leg. So much for money taking the strains of life away!

If you are in this area and are not too fed up with all these churches, try St. Peter & St. Paul at *Kedington*. Things to look out for include the Anglo-Saxon cross installed in the chancel window (dug up in the vicinity in 1860), the Roman bricks, and a notable three-decker Puritan pulpit complete with wig and hourglass stand. The infamous Fairclough is said to have thundered his preachings from here, but it was John Tillets, the first priest ever to wear a wig, who hung his ludicrous accessory off this stand.

# Sudbury

Sudbury was one of the largest of Suffolk's wool towns but it has not retained the picturesque charm of the likes of Lavenham and Hadleigh, no doubt because it continued as a manufacturing town long after their trade declined. Flemish weavers originally settled here during Edward III's reign (1327-1377) and it is they who taught local inhabitants their cloth making skills especially those connected with the making of crepe. All manner of cloth continued to be produced here and as late as 1724 Daniel Defoe is able to record '... a great manufacture of says and perpetuanes.' Indeed weaving still continues in the town today; Ralph Lauren, for example, uses Sudbury woven silk for his luxury ties, and two other textile mills are also well respected.

Sudbury is a market town of ancient origin, once known as *Southburgh* to distinguish it from *Northburgh* (Norwich) and later immortalised in Charles Dickens *Pickwick Papers* as *Eatanswill*. It was here that Mr. Pickwick stood for Parliament and it is here that we learn every trick in the trade to catch the voter's favour!

The town owes much of its later success to an Act of Parliament (1705) improving the navigability of the River Stour. In its heyday as much as 12,000 tons of coal per year were moved by barge from Manningtree to Sudbury. This practice continued well into the 1900's, the last barge delivering its load to Dedham in 1930.

*The bronze statue of Gainsborough, Sudbury*

Places to visit in the town include St. Gregory's Church, rebuilt in the 14th Century by local man Simon of Sudbury, Archbishop of Canterbury (1375-81) and also Chancellor of England. His own fate though was not so dignified being executed by Wat Tyler's rebels during the Peasant's Revolt for, amongst other things, imposing a savage poll tax on labourers. His skull, rather bizarrely, is preserved in the Church vestry. The other item of real merit is the medieval, telescopic font cover.

Now to **Gainsborough's House** *(01787 372958), 46 Gainsborough Street,* to see a collection of his and his contemporaries paintings. The house itself is a half-timbered 15th Century structure with mainly Georgian modifications. It is also Gainsborough's birthplace. *Open daily, excluding Mondays. Admission charge.* Note also Sir Bertram Mackennal's bronze statue to the great man on Market Hill.

**Thomas Gainsborough** (1727-88) was the youngest son of a woollen crepe maker. From an early age he copied the works of Dutch landscape painters until, aged 14, his father sent him to London to learn the art of rococo decoration under the masterly tutorship of Gravelot. This complete he returned to Sudbury where he took up portraiture, married Margaret Burr, the Duke of Beaufort's daughter, and on her dowry was able to move to Ipswich and later to Bath where he settled into a life as both a landscape artist and portrait painter. It is for his portrait work that he is especially known and this despite the fact that his real passion was for a nostalgic Arcadian styled landscape. Of the former category his best works are perhaps typified by those of *Lord & Lady How, Mrs Portman, George III, Mr Truman* and *Mrs Graham.* As for his great landscapes, we should include *The Harvest Wagon, The Watching Place, Cottage Door* and *Cattle Crossing a Bridge.*

A few miles south of Sudbury at Lamarsh is the **Paradise Centre** *(01787 269449)), Twinstead Farm Road, Lamarsh, near Bures.* Go here if you are looking for an unusual choice of rare bulbous and tuberous plants including fritillaries, alliums, and erythronicums. The nursery also specialises in damp and shade loving plants, as they do in miniature and short-growing plants for smaller gardens. The Centre's own landscaped garden, with its panoramic views over the Stour Valley, is also open to visitors. ***Open weekends only, Easter to October.***

## Food & Accommodation

**Mabey's Brasserie,** *(01787 374298), 47 Gainsborough Street, Sudbury.* As its name advises this is a brasserie styled restaurant where some of the food is pre-prepared (starters and deserts) but the main courses are cooked to order and often very imaginative. It is a cosy, laid back atmosphere where booth-styled seating affords a pleasant degree of privacy.

**Red Onion Bistro** *(01787 376777), 57 Ballingdon Street, Sudbury.* A cheap and cheerful bistro making use of what would appear to be an old barn and to be found on the outskirts of town. The menus change daily, the produce is locally sourced, the choice wide and fun, and the decor is colourful. A good choice of wines is available by the jug.

*Boxford,* still further south-east, is an attractive village known to have once been much larger. In 1600, for example, four weavers guilds are known to have been extent - opposite the Church, a characteristic weavers hall with its high latticed window still survives - and in 1684, the local building company of W.B. Kingsbury & Son, employed an incredible 200 workers. Today, the family run business of *Copella Fruit Juices* (01787 210496) operate from Hill Farm, producing a range of different blends of quality juices. Their outlet is *open to the public during the week.*

If you wander around the village, note the pretty row of timber-framed houses in Church Street, additional timber-framed houses with oversailing upper floors in Butchers Lane, and in Riverside early Georgian properties as well as the Gothic arched Engine House. Passing the White Hart note the curious representation of a lion on the opposite side of the pavement. This commemorates Briton, the side-car partner of Wall-of-Death motor-cyclist, Tornado Smith, who used to stroll around the village with his pet lion at his side.

As for the Church, the 14th Century porch belonging to St. Mary's is wood and is probably the oldest timber porch in England. Also in the Church is the unusual 17th Century font-cover with its little doors which open up to reveal panels of printed texts.

# The North Coast

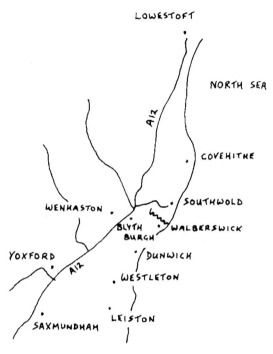

In the extreme north of the county and bordering the Waveney Valley, Lowestoft is Suffolk's principal fishing port, with a colourful quay to boot. We thus begin our exploration of Suffolk's beautiful coastline here, visiting the odd hamlet along the cliff edge before we arrive at Southwold, the most charming of all the county's seaside resorts. From Southwold we cross the River Blythe first to neighbouring Walberswick then to Dunwich where only a few vestiges of probably Suffolk's once wealthiest port remain. From here we go inland skirting the likes of Yoxford and Saxmundham before concluding our tour in the town of Leiston.

## Lowestoft

Referred to in *Domesday* (1086) as *Lothu Wistoft*, Lowestoft rose to become a Royal demesne which attracted vast privileges. So Royalist did it remain that during the Civil War, Cromwell was forced to march against the town in 1643. Today, it is one of East Anglia's main holiday resort areas but, unlike others along this coast, it has managed to retain a fairly decent sized fishing fleet and

137

*A typical catch of herring at the end of the last century*

also acts as a harbour for cargo ships carrying timber and grain. ***Tours around the quay are organised by the Tourist Information Centre*** *(01502 523000)* and are well worth the effort.

During the early 1900's, over 700 trawlers operated out of Lowestoft alone, their main catch herring and mackerel, and much of this exported to Russia, Germany, Belgium and Italy. Today, this has decreased to around 40 boats, their quotas heavily restricting the size and nature of the catch. Particularly recommended though is the locally caught cod and sole. Another way to familiarise yourself with Lowestoft's fishing industry and how it made the town prosperous is to visit the ***Maritime Museum*** *(01502 561963), Sparrows Nest Park, Whapload Road.* Housed in former fishermen's cottages, it holds the Cox Collection of model lifeboats. Lowestoft's first lifeboat was granted the town in 1801 and in 1807 its crew commanded the first lifeboat in the world to use sails.

**Lowestoft's trawler fleet today**

*The Lydia Eva*

The town has grown up along the northerly and southerly banks of the River Lothing. To the south can be found the beach, two piers - Claremont Pier and South Pier - parks and hotels and the newly built Edwardian styled East Point Pavilion housing the Tourist Information Centre, a restaurant and heritage exhibition. Also here, in the outer harbour, is the famous Royal Norfolk & Suffolk Yacht Club, additionally the *Lydia Eva*, the world's last steam drifter to be built, can usually be found in the Yacht Basin during the summer months.

To the north, over the bascule bridge, finds us in the town's shopping and commercial centre. This northerly aspect rises towards the Lighthouse and the Ness, the most easterly point in the British Isles and one which can be extraordinarily cold and windy should the necessary conditions prevail. From this main northerly street run a series of narrow, steep lanes or 'scores' down to the Denes at sea level. Some of these scores have even retained their original names, for example, Lighthouse Score, Gallows Score and Mariners Score.

Lowestoft was also once well known for its benchmen, salvagers who would launch their yawls to the rescue if a ship ran aground or struck one of the many sand banks off this coast. Organised in bands, and variously called for example The Old Company, the Young Company and The North Roads Company, the benchmen were often unpopular considered to be sharks feeding off others misfortune. But there again someone had to do the job and why not these men who also manned the lifeboats when lives were considered to be at risk. By the laws of salvage, the first boat to establish direct contact with a distressed vessel is entitled to a reward and many were the criticisms of these benchmen:

> *'A bold, artful, surly, savage race,'* [who]
> *'Wait on the shore and as the waves run high,*
> *On the toss'd vessel bend their eager eye:*
> *Which to the coast directs its vent'rous way*
> *Theirs, or the ocean's miserable prey.'* (George Crabbe)

The benchmen are no longer but a few lines from W.A. Dutt's *The Norfolk and Suffolk Coast* (1909) leaves us with a colourful picture of the Old Company's beach shed:

> *'... a tarred and red-tiled building standing near the coastguard station*
> *has its exterior adorned with the figureheads and name-boards of*
> *several ships that were wrecked on the coast, and in it, on winter*
> *days, when storms are raging, the older members of the company*
> *sit around a glowing fire, talking of the wrecks, the*
> *rescues and the salvages of fifty more years ago.'*

Other places to visit in and around the town include St. Margaret's Church, a spacious 15th Century flint building set well back from the sea and containing many memorials to men who distinguished themselves in Royal Navy Service. And on *Raglan Street*, a visit to the 200 year old **Raglan Smokehouse** *(01502 581929)* will enable you not only to see the operations of a traditional smoke-house in full swing but also allow you to take away whatever you fancy - cod, haddock, trout, sprats, kippers or herring. This is the one of the last two sur-viving smokehouses in the town, the only ones of 135 houses to withstand the ravages of time. The other operation can be found at *J.T. Cole's (01502 574446), November Road.*

At **Broad House** on nearby *Oulton Broad (01502 511457)* is the **Lowestoft Museum** which documents the history of the town admirably well and further contains a large collection of important Lowestoft Porcelain. ***Open variously from the end of March to the end of October. Admission charge.***

In 1756, a gentleman by the name of Hewlin Luson discovered a fine clay on his Gunton estate. He duly sent a sample of the same to a London china manufac-turer who considered it to be finer than that used for Delft ware. Within a year of his initial find, Luson had set up, with four other partners including the most active Robert Brown, the first Lowestoft producing factory. Bit by bit, operating from premises in Bell Lane, the company became known for this soft porcelain which usually in the early days was decorated in blue and white oriental style. Later pieces were moulded and a red tone, peculiar to Lowestoft, was added. Through 1768 to 1784, the firm of Robert Brown & Co. flourished, but by the turn of the century various problems hampered manufacture not least the tran-sition from wood to coal firing. The much larger Staffordshire potteries also left Lowestoft at a distinct disadvantage, their operations much more competitive and influential; so much so that by 1803 the Lowestoft factory was no longer.

Nonetheless, Lowestoft Porcelain remains highly collectible today and where better (probably only Norwich Castle Museum) to see it then in the town itself.

Lowestoft enjoys many literary associations not least with native born **Thomas Nashe** (1567-1601), the brilliant but dissolute 16th Century dramatist and satirist Other well known writers who spent much time here include **Edward Fitzgerald, George Crabbe** and **George Borrow**, the latter living at Oulton Broad from where he wrote his masterpieces of Gypsy lore *Lavengro* and *Romany Rye*. Then in June 1878, a young Polish immigrant docked here on a boat from Marseilles, his name Jozef Konrad-Korzeniowski. He later became a Captain in the British Merchant Navy but is best known for his works *Heart of Darkness* and *Lord Jim*, penned under **Joseph Conrad**, a close rendition of his original name. Involved in an altogether different art form was **Benjamin Britten**, born in Lowestoft, appropriately enough on the 22nd November 1913, the feast day of St. Cecilia - the patron saint of music.

Another nearby museum, *The East Anglian Transport Museum (01502 518459), Chapel Road, Carlton Colville,* holds a large collection of street and commercial transport vehicles both static and operational. You can for example take a trip on a traditional trolleybus or on the Museum's 2" gauge railway. *Open variously Easter to September. Admission charge.*

Also in the vicinity is *Carlton Marshes Reserve*, a dyked grazing marsh with much wet woodland and a number of peat diggings. Managed by the Suffolk Wildlife Trust, this is a breeding ground for many species of bird and is also an area rich in plantlife including water-soldier, marsh-pea, cowbane and frogbit.

## Entertainment:

*Piers: Claremont Pier* provides amusements, angling, games and a licensed bar and the *South Pier* amusements, angling and cafes.

*Pleasurewood Hills Theme Park (01502 508200), Corton,* provides fun for the whole family whether it be the circus, Punch & Judy, or the myriad of rides from juveniles to a white-knuckle roller-coaster. *Open daily, mid May to mid September and some weekends either side of these months.*

*Theatres:* a number of theatres offer a varied programme including the *Marina Theatre (01502 573318)* and *The Seagull Theatre (01502 562863).*

## Sports Venues:

*Boat Hire:* motor launches for Broads use can be hired from *Day Launch Hire (01502 513087), The Yacht Station, Oulton Broad.*

*Horse Riding: Pakefield Riding School (01502 572257), Carlton Road, Lowestoft* is

BHS approved.

*Sailing:* the historic Lowestoft built sailing trawler *Excelsior* can be joined for trips to Europe lasting between two days and a couple of weeks. Summer season only.

*Walking: The Suffolk Coast Path* runs between Lowestoft and Felixstowe taking in a stretch of about 45 miles over crumbling cliffs, mud flats, shingle banks, estuaries, marshland and nature reserves. A leaflet describing the walk is available from the Suffolk County Planning Department, Suffolk County Council, Ipswich.

*Watersports: Wayman Outdoor & Leisure Activities Centre (01502 564621)* run a number of windsurfing courses on Oulton Broad. There is also an *indoor climbing wall* here available to visitors Monday to Saturday (daytime only).

## Food & Accommodation

**The Plough** *(01502 730261), Market Lane, Blundeston.* An old country pub built in 1701, but smartly modernised. Dickens is thought to have supped here and indeed this is *The Blunderstone* of *David Copperfield* fame, and The Plough, the inn from which Mr. Barkis set off from. Retention of the original oak panelling, exposed beams, open fires and high back settles means we can enjoy good ale in an atmosphere not that dissimilar from that which Dickens must have found, though naturally now equipped with all the necessary mod cons. Dickens fans should also note the sundial over the old church porch.

A southerly outcrop of Lowestoft, **Pakefield** was once known for its 'Roaring Boys', male villagers noted for their smuggling prowess and about whom an old son was written:

> 'The roaring boys of Pakefield
> Oh, how they do thrive!
> They had but one poor parson
> And him they buried alive.'

This last line does not ring quite true, for it was the Rev. Francis Cunningham, Rector from 1814-1830, who on many occasions assisted the 'Roaring Boys' exploits. Indeed, he even held a burial service in full view of the excise men, only the coffin was minus a body and packed full instead with contraband which was later distributed amongst the villagers.

The almost unbroken line of cliffs between Lowestoft and **Kessingland** is the most imposing along the Suffolk coast. Nonetheless, they are still barely more than 70 feet high. The sea's encroachment here seems to have been less damaging than at southerly Covehithe but as Rider Haggard recalls the great gales of winter 1897 we should not be complacent: '... [it] *will long be remembered on the east coast for its terrible amount of damage ... for here* [Kessingland} *and at Pakefield the high cliff has been taken away by the thousand tons.'* (*Farmers Year.*)

Today, Kessingland is home to the **Suffolk Wildlife Park** *(01502 740291)*, where an African Safari like experience can be enjoyed in over 100 acres of countryside. A special entertainments programme for children is run during the school holidays. *Open daily. Admission charge.*

*Covehithe*, a little further south of Lowestoft, was once as its name suggests a small port equipped with a hythe or staithe. Serious cliff erosion along this part of the coast has seen much of the original village disappear into the sea, and what is left - mainly the church and a couple of farmsteads - face further uncertainty.

The original church here is thought to have been built in the 15th Century, its vast scale out of all proportion to the village's population. Finance for the same is thought to have come from William Yarmouth and the first cleric was appointed in 1459 under the patronage of Norfolk's Prior and Monastery of Thetford. Dowsing, however, destroyed over 200 monuments here at St. Andrew's alone and all that is left of the original church is the large west tower and the walls. The current and quaint, small, thatched Church was built in what was left of the nave in 1672.

Covehithe is also thought to have been the birthplace of the Protestant Bishop of Ossory, John Bale (1495-1563). Not only was Bale a weighty defender of the principles of the Reformation but he also played a major part in establishing the importance of English drama. He wrote a number of Morality and Historical Plays and in one, *King John*, he ridiculed the Catholic Church in Rome for having divided itself into a multitude of 'holy religions'. Nick-named 'Bilious Bale', he offended the Catholics to such a degree that they attacked his home killing all of his servants.

**The crumbling cliff line at Covehithe**

# Blythburgh

Until the 16th Century, Blythburgh was a bustling sea port but then the river silted up and put paid to most seafaring trade, except that is the smuggling which was at its height during the 18th Century. So important was Blythburgh that it even had its own mint, two annual Charter Fairs, and a jail standing in the shadow of Holy Trinity Church. Today, it is this majestic 15th Century Church which attracts our attention and which is rightly considered one of Suffolk's finest, often referred to as 'The Cathedral of the Marshes'. Holy Trinity was built on a site where Christians are believed to have worshiped since 630 AD, and in the *Domesday* survey, Blythburgh, as a Royal burgh, is listed as having one of the richest churches in Suffolk. The Priory itself was founded in 1130 and it is to this that Henry IV granted the right to build the current structure in 1412. What scanty remains there are of the former Augustinian Priory can be found in the gardens of Priory House (private).

As for Holy Trinity, there is so much to see that the following description of some of the more important items barely does it justice. One of the first sights you will see upon opening the door is the angel roof, a huge unbroken, tie-beam roof which spans from the nave to the chancel carrying 18 pairs of angels painted in red, green and gold leaf. The angels hang in pairs back to back, facing east and west and each has a different countenance. The light which streams in the clerestory windows is such that you cannot but hold this remarkable craftsmanship - using neither nails nor bolts - in awe.

Next, look for the 15th Century poppyhead carvings on the bench ends, and which depict the Deadly Sins: Drunkenness is in the stocks to sober up, Sloth is in bed, Avarice sits on a chest of money, Hypocrisy prays with open eyes, Gluttony has a rather distended belly and Slander reveals a split tongue, remind

**Blythburgh's Holy Trinity Church**

*Jack-o'-the-Clock*

ing us of the punishment which awaited those of this bent. The rood screen is typically late medieval and the pulpit, a superb example of 17th Century Jacobean work. As for the choir stalls, their carvings depict the apostles, saints and a king. But perhaps one of the most favoured items is the Jack-o'-the-Clock, one of few to survive in England; ironically, there is another in Southwold's Church. Dating from 1682, this wooden man painted in his armour originally struck the hours of the clock with his hatchet hitting the bell, but now is only used to announce the beginning of the service. These are amongst the more important of Holy Trinity's contents but perhaps its size and simple majesty and the exquisite light which streams through the windows here is all we need to appreciate its true beauty and uniqueness.

*Detail of the tie-beam roof*

## Food & Accommodation

**The Queen's Head** *(01502 478404), Blyford, near Blythburgh.* A 15th Century, thatched pub which has been attractively furnished and which still retains its low beamed bar, antique furniture and open fireplace. Noted for its fine food - choose from an elaborate evening menu which features fish and game or a simpler lunchtime offering - and hand-pumped ales.

**The White Hart** *(01502 478217), Blythburgh.* With its Dutch gables, moulded and carved ceilings, Elizabethan beams and Stuart staircase, The White Hart was once a court house bearing further testimony if any is needed to Blythburgh's former importance. Although on the side of a busy road, it enjoys a position opposite the Church and to the other side a spacious lawn looks over the tidal marshes here. The pub is known for its well kept Adnams ales and a decent offering of wines.

Just beyond Blythburgh, **Wenhaston** is known for its *Doom*, a large painted panel of The Last Judgement to be found in St. Peter's Church. Dated variously between 1480 and the early 1500's, it survived dissolution as it had earlier been white-washed to comply with a 1545 Parliamentary Order. The architect Sir Nikolaus Pevsner does not find anything about it to like, calling it '... *distressingly rustic.*' Individual tastes being what they are, I found it a quite splendid, vibrant offering where the Divine Judge sits upon a rainbow his hand raised in the form of a blessing, St. Michael weighs the scales, St. Peter holds the key to the gates of a castle, Satan holds a scroll and the fish' head presumably serves to remind us of the jaws of Hell.

*Detail from Wenhaston's Doom*

146

# *Walk 18: Blythburgh and the River*

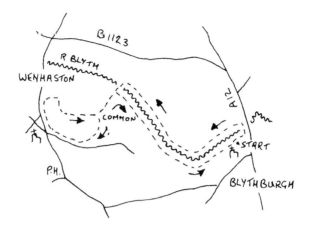

## *Directions:*

1. From your park at Blythburgh Church, go into a narrow lane and turn left. Go right by a small green to pass two timber-framed houses. At the main A12, go left and cross the bridge over the marsh. Look for a signed footpath on your immediate left which will take you to the River bank. 2. Continue along the banks of the River Blyth for approx. one and a half miles - note this stretch can be quite overgrown especially in summer so stout shoes and sensible clothes (not shorts) are recommended. The occasional stile will be encountered along the way as will a bridge but always return to the River bank once you have negotiated any channel cuts. 3. Cross over the second bridge and follow the path over some pasture land plus the small bridges in front of you. Go through the first farm gate and the next one on your right which leads into a lane. At a cottage, go left to pass a farm on your right. Go right along a track to a road and then right again into Wenhaston. 4. Continue along the road into Wenhaston, past the Church, keeping to the right and heading towards Blyford. Look for a path (signed) on your right and walk along the edge of a field. Turn right at a track, and just before the farm go left on a path leading to Blowers Common. Keep left at the next farm to retrace your steps back to the River Blyth. 5. Do not cross the River but instead follow the path on your right back to Blythburgh Church (approx one and a half miles).

**Start: Blythburgh Church**
**Approx. Distance: 5 Miles**
**Approx. Time: 2.5 Hours**
**Map: Landranger 156**

## *Southwold*

Southwold is the most alluring of Suffolk's coastal towns with an air of grace and tranquillity all its own, and standing proudly sentinel over Sole Bay. Much of the town was destroyed by fire in 1659 so today we find an amalgam of Dutch and Flemish influenced, Regency and Victorian buildings set around greens and squares and some facing eastwards over the North Sea. Along the beach is as colourful array of beach huts as you will find anywhere.

Southwold has for centuries been known for its fishing industry with *Domesday* (1086) recording an annual rent of 25,000 herrings per year and further documenting a sea weir: what was probably a wicker fence like structure built out to sea to entrap the fish. It remained an important port through to the 16th Century sending more fishing and merchant ships to Iceland than any other English port. Then came the Battle of Sole Bay off this shore in 1672, against the Dutch fleet, and with no real victor. One can only imagine that much of the town's own shipping was lost as a consequence as too a large proportion of its male population. Ironically, 17 years later, Britain had a Dutch King in the form of William of Orange. Attempts were made to seize back the monopoly the Dutch had gained over herring fishing, and to this end the Free British Fishery Company was set up in 1750, its headquarters in Buss Creek. At its height, the Company had over 50 square-rigged vessels under its authority, but by 1792 it was no longer and the fishermen were once again reduced to their beach punts. Only in the late 19th and early 20th Centuries was there any significant return to large scale fishing with Southwold harbour enjoying the seasonal occupation

**The Swan Hotel**

*Southwold*

of the Scottish drifters and their large entourage of workers. This too was fairly short-lived, the herring industry finding better anchorage at the more northerly ports of Lowestoft and Great Yarmouth. Southwold's hopes were thus finally dashed and today only a handful of fishing boats are still in operation. Their catch highly recommended and available from either **John's** *(01502 724253)* on *East Street* or alternatively direct from the fishermen's own huts which flank the harbour entrance to the south of the town.

Much of the town's history is preserved in the **Southwold Museum** *(01502 722711)*, *Victoria Street*, **The RNLI Lifeboat Museum** *(01502 722422)* and **The Sailors' Reading Room** on *East Cliff*. The latter was originally financed by the widow of a ship's captain in 1864 in an attempt to encourage the fishermen to give up drinking in favour of reading. It is a truly charming place, its walls adorned with paintings, prints, photographs and with a number of model boats and other memorabilia on display including one of the last yawls to be built, *The Bittern*. The old fishermen do use the place but perhaps not as intended finding billiards, poker and a good ol' yarn amongst their favourite poisons. Still, do go in as it is a most unusual and eccentric meeting place.

St. Edmund's Church built in the 15th Century on a much earlier site also deserves a visit not least to admire the rood screen with its 30 or so figures, the magnificent carvings on the choir stalls, the equally superb and colourful hammerbeam roof, and the colourful 'Southwold Jack' that now rare medieval striker of the bell heralding the services start (see also an equally rare example in Blythburgh Church). In 1643, Dowsing, Cromwell's henchman and iconoclast, was to find much to occupy himself with here writing in his diary: *'We broke down 130 superstitious pictures, St. Andrew and four crosses on the four corners of the vestry, and gave orders to take down thirteen cherubims, twenty angels and the cover of the font.'*

The best way to appreciate Southwold is simply to wander around its many streets and then take a southerly course along the beach towards Walberswick where, once at the harbour, you can either take the little ferry (summer only) to the other side or the footbridge further along. Retail outlets worth investigating in the town include *The Amber Shop* (01502 723394), *15 Market Place*, with its large collection of amber jewellery - Southwold beach was once known for its raw amber - and Adnams *Cellar & Kitchen Store* (01502 722138), *Sole Bay Brewery*, with its large selection of wines sourced direct the world over; Adnams are regularly voted Wine Merchants of the Year so you will not be disappointed about the choice on offer. Adnams also continue to brew an excellent range of local ales in Southwold and you can often still see these being delivered by horse and dray to various establishments around the town. Also well worth a try is Adnams own very affordable Champagne, bottled especially for the Company.

*The Sailors' Reading Room*

# Food & Accommodation

**The Bell** *(01502 723109), Ferry Road, Walberswick.* The Bell can date its origins way back to the 1300's, and can be found only a couple of minutes walk from the beach and harbour. It is a rambling, Grade II listed, oak-beamed pub with high backed settles, stone and tiled floors and some interesting items of wall decoration. Generally unspoilt and unpretentious, it does get very busy with locals and visitors alike.

**The Crown** *(01502 722275), 90 High Street, Southwold.* Owned by Adnams, this is a well-run, comfortable inn especially noted for its imaginative and well-preserved food and where the menu changes daily. To be expected, the range of wines on offer is also extensive. The decor in the main is rightly simple but nonetheless exudes a rustic elegance: settles, wooden tables and a fine carved fireplace. Plus a small restaurant leads off to a rather quieter area. If you intend to eat here, it is best to arrive early (or book the restaurant) as it does get very busy. Accommodation is also available.

**The Lord Nelson** *(01502 722079), East Street, Southwold.* A good solid pub with a traditional old atmosphere. Low ceilings, tiled floors, wood panelling and interesting bric a brac items create the setting for what can also be a very busy drinking place, especially at weekends. Good lunchtime food.

**Mary's** *(01502 723243), Manor House, Walberswick.* You can choose to enjoy either your morning coffee, lunch, afternoon tea or evening dinner here, though lunches are generally the main attraction. The menus are good, simple and wholesome and there is a preponderance of fresh, locally caught fish. A cheerful spot not afraid to make use of maritime paraphernalia in its decor. Evening meals are only available on Fridays and Saturdays.

**The Swan** *(01502 722186), Market Place, Southwold.* A notable and stylish landmark, The Swan (Adnams controlled) has a brick and white painted facade, railed balconies and symmetrical three-storey bay windows. Although rebuilt in 1660 it was remodelled in the 1800's with some further enhancements this century. The high ceilinged drawing room is comfortably furnished in well balanced plain and floral fabrics. The carved wooden panels have also been retained above the doorframes, windows and mantelpieces, and the walls are decorated with prints and paintings. The formal dining room is especially elegant and here you can choose anything from traditional fare to English classics, with much local fish and game on offer. Again, to be expected the choice of wines is excellent. Many of the bedrooms enjoy glimpses of the sea and superior rooms are well worth the extra in terms of space and antique furnishings; best of all, if funds allow, treat yourself to one of the suites. You will not regret it.

*Walberswick* today is very much inhabited by second-homers, artists and media personalities but before all this it was home to the 'Walberswick Whisperers', so called because their loud voices could be heard across the marshes and river in Southwold.  It is an attractive place but now much smaller than it was even in the 14th Century when it was one of the main exporting ports for Suffolk cheese and butter, and could count amongst its fleet 13 barks trading the Iceland and Faroe Isles route plus another 22 fishing vessels.  Even at the beginning of our own century, it bustled with the merry activities of the Scottish 'fisher girls' who boarded in the village during their three month stint at the Southwold fish wharf:

> *'These buxom lassies, clad in glistening oilskin overalls*
> *and wearing heavy, high-topped boots, considerably*
> *enliven the village during their stay in it.  No one*
> *can watch them at work upon the herrings without*
> *being amazed at their dexterity, nor can one*
> *listen to their singing ... without  wishing*
> *they were always here ...'*
> (W.A.Dutt, *The Norfolk and Suffolk Coast*, 1909).

Today, there are only a few fishermen operating out of the village, and many of these only part-timers.

Sheep rearing around the heath known as Tinkers Walk was also once a prosperous enterprise recorded in *Domesday* but reaching its heyday sometime around the late 17th and early 18th Centuries.  Increasingly, the practice is now being reintroduced encouraged in part by EC farming initiatives and subsidies.

Artists too have found much to celebrate in this picturesque corner of Suffolk's coast, most notably Philip Wilson Steer, whose paintings of the locality can be found in the Tate Gallery, London, as also Charles Rennie Mackintosh with his exquisite plantlife watercolours, over 40 of which can be attributed to his sojourn in Walberswick. It is certainly a lovely corner of Suffolk, best explored on foot, whether via the ferryman over the River Blyth to Southwold, south along The Flats and through the marshes or generally within the **Walberswick Reserve**.  Managed by the Nature Conservancy Council, the Reserve is known especially for its large numbers of rare and local moth species.

*Scottish Fisher Girls*

# *Walk 19: Southwold and Walberswick*

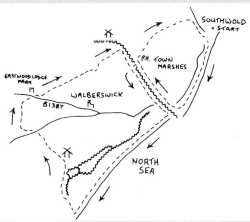

## Directions:

1. From your park in Southwold, head towards the sea and walk in a southerly direction along the shore (approx. one mile), passing the pretty beach huts and chalets and so to Southwold Harbour. 2. Go right here along a rough track which leads past the boats and boat-sheds. In summer look for a little rowing boat ferry which will take you across the River Blythe to Walberswick; otherwise continue along the track passing the pub until you come to a bridge. Cross over this and go left along the Blythe's opposite bank until you reach the same point as the ferry would have deposited you at. Continue to follow the River Blyth to its sea mouth, crossing next the River Dunwich by a footbridge and then turn right along the southerly shore again. 3. Continue along the shore for just under two miles, turning inland along a path nearly opposite a stretch of land reaching into the marshes and known as Dingle Great Hill. 4. Make sure you follow the left-hand bank along the creek which will take you to a windmill, now minus its sails. Near the windmill, another path joins in from the left; do not go left but instead follow what is now a single path straight ahead. 5. At the next meeting of paths, go left leaving the River Dunwich to head across the marsh. This path leads to East Hill on your left and passes the extreme fringe of Hoist Covert on your right. The pathway changes from reedbed to heathland and then to sandy track. 6. At the road, go slightly left to follow a path on your right leading across East Sheep Walk and along a belt of pine and birch trees. At the end of this, go right along a path to Eastwood Lodge Farm. 7. At the road (B1387), go right for a short distance and then left through a farm gate into a meadow. The path you now take runs parallel, in places, to the dis-used railway line. Go straight ahead ignoring left and right intersec-tions and so to Squires Hill. 8. Continue straight ahead to the bridge across the Blythe once more. Once over this, go right as far as the pub and just before this take the left track across Town Marshes to return to Southwold.

### Start: Southwold Shore
### Approx. Distance: 8.5. Miles (7 Miles if you catch the ferry)
### Approx. Time: 4 Hours  Map: Landranger 156

# Dunwich

Our last coastal stop in the more northerly part of the county is Dunwich, which derives its name from the Celtic *Dubno* or deep water and the Saxon *wic* meaning port. Today, most of it lies buried under sea and sand but not before it became one of the greatest and most prosperous ports in England. It is also claimed that Christianity first made its way to the British Isles via Dunwich, Saint Felix, a missionary from Burgundy, arriving here in 632 AD. Here he crowned the Saxon Sigebert as King of East Anglia and it was at Dunwich that Sigebert built his palace.

Even the Norman *Domesday* (1086) record reports Dunwich with 3,000 inhabitants (Ipswich's population at this time less than half this figure), three churches, 236 burgesses, 178 poormen, 80 mere men, and rendering 68,000 herrings per year as tax. Dunwich's importance as both a fishing and trading port was at its peak during the 13th Century when it was classed as East Anglia's second largest town, Norwich being just that bit bigger. An incredible 18 churches and monasteries are recorded at this time and trade supported by 80 vessels - among them 11 men o' war, 20 barks trading the North Sea and Iceland, and 24 smaller boats for the home fishery - as compared with Ipswich's 30. But then came a devastating storm in 1328 which saw over 400 homes and three churches lost to the ravages of the sea and the port itself blocked, a victim of the silting caused by the movement of shingle and sand.

> **John Daye** (1522-84), the printer and inventor of the Saxon typeface, was born in Dunwich although he later set up his press in London; he is buried in the churchyard at Little Bradley near Newmarket. Daye was one of the first English music printers, producing in 1560 the earliest church service book complete with musical notation. He is perhaps best known though for the celebrated publication in 1563 of Foxe's *Actes and Monuments*, commonly known as the *Book of Martyrs*, and for being the first to publish the *Psalms* in English.

Dunwich's problems did not end there for, bit by bit, more of the town was lost to the sea and by the end of the 17th Century even the Market Place was no longer. Although fishing and trade continued on a smaller scale, Dunwich's prosperous heights were over. Visiting the town in 1724, Daniel Defoe was still able to record the export of butter, cheese and corn, the ships though having to use Walberswick's more northerly port, as he was one element of the fisherman's trade: '... *they use sprats in the same manner as they do herrings at Yarmouth, that is ... they make sprats red.'* (*Tour Through the Eastern Counties.*)

As for later documentors of Dunwich's story, perhaps the poet Swinburne (1837-1909) captures its sad fate best. Contemplating All Saints Church, which had begun its slippery descent into the North Sea at the beginning of this century, he wrote:

> *'One hollow tower and hoary,*
> *Naked in the sea-wind stands and moans*

*Filled and thrilled with its perpetual story;*
*Here, where earth is dense with dead men's bones.'*

Today, Dunwich is little more than a small, quaintish village with a fairly modest Victorian Church, and little more than one hundred inhabitants. The fishermen still draw their boats up onto the shingle bank and if you catch them at the right time, you can buy their fresh catches there and then. Alternatively, the beach cafe serves some good fish and chips. Do take the trouble to visit the small *Dunwich Museum (01728 648796), St. James Street,* which illustrates the history of Dunwich from Roman times to the present day. The displays also cover the natural history of the area. *Open variously March to October. Admission charge.*

You can also visit the scanty ruins of the leper hospital of St. James, and those of the Franciscan Friary of Greyfriars, rebuilt with Edward I's permission in 1289 after the first building was lost to the sea. Like other monasteries, it too was suppressed during the 1538 dissolution and now only the 13th Century gateway and ruins of the refectory and precinct walls remain.

## Food & Accommodation

**The National Trust** *(01225 791199)* have three self-catering holiday flats at Dunwich Heath, **one of which is equipped for disabled visitors.** All form part of a row of former *Coastguard Cottages* used for that purpose until 1907. Superb views can be enjoyed over the Minsmere Reserve as they can out to sea. The National Trust tea room occupies part of the ground floor and a look-out-room part of the first floor. ( **Sleeps 4/2/2.)**

On the outskirts of Dunwich village, *The National Trust (01225 791199)* have also recently made available *Bridge Farm Cottage* for holiday rental. This pretty semi-detached cottage is situated in a quiet lane close to all amenities. **(Sleeps 4.)**

*The Ship (01728 648219), St James Street, Dunwich.* This is an atmospheric inn where not unexpectedly a nautical theme pervades and where the furnishings are traditional. Close to the beach, the Heath and Minsmere this is a great place to rest weary legs and enjoy some good ale and tasty food.

Surely though the main purpose of any visit to Dunwich must be to enjoy either a ramble around *Dunwich Heath* - managed by the National Trust - or a visit to *Minsmere RSPB Reserve. Note the latter is closed on Tuesdays and is for members only on Sundays.*

The 215 acres which make up *Dunwich Heath* are an excellent example of sandlings, heather and scrubland. Look out for a wide variety of grasses and sedges as also for linnet and yellow-hammers, and you might just hear the

**Dunwich Beach**

nightjar at dusk on summers evenings. This gently rolling heath is stopped at the beach by the low sand and gravel cliffs; all in all, very picturesque. You can even take advantage of the National Trust's Information and Observation Room which can be found in the former Coastguard Cottages, as can The Trust's Cafe. *The Heath is open all year, dawn to dusk. Nominal car park charge only.*

Bordering onto the Heath is *Minsmere Reserve* one of the RSPB's most significant holdings and noted for its exceptional variety of wetland species. An important feature here is the scrape - shallow lagoons constructed from derelict marshland. Over 280 species of bird have been recorded on this site alone including the spoonbill, osprey and purple heron. The plantlife is also very varied and amongst those to be seen are the rare marsh sow-thistle, hemp agrimony, yellow iris and orchid. The Society has constructed a number of observation hides and *access is by permit only available to non-members at the site.* Lovers of P.D. James work may also be interested to know that she drew upon Minsmere Reserve and one of the hides here as the setting for the murder committed in *Unnatural Causes*.

*Westleton*, just beyond Dunwich, is a fine, proud village standing around the pond and green, referred to locally as Green Ditch. Most of the cottages are 19th Century but thatched St. Peter's Church was built by the monks of Sibton Abbey as early as 1340. Story goes that there is a piece of stone near the priest's door over which no grass will grow, in other words it is a witch's stone. Supposedly, if you place a handkerchief in the grate of the wall and run round the church in an easterly, anti-clockwise direction you will hear the Devil's chains clanking below the grating. Not to be recommended!

The village is more popularly known though for its nationally acclaimed *Fisk's Clematis Nursery (01728 648236)*. Here you will find any amount of clematis varieties to choose from, and if you need a little help or inspiration then take a look in their own display garden. *Open during the week, plus weekends during the summer months.*

# *Walk 20: The Lost Town of Dunwich*

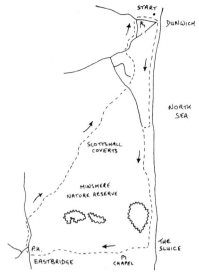

## *Directions:*

1. From your park near the beach at Dunwich, turn right along the beach and walk in a southerly direction for approx, one and a half miles. Go up the third set of steps up the cliffs. Continue along the cliff path through the car park, past the Coastguard Cottages and National Trust Centre, past a series of World War II concrete tank defences and past Minsmere Nature Reserve. 2. At the sluice gate, go right, but taking the left hand path (signed) through a gate to go inland following the drainage channel. (The path further to your right leads through Minsmere Reserve.) Continue along this path (following the yellow waymarker signs) to Eastbridge passing the remains of a Premonstratensian Chapel on your left, and where you meet a track on your left continue along the footpath to the right of some trees. After another grouping of trees, cross over a track to get into Eastbridge. 3. At the road, go right to walk through the village and past the pub. Cross the bridge and after approx, a quarter of a mile look for a tarmac track through the trees on your right. Where the track later leads off right, continue straight ahead along a bridleway. 4. Walk through the edge of Minsmere Reserve/Westleton Walks and when after three-quarters of a mile you come to a private road on your right continue straight ahead (signed Bridleway) into Scottshall Coverts. 5. Continue straight ahead for approx. two miles, ignoring all left and right intersections, until your come to the road. 6. Cross the road to take the path ahead of you through the woods. Cross over a track and where the path forks, keep to the right. Once at an unmade road, go left to another road. 7. Go right here and then left, and where the road forks again go left. At the corner with the Church, go right to return to Dunwich beach.

**Start: Dunwich Beach  Approx, Distance: 8 Miles**
**Approx. Time: 4 Hours  Map: Landranger:156**

*Yoxford* is an attractive village just a few miles from the coast and unusually well graced with general provision shops, restaurants, galleries, antique shops and a secondhand bookshop. Particularly good is *Susan Wells Antiques*, specialists in 18th and 19th Century period furniture. An extraordinary mix of architectural styles can also be found here from Tudor cottages to a Trafalgar styled balcony and a house with a *tromp l'oeil* facade. At nearby **Darsham**, you can hire bicycles from *Byways Bicycles (01728 668764), Priory Farm,* who have a fleet of over 100 bikes and can also offer a number of pre-planned routes if you are uncomfortable designing your own.

## Food & Accommodation

**Darsham Old Hall** *(01728 668514), Darsham.* Here you can enjoy B & B styled accommodation with a difference for parts of this building date back as far as the 11th Century. Later 17th Century additions are obvious and many of the oak beams and sloping floors have been retained. The bedroom accommodation is of an especially decent size and guests can also use the conservatory and galleried hall. Alternatively, there is croquet on the lawn or just enjoy the quiet landscaped garden. Packed lunches are also available.

**The Old Chequers** *(01728 688270), Aldeburgh Road, Friston.* Pine furniture, exposed brickwork, beams and wood burning stoves greet visitors to this pub. The emphasis here though is on food and the choice excellent (especially in the evenings); anything from locally caught fresh fish to locally shot game.

**The Parrot & Punch Bowl** *(01728 830221), Aldringham.* A rich history surrounds this 16th Century establishment, no stranger to the smuggling activities of its former locals. A typical colour-washed Suffolk building with a traditional interior of exposed timbers and split levels. Well kept ales, a good choice of wines, and a very busy dining room at weekends when you must book your table if you intend to eat here.

Next, to *Saxmundham*, a small market town which unfortunately has little to commend itself save perhaps the 16th Century glass in St. John the Baptist's Church. Lovers of herbs though may like to try **Laurel Farm Herbs**, *Laurel Farmhouse, Main Road, Kelsale,* who grow over 100 varieties and a particularly good selection of rosemary, lavender, thyme, basil, and mint. *Open daily, April to October.* Alternatively, at nearby **Knodishall** is **Good Food Growers** *(01728 830620), Green Trees,* specialist growers of figs and grape vines. Although they are primarily wholesalers, callers are welcome by appointment. Also in Knodishall is potter **Jonathan Keep** *(01728 823901), 31 Leiston Road,* best known for his large range of kitchen and tableware but equally adept at large sculptural pots. Visitors are welcome but *please phone before turning up.*

# Leiston

The larger and more interesting town to be found at Leiston was once home to an important engineering company manufacturing agricultural implements. Established in 1778, Garretts originally were little more than a blacksmith operation making horseshoes and grills. From these early beginnings, they moved on to the production of threshing machines, steam rollers, traction engines, ploughs and tractors and were even commissioned by the Tsar to build many of Russia's railway engines. So successful were Garrett's skilled labourers that over 1,000 were employed by the company at the end of the 19th Century. Success continued throughout the first half of the 20th Century, with Garretts manufacturing thousands upon thousands of grenades used with devastating effect during the two World Wars. Then in 1980 the company closed, to be restored three years later as an industrial museum. Today, the *Long Shop Museum (01728 832189)* - the Long Shop originally built in 1853 as an erecting shop for traction engines and one of the earliest British examples of an 'Assembly Line' production - houses three exhibition halls and a gallery where the whole range of Garrett produced machinery can be seen. *Open daily, April to the end of October. Admission charge.*

Just north of the town are the imposing ruins of *Leiston Abbey* founded for Premonstratensian Canons by Sir Ranulf de Glanville in 1182 and moved here from Minsmere in 1363. The brick and flint built remains are amongst the most extensive in Suffolk and include the Church transepts and cloisters and the restored (1920) Lady Chapel which is still in use. The site is managed by English Heritage and is *open all year, free of charge.*

*A Garrett Showman's Engine used by J Cottrell to power his Picture Show.*
*Seen here at the Leiston Works*

Also on the outskirts of the town is ***Summerhill Boarding School*** founded by Neill Alexander Sutherland in 1924 and now run by his daughter. Summerhill is something of a 'revolutionary school', one where the pupils do not have to attend classes unless they want to although the majority do do so on a voluntary basis. The school has met with much criticism for its overly flexible and 'free' stance but the pupils it turns out appear fairly well-rounded individuals. In his *Summerhill: A Radical Approach to Child Rearing* (1960), Sutherland summed up the sentiment behind the School's founding as follows: *'I would rather see the school produce a happy street cleaner than a neurotic scholar.'*

Close to Leiston, a visit of a different kind can be made to the ***Sizewell Visitor Centre*** *(01728 831654).* Situated alongside Sizewell A and B nuclear power stations, the purpose built Exhibition Hall seeks to inform us about the whole process of electricity generation, including nuclear; the stations themselves channel power to the Midlands along pylons and cables. The Exhibition is accompanied by a high-tech light and sound show. ***Open daily for guided tours which should be pre-booked. Admission free.*** Devotees of P.D. James work will be interested to learn that Sizewell was featured as *Larksoken* in her crime novel *Devices and Desires* (1989), and its situation moved to the Norfolk coast.

# The South Coast

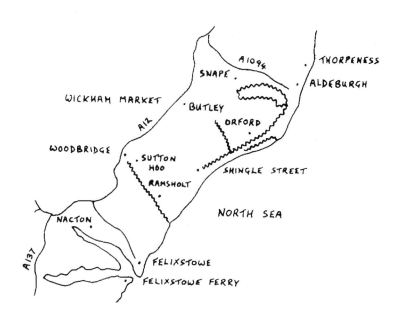

S uffolk's more southerly coast begins for our purposes at least at Aldeburgh which offers a different more open sort of charm than that to be found in its northerly equivalent Southwold. From Aldeburgh and its northerly outpost Thorpeness, we follow the marshy reaches of the River Alde to Snape, the home of the Aldeburgh Festival begun by Benjamin Britten. Then to Wickham Market before a visit to Butley and on to Orford sheltering from the North Sea behind a constantly extending shingle bank. Back inland thereafter to the delightful market town of Woodbridge, and along the northern banks of the Deben Estuary to the likes of Sutton Hoo. Given the nature of Suffolk's estuaries, we then have to retrace our steps to journey the northerly banks of the Orwell Estuary to the vast container port of Felixstowe. The southerly banks of the Orwell, however, are left to our last Chapter for they are best pursued via the county's capital, Ipswich.

## Aldeburgh

Aldeburgh was once an ancient port which rivalled the likes of Dunwich to its

**Aldeburgh Beach**

north and Orford in the south. It was left to the Saxons, however, who invaded the shore after the Romans departed to give the town its name of *Aldeburc* or old port, suggesting the existence of such a defensive structure even then. The fact that three Roman roads lead towards Aldeburgh perhaps provides some weight to this theory. Under the Saxons, the manors of Aldeburgh and Snape were combined and formed part of the possessions of the See and Priory of Ely. By the time the Normans had arrived though this manor had clearly become rather depleted.

Little more of substance is known until Edward VI granted the town a Charter in 1547, with the right to hold a Wednesday Market. Thereafter, Aldeburgh went on to become one of the largest ports along the East Coast but like Blythburgh and Dunwich amongst other great trading centres, it too was to suffer heavily from the ravages of the encroaching North Sea. The Moot Hall, for

**The Martello Tower at Slaughden**

example, was once in the centre of town and the site of an open market instead of occupying a spot today just inside the shoreline. Even during Queen Victoria's reign, the town retained 200 licensed fishing vessels, their main catch 'long-shore' herring and sprats, and was further known for its imports of coal and timber and exports of wool and corn. With the arrival of the railway around 1900, Aldeburgh was to become the popular, seaside town it is today, one hugely dependent upon this regular influx of visitors for sustaining its local economy. A fair amount of fishing though is still done off the town's shore, and a great proportion of the catch sold from the rickety black huts which flank the sea; do buy from the fishermen as you will not have tasted fresh, succulent cod, or whatever your fancy, like it, accustomed as we are to the immediate freezing of our sea catch.

*The Moot Hall*, built between 1520 and 1540, is now a Museum of Local History, *open daily from May to September. Admission charge.* It is a beautiful little building with its brick nogging on the upper floor, original timber arches on the ground floor and two typically 16th Century circular, ornate chimneys.

The only other building of real note is the *Martello Tower* at adjoining Slaughden and built between 1810 and 1812 by Royal Engineers as a defence against any Napoleonic invasion. A total of 74 Martello Towers were built along the English Channel and East Coast during the early 1800's, designed along the lines of the Torra della Martello in Corsica which so impressed the British Navy during their 1794 campaign against the French. The Slaughden Tower is exceptional in that it is rather larger than the others in the chain - requiring almost one million bricks - but like them it would have had a platform to house an arsenal of guns. It is now a holiday let managed by the Landmark Trust; for more details of the same see below.

*Aldeburgh Moot Hall*

Near the Tower you cannot help but notice the plethora of yachts along the safe harbour which was once Slaughden Quay. The Quay itself together with the many houses which once surrounded it is now buried in the sands. The marshy estuaries around here though remain a haven for local fishermen, one of whom, Peter Grimes, was first immortalised in George Crabbe's poetic creation and later by Benjamin Britten's opera of the same title.

Born the son of an Aldeburgh salt-tax collector, George Crabbe was early on to sail aboard a fish carrier to London to seek his fortune as a poet. Although Crabbe almost seemed to hate Aldeburgh, he nonetheless wrote some of his best verse about the town and its inhabitants, the latter depicted as ' *... a wild amphibious race, with sullen woe displayed in every face ...*' As for Aldeburgh itself, perhaps some empathy in ' *... the ocean roar, Whost greedy waves devour the shore ...*'

He was later to return to Aldeburgh to become first the parish priest and then the Duke of Rutland's private chaplain. Perhaps no other poet can better capture the grim reality of coastal life than did Crabbe, and in particular of this menacing stretch of the North Sea:

> *'Thus by himself compell'd to live each day*
> *To wait for certain hours the tide's delay;*
> *At the same times the same dull views to see,*
> *The bounding marsh-bank and the blighted tree;*
> *The water only when the tides were high,*
> *When low, the mud half-cover'd and half-dry;*
> *The sun-burnt tar that blisters on the planks,*
> *And bank-side stakes in their western ranks;*
> *Heaps of entangled weed that slowly float,*
> *As the tide rolls by the impeded boat.'*

**Memorial Bust to George Crabbe in the
Church of St. Peter & St. Paul**

With Crabbe's lines in mind we should also recall Aldeburgh's famous lifeboat coxswain, James Cable, who was responsible for saving many lives along this shore and who received the Lifeboat Institute's Silver Medal for his extraordinary bravery. On one remarkable occasion, for example, he and his men were at sea for a stretch of over 100 hours without a break, saving three crews from three different boats in the process. The RNLI still operate a lifeboat from Aldeburgh's shore and just south of this are two unique beach towers of the former 'beach companies' salvage operation which pre-dated the RNLI's exemplary rescue service. Watch would have been kept from these towers for possible and actual wrecks during heavy, stormy seas.

Other interesting personalities who found their home in Aldeburgh include the Garrett family, the father, Newson Garett, a prosperous merchant of whom we shall learn more about from a visit to Snape. It is his daughters, however, who receive our attentions here. The eldest, Elizabeth, being the first woman in Britain to secure a right to a medical education and who went on to pioneer the first hospital (Marleybone, London) in Europe staffed by and for women. Only after a long and bitter struggle was the British Medical Association to relent and finally admit her to its membership. Of equal pioneering stature was her younger sister, Millicent, who was to champion women's suffrage. Perhaps an early life by the sea was to instill such selfless determination into these two brave souls.

Talking of souls, a visit to the medieval Church of St. Peter & St. Paul which overlooks Aldeburgh from something of a ridge is a must. It was once topped by a lantern house in which a warning beacon could be lit for the benefit of shipping operating along this perilous coast. Somewhat unusually, ship auctions were once held in the Church just as it also played host to a number of theatrical performances; as late as 1573, the Earl of Leicester's troope of actors were to play here.

Of particular interest today are the memorial bust to George Crabbe, poet and Church Curate (1781-2), and John Pipers window (1980) commemorating his friend Benjamin Britten. The latter depicts three parables from Britten's church operas, namely *Curlew River, The Prodigal Son* and *The Burning Fiery Furnace.* In typical Piper fashion, the colouring of the stained glass is extraordinarily rich and vibrant.

Founded by Benjamin Britten, Peter Pears and Eric Crozier, the first Aldeburgh Festival was held in 1948 in response to lack of support from London, Manchester and Edinburgh for performances of British operas. The Festival was intended as a modest, musical affair with early events being held in Jubilee Hall, the Church and other locations around the town, but as the event grew, becoming ever more popular, a large permanent site was clearly needed. Consequently, in 1967, Snape Maltings, a few miles away on the banks of the River Alde were converted for this purpose. Both Britten and Pears are buried in Aldeburgh churchyard and their house in Golf Lane is now an international

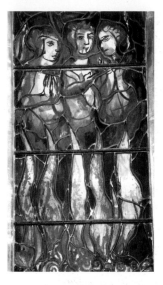

*Detail of John Piper's Stained Glass Window*
*celebrating the work of his friend Benjamin Britten*

research centre holding the Britten-Pears Library of original scores, letters and diaries, together with a collection of old-English songs dating from the 16th Century. For details of the *Aldeburgh Festival* as well as other events held throughout the year, contact the *Box Office (01728 453543)*, on the *High Street*. The Suffolk Craft Society also hold an annual Summer Fair next to the Box Office, the high quality works displayed ranging from hugely competent ceramics to one-off jewellery and furniture, all for sale.

> Eight of **Britten's** operas were given their first hearing in Suffolk with Pears usually singing the title role, and Piper creating many of the sets. Britten and Pears lived together for over 40 years and were both knighted for their outstanding contributions to British music. But perhaps more important, we should recall the way in which Britten's music is derived from a real communion with the countryside, this is its spirit, and maybe this is due to the fact that Britten never seemed to lose sight of his audience, the people.

As for shopping in Aldeburgh, try *Harvey's Wet Fish Shop (01728 452145), 115 High Street* for a range of wet, smoked and shell fish; alternatively fish can sometimes be bought direct from the fishermen from their huts along the shore; *Salters Family Butchers (01728 452758), 107-109 High Street* for their locally farmed meats and home made sausages; *Stephenson's Jewellers (01728 452431), 122 High Street*, a sister operation to the Amber Shop in Southwold; you might also like to try potter *Gary Wornell (01728 453315), The Old Slaughterhouse, Park Road, Aldeburgh* who works primarily in terracotta using burnished slips for simple but exotic decoration - *you must phone first.*

Golfers may like a round at the *Aldeburgh Golf Club (01728 452890), Saxmundham Road, Aldeburgh*. Choose from either the 18-hole or 9-hole heath and parkland courses overlooking the River Alde.

# Food & Accommodation

**The House-in-the-Clouds** *(0171 252043), Thorpeness*, is a holiday self-catering let of an altogether different kind. For more details see the details under Thorpeness.

**The Lighthouse** *(01728 453377), 77 High Street, Aldeburgh*. A recent addition to the town's eating establishments, The Lighthouse has been converted from a former high street shop. Choose from coffee, lunch, afternoon tea or dinner, and know that all ingredients have been locally sourced and with seafood inevitably receiving special attention. Although it can get pretty busy, especially in high season, it is nonetheless a restful place whatever your purposes and desires.

**The Martello Tower** *(01628 825925), Slaughden, Aldeburgh* is managed by the Landmark Trust and also offers unique self-catering holiday lets. So spoil your self in this the largest and most northerly of all the Martello Towers built to keep Napoleon off England's shores. For more details on the Tower see the main body text. **(Sleeps 4.)**

**Regatta** *(01728 452011), 171-173 High Street, Aldeburgh*. A restaurant and wine bar each with their own separate menus and separate entrances. Although standards can be a little up and down, when on form it is a generous and civilised place to spend the evening and the decor nautically themed.

**Cross Keys** *(01728 452637), Crabbe Street, Aldeburgh*. A 16th Century establishment close to the sea front where woodburning stoves warm you from the worst of the blustering winds and which divide the two bar areas. Good real ale and simple, good, wholesome food are a plus whether for lunch or supper.

*Thorpeness Post Mill*

The unusual village of ***Thorpeness***, just north of Aldeburgh, was the brainchild of playwright and barrister Glencairn Stuart Ogilvie, his dream to create a corner of 'Merrie ol' England' by the sea. Built between 1910 and 1930 it is a small, well-planned resort, neatly designed, and with some unassuming deployment of timber-framing and weatherboarding. There is also an artificial lake called The Meare.

Two buildings which deserve special mention are the well-restored ***Post Mill*** built around 1803 and moved from Aldringham to Thorpness, its corn-grinding machinery removed so as to enable it to pump water into the curious ***Watertower*** next to it. The latter is probably one of the most unusual buildings you will encounter for a long time. Called the ***House-in-the-Clouds***, it was built in 1925 as a watertower concealed behind timber-framing and later converted to residential use. It is now a holiday 'cottage' and for letting details see the boxed item above.

Keen golfers, may enjoy a round on ***Thorpeness Golf Club's*** *(01728 452176)* 18-hole moorland course, which adjoins the hotel here. You must take your handicap certificate with you.

**House-in-the-Clouds**

# Walk 21: Aldeburgh and Thorpeness

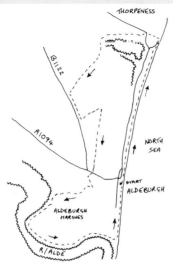

## Directions:

1. From your park near Aldeburgh Coastguard Station, climb the sea wall in front of you near a converted windmill. Once on the bank, go left along the shore heading back towards Aldeburgh proper. Continue along the shore for approx. two miles until you reach Thorpeness.
2. Leave the beach in between two brightly painted green and white chalet bungalows. Bear right slightly, and then left into a lane called The Dunes. Go right at the junction keeping The Meare on your left and ignoring the private road to the Golf Course on your left, and take the public footpath/track next on your left (signed incorrectly B1122).
3. Pass the Post Mill and the elaborate House-in-the-Clouds. At the Golf Course, continue along the left hand edge of the Course, The Meare on your left. 4. Go left at Sheepwash Crossing into a narrow path which runs beside the old dismantled railway line. Cross a bridge and take the left hand fork where two paths splinter off - this leads through North Warren Nature Reserve managed by the RSPB. Continue along this path until you reach the B112. 5. Turn left onto the road, and after approx. half a mile, take the lane on the left which leads past a number of large properties. Once back to the railway line, turn right and continue along here until you come to a modern bungalow on your right (approx. half a mile). Go left here onto a path running into Aldeburgh. 6. At the junction, cross the road and aim for the Fire Station, and at the recreation area, go straight on along a path running beside a wall. Next, take the path beside the allotments and go through a gate on the right along a path (signed) heading towards the River. Follow the footpath signs which eventually lead up the River bank. 7. At the River, go left and follow Aldeburgh Marshes round Short Reach and Westrow Reach. Where the River and sea walls meet (the Martello Tower to your right), go left to return to your start.

**Start: Aldeburgh Beach  Approx. Distance: 9 Miles**
**Approx. Time: 4-5 Hours  Map: Landranger 156**

# *Snape*

Snape Maltings, now the main centre for the Aldeburgh Festival, were as their name identifies a malting operation first begun in 1854 by Newson Garrett. Garrett had originally bought a corn and coal business at the beginning of the 19th Century but needed to expand the maltings side of his business. Story has it that he marked out the site for his new premises with a walking stick and that this accounts for the slight curve in their structure. Nevertheless, they form an attractive collection of buildings, employing red and yellow bricks, a considerable amount of weatherboarding and a number of imposing hoists. The Maltings continued to be worked as intended until 1965.

The following year they were taken over by Benjamin Britten and Peter Pears to house their ever expanding music Festival. Opened in 1967 by the Queen, two years later the interior was badly damaged by fire and this on the seasons opening night. A year later they were back in business growing from strength to strength thereafter. Concerts during the Festival season and occasionally at other times are still held here in the Concert Hall, and despite the latter's modest appearance it is renowned as one of the finest in Europe for its acoustics.

Furthermore, a considerable part of the complex here is given over to the School for Advanced Musical Studies, a piano workshop, art gallery, antiques centre, a gift shop and cafe. For details of the *Aldeburgh Festival* programme contact the *Box Office* on *01728 453543*. Finally, on the lawn in front of the Concert Hall is a fine piece of sculpture by Barbara Hepworth (1903-75).

Snape means *boggy place* and to be expected the Maltings stand on the banks of the River Alde. You can take a stroll along 'Sailors Walk', the north bank to Aldeburgh but this can be fairly dangerous if the water level is high. Better still is the path which takes a south easterly course to Iken and is covered in part by the walk described below. Alternatively, try a *boat trip along the River* from Snape Quay beside the Maltings. Departure times are posted daily on the Quay itself.

In 1862, Aldeburgh historian, Septimus Davidson, discovered an Anglo-Saxon ship at Snape. Unfortunately, the grave had been robbed when opened and only the remains of a 46 feet long clinker-built longboat were unearthed together with a Saxon ring dated circa 635-50 AD and engraved with onyx. There was no sign of a body but the individual must have been a wealthy one. Subsequent excavations in the 1980's revealed a second burial ground and this not plundered. The boat, body and artefacts this time well preserved in the sandy acid soil. This second burial is thought to date from 550 AD.

## *Food & Accommodation*

*The Plough & Sail* (01728 688413), *Riverside Centre, Snape Maltings.* A friemdly atmosphere awaits visitors to this establishment where the emphasis is on food and all of it excellent. Well kept ales and a good choice of wines some of which are available by the glass.

# *Walk 22: Snape Maltings and Tunstall Forest*

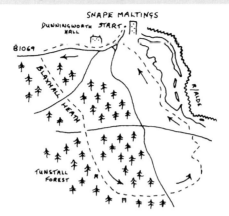

## *Directions:*

1. From the car park at Snape Maltings, go back to the B1069 and walk the short distance south along the road, the Maltings on your left, to a junction. Go right here continuing along the B1069 to another junction where you again go right (signed Blaxhall). 2. Continue along this lane - it is usually very quiet - for approx. half a mile until you reach a right turning. Opposite here, on your left, look for a footpath sign leading through the woods. Continue along this path for a short distance until you reach a pit - keep left of this and then right using a sandy track and keeping the woods on your left. 3. Continue along Blaxhall Heath using a broad track at the edge of the forest and over Rimple Hill. 4. On reaching the Snape to Tunstall road again (B1069), cross straight over. (To be sure you have your bearings correctly as there are many paths along the Heath, look for a cottage on your left just before you cross the road.) Continue straight along this path, ignoring all left and right intersections until you reach a minor road. 5. Cross straight over the road along a track immediately in front of you and which leads across Tunstall Forest (signed footpath). Again, ignore all tracks running in from the left and right and head for a house in the distance. 6. Walk past the house (on your right) for a few yards until you come to a meeting of tracks. Go left here and at the corner of this note another cottage which should now be on your right. 7. Continue along this track until you reach the Snape to Sudbourne Road. Go straight across and to your right for a couple of yards to pick up a path (signed) on your left leading beside the edge of a field and with the woods on your left. 8. Go left at the end of here following a yellow Heritage Coast sign, and then right and then left, following the yellow signs around the edge of the wood. Keep following the signs left and then right around the edge of a field and at the end of a stretch of water go left, and left again heading towards a group of farm buildings. Look for a footpath sign on your right after approx. 40 yards which takes you left across a field. 9. Once over the stile and at the other end, go right for a short distance and then left (signed footpath to Snape). 10. After a short distance take a signed a path on your right leading down to the marshy reach of the River Alde. Note Iken

Church in the distance over the marsh on your right, and go left at the bottom of a series of steps. 11. Follow this path round the marsh fringe and then go up a few steps in between some cottages and right at the top of here. 12. The path leads you across Iken Cliff Picnic Site and then round through the marsh - there are boardwalks in some stretches making the going easy in winter - and so to Snape. 13. Once you reach the first buildings at Snape, go right following the path behind them and so round to your starting point.

**Start: Snape Maltings  Approx. Distance: 5.5 Miles**
**Approx. Time: 2 Hour  Map: Landranger 156**

Just south of Snape, *Blaxhall* is something of a remote village scattered around former common land. Perhaps conscious of how untouched the village was, George Ewart Evans, the unique chronicler of the East Anglian countryside, wrote about the villagers early memories in *Ask The Fellows Who Cut The Hay*. Go to St. Peter's Church to see the various Arts & Crafts works by the Rope sisters. Foremost amongst these are there War Memorial and Bates Monument by Ellen Mary (d.1934), the stained glass in the east window by Margaret, and the Wilson Monument by Dorothy.

The coastal heath, known as the sandlings, near the village is worth a wander and although it is constantly invaded by the likes of pine and bracken, the open areas are dominated by sand sedge and acid grassland. On summers evenings, keep your ears tuned for the sound of nightjars. Tunstall Forest also close by was once much more attractive than is the case now, the area being severely damaged by the 1987 hurricane, but replanting is well under way and the area still pleasant enough to stroll across.

*Snape Maltings*

Inland and now by-passed by the A12 is **Wickham Market** once a main coaching stop on the route south and north from Lowestoft and the village would appear to have taken full advantage of the additional trade this would have generated. The small square, known as Market Hill, has retained a good deal of its medieval character and is dominated by its tall, spired Church.

## Food & Accommodation

**The Old Rectory** *(01728 746524), Campsea Ash, near Wickham Market,* is a private house dating from the 17th Century and offering friendly hotel-like facilities. Standing in four acres of garden, a quiet atmosphere pervades. Although the bedroom accommodation, all en-suite- is simply decorated, some is more interestingly appointed. Note, for example, the room at the top approached via two doors and a spiral staircase and the garden room with its Gothic arched windows. The food is served in the restaurant and is usually of a high standard and to a three-course, fixed-price, set menu

# Butley

Just beyond the reaches of the River Butley, **Butley Priory** was founded in 1171 for Augustinian Canons by Ranulf de Glanville, a Suffolk man, who was also Henry II's Lord Chief Justice (de Glanville was also responsible for the slightly later Leiston Abbey). With the Reformation, most of the monastic buildings were destroyed but the **Gatehouse** remains pretty well in tact, and represents one of the best pieces of flushwork in East Anglia and probably the earliest example. Furthermore, evidence also suggests that the freestone was brought in for the job especially from France; the line of a canal has been traced from the former Priory to Butley River. Although the Gatehouse is now a private residence and can only be viewed from the lane, sufficient detail can still be made out to make the effort worthwhile. From the heraldic decoration on the north aspect a total of 35 coats of arms displayed in five rows can be made out, all of which date from 1320.

These are thought to represent on the top row amongst others the Holy Roman Empire, France, St. Edmunds Bury, Christ's Passion and England. The next two rows bear the shields of English baronial families such as the de Vere's, Warenne's, and Clare's, and the last two rows depict East Anglian gentry including de Glanville's own in the middle of the bottom row. Those wanting to know more about the Priory should consult a very interesting document providing an account of everyday life in a religious order just before the Reformation, namely the *Register or Chronicle of Butley Priory, Suffolk 1510-1535,* a copy of which can be found in some local libraries.

Just beyond the site of the former Priory is a dense and ancient wood of oak and holly known as Staverton Thicks. Some believe the Druids began this planting but others suggest it was the monks who would probably have been given permission to take 'one crop' off the land and so opted for oak. Whatever the real story, the oldest recorded trees still around here date from as early as 1540. A public footpath can be used around the edge of the Thicks.

Another unusual planting of trees known as Butley Clumps was begun by the Marquess of Donegal in 1790 and who was then living at the Gatehouse. Seeking to enhance the approach to his home and create a woodland which would not take away his view, he planted an avenue of trees but one which was always clumped in fives. In other words a quincunx was formed from a pine tree in the middle of a square of beech trees. Although these ancient beeches are no longer, they have nevertheless been replanted to the same scheme.

A tiny hamlet straddling the Butley is *Chillesford* included here as much for its unusual geology as for its former brick industry. For in the Coralline Crag around here 400 species of mollusc have been identified, over 140 of which are now extinct. The micaceous sand and clay Chillesford Beds have also proved rich in estuarine fauna. (Remember, Butley too was once not so long ago famous for its oysters, and the same can be bought from nearby Orford.)

As for the village, many of the old houses were built from the output of the ancient brick and tile kiln, worked until World War I and to be found just beyond the Church. It was in these old brick works that incredibly a whale's vertebral column, 31 feet long, was found.

# Orford

Orford, our main purpose along this stretch, is an especially charming and picturesque old sea port worthy of a whole day spent exploring its many secrets. First to the *Castle*, with its 90 feet high keep and one of England's finest surviving medieval fortresses. Construction of the Castle can be dated to 1165, and this was just one of a network of coastal defences ordered by Henry II. Revolutionary in its shape, it was the first Castle to be built as an irregular polygon of 18 sides reinforced by three battlemented turrets. The idea being to prevent any invading force from undermining (sapping) the corner of a square keep and thus bringing about the structure's collapse. That it still stands is testimony itself to the effectiveness of its overall design.

Inside, however, a cylindrical practice has been followed and here we find the ruins of the chapel, garderobes and great hall. Climb the battlements for some truly spectacular views of the surrounding countryside as out to sea. No wonder it was used by the Army as an observation point during the two World Wars, you can literally see for miles and miles. Managed by English Heritage *(01394 450472)*, *the Castle is open daily. Admission charge.*

> During the 15th Century, a *wild man* caught in the fishermens nets was held in the Castle's dungeons. Described as half man and half fish, little sense could be made of the creature and even under duress his torturers were unable to establish 'anything Christian' from him. Eventually the 'merman' was returned to the sea (some say he escaped) never to be seen again and who can blame him!

# *Walk 23: Butley Priory and Orford Ness*

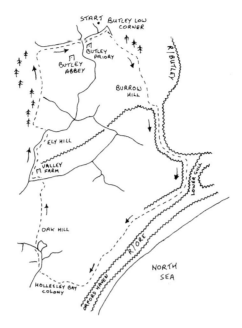

## Directions:

1. From your park at the end of the lane at Butley Low Corner, turn right along a wide track which takes you to a copse of trees. Continue along the edge of that wood to a stile. Once over the stile, continue along the path over Burrrow Hill, down to another stile, to another and so to the River. 2. Once at the River Butley, go right along the River wall, continue along here, round Lower Gull and along the River Ore. (Approx. three and a half miles.) 3. Just before Orford Haven and once you have reached an old wartime pillbox, follow the track which bends right to pass Hollesley Bay Colony. 4. At the road go right, up the hill, to a post box. Look for a track on your right near the bus shelter. Continue along that path for approx. one mile where it bends right and left to meet the minor road to Boyton. 5. Turn left along this road and at the crossroads go right. This lane leads past Valley Farm and up Ely Hill. 6. Where the lane bends sharp right, follow the track on your left leading to a forest devastated by the 1987 hurricane. Once at the forest fringe, go right along a track to join a lane. 7. Continue straight ahead i.e. do not via right, passing Oak Wood on your right and up to Capel Green. 8. Take the first right after a cottage and keep right at the junction to go along a minor road leading past the site of Butley Priory. 9. At the next junction, go straight across, and at the next also straight across to return to your starting point.

**Start: Butley Low Corner**
**Approx. Distance: 9.5 Miles**
**Approx. Time: 4-5 Hours˙**
**Map: Landranger 169**

Now to St. Bartholomew's Church with its ruined Norman chancel of 1166, but retaining the excellent dog-tooth decoration on its piers. Look to the altarpiece, a *Sacra Coversazione,* an important Renaissance work by Bernardino Luini (1520). The Church has seen some of Benjamin Britten's works given their first public performance, perhaps most notably those of *Curlew River* and *Noye's Fludde.* In fact the Aldeburgh Festival, first begun by Britten, continues to hold some of its concerts at St. Batholomew's.

**Orford Castle**

Passing the charming timber and brick built cottages and stretched out village green along Quay Street, we arrive at the Quay itself. Orford was during the Middle Ages through to Elizabeth I's reign an important port and remained a sizeable operation well into the 17th Century. Into the 18th Century and the picture was not so cosy for in his *Tour Through the Eastern Counties* Defoe recorded that the town '... is now decayed. The sea daily throws up more land so it is a sea port no longer'. (1724). Indeed, the River Ore today runs parallel with the coast for a distance of ten miles separated from its salty counterpart by only a narrow shingly spit; all this the consequence of Longshore Drift.

A crucial export when times were good, however, as for many other ports along this east coast were the shipments of wool to Continental European markets. Much trade though was lost in later periods to ships of deeper draught and Orford was left to find alternatives. Coal was one such commodity brought up stream by barges to the Quay in the early 1900's and stored in the warehouse (now a tearoom). The same barges would also continue further along the Rivers Ore and Alde to the likes of Snape where customers would line the banks ready to unload their purchases into carts and then away home.

Orford's Town Regalia comprised of two miniature silver oars is unique in England and was once carried by the portmen in ceremonies designed to enforce their rights over the fisheries in the River Ore. Fishing continues today, albeit on a much smaller scale, and is probably best enjoyed at the **Butley Oysterage** (see below) or alternatively buy some fresh to cook at home.

During World War II, the Quay was also busy with river traffic to and from Orford Ness where the Secret Weapons Research Establishment had a base. Here, early experiments in radar, which proved vital during the early years of the War, were carried out by scientists working under the command of Sir Robert Watson-Watt. Although the Ness is connected to the mainland by a shingle bank it has nevertheless been 'out of bounds' until today when a plan to turn it into a Nature Reserve is under serious consideration.

There is another Reserve already at Halvergate Island, and this managed by the RSPB. Here the largest breeding colonies of avocet in the British Isles can be found and other breeding species include the short-eared owl which can regularly be seen hunting its prey in broad daylight. Boat trips to the Island can be taken from the Quay.

Alternatively, why not take a four-hour trip aboard *The Lady Florence (0831 698298)* as she cruises you up river whilst you enjoy lunch or evening dinner. All the food is freshly prepared on board and naturally there is an extra charge for this. Trips are run all year round and booking is advisable.

*Orford*

# *Food & Accommodation*

***Butley-Orford Oysterage*** *(01394 450277), Market Hill, Orford.* A down to earth bistro-cum-restaurant in the middle of the village square. Fish predominates and it is usually prepared to a high standard. There is also a smokery at the back where you can buy your own fresh oysters and smoked salmon among many other fine delicacies.

***The Jolly Sailor*** *(01394 450243), Quay Street, Orford.* A short walk from the Quay, The Jolly Sailor was once a port side inn, that is until the sea retreated somewhat during the 18th Century. The pub's origins can be dated to the 16th Century when it was a favourite retreat of the many smugglers who worked this shoreline. Tradition even has the body of Will Land, a well-known smuggler in these parts, laid out in the pub's 'Captain Room' after he had been shot by excise men on Orford beach. Today, stone floors, exposed beams, cosy rooms and secret cupboards abound, and service can be had from an old-fashioned central bar area complete with hatches. Accommodation is also available.

***The King's Head*** *(01394 450271), Orford.* Of even earlier 13th Century origin, The King's Head was also once well frequented by smugglers. Perhaps its situation close to the Church afforded alternative avenues of retreat and concealment. Oak beams and cushioned wall settles make for a comfortable atmosphere. Accommodation is also available.

## *Walk 24: Ancient Orford*

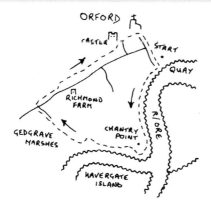

### Directions:

1. From your park near the Quay at Orford, go down to the Quay and bear right along a footpath running alongside the River Ore. Go through a gate, up a series of steps to the path along the River's bank and turn left. Continue along the path which curves round with the River - occasional stiles will be encountered - round Chantry Point, where it goes inland slightly to curve back to the shore. 2. Almost as you pass near the north-westerly point of Halvergate Island, look for a footpath sign on your right taking you over Gedgrave Marsh for just under a mile. 3. At the minor road, turn right and after a short distance just before Richmond Farm, go left along a sandy track. After a short distance, just beyond an open barn, go right up some steps and onto a path skirting a field. 4. Continue along this path for three-quarters of a mile until you reach the outer grounds of Orford Castle. 5. At the main entrance to the Castle, cross the road and go up a slight hill on your left past the Hotel and onto the Market Square. At the Church, go right along the road heading back to Orford Quay.

**Start: Orford Quay**
**Approx. Distance: 3.5 Miles**
**Approx. Time: 1.5-2 Hours**
**Map: Landranger 169**

Back to the A12 now and first to **Ufford**, something of a show village restored by wealthy Woodbridge people wanting a more rural location. The village name is derived from the ancient Uffinga's or Wuffinga's, the royal line of the East Angles. The village sign, however, depicts the famous Suffolk Punch, the original horse foaled here and from which virtually all Suffolk horses to the present day are said to be descended.

A number of interesting buildings make up the village not least the Rectory - one of few medieval priest's houses to survive in the county, also the 1690 almshouses built by Bishop Wood and Dewer House built in the early 1700's.

To St. Mary's Church though to see probably the finest font cover in England dating from the second half of the 15th Century. Telescopic, it extends to a height of 18 feet and is topped by a carved pelican. Church Wardens managed to stave off 'Smasher' Dowsing's men, forcibly preventing them from entering the Church. Otherwise it too would have been lost to the vagaries of history.

# *Woodbridge*

Woodbridge itself is a particularly agreeable town at the head of the River Deben, and was for many centuries both a noted shipbuilding centre with easy access to the oak forests of High Suffolk, and a port renowned for its exports of timber, corn and butter. Of the latter, Daniel Defoe tells us: *'The butter is barrelled or often pickled up in small cases and sold, not in London only, but I have known a firkin of Suffolk butter sent to the West Indies ...'* (1724). Defoe's claim is not so unrealistic when one considers that over 350 ships were registered in Woodbridge alone during the mid 17th Century. Silting up of the River Deben was to halt both the ship building industry and the town's principal trading activities but the Quay area still sees ample use from the yachting fraternity. It is also a very attractive end of town dominated by the weatherboarded *Tide Mill*, restored in 1982 with fully operational machinery. The first mention of a mill on this site was during the 1170's but the present one is probably 17th Century in origin. *Open during the summer months and also occasionally at other times. Admission charge.*

Woodbridge has also variously been known for its weaving and rope-making industries as also for its salt manufacture; all this especially evident during

*Woodbridge*

*The unusual Steelyard at Woodbridge*

Elizabeth I's reign. On Bell Street there is also a curious 18th Century Steelyard complete with its balanced overhanging timbers and presumably used for weighing commodities such as wool, hides and hay. But it is to Thomas Seckford, Master of Court Requests in Elizabethan times, that we should look to as the town's real developer and benefactor.

Seckford had amassed a considerable fortune from overseas trading - his brother incidentally was a notorious pirate - and he financed first the almshouses which subsequently gay way to a hospital bearing his name, and the **Shire Hall**, originally built in 1575 but its lower floor bricked in during Regency times and so converted first to a corn exchange, then a court room. Seckford Hall on the outskirts of town though is thought to have been built by Seckford's father in 1530.

All in all, Woodbridge is a delightful little spot, dominated at its centre by Market Hill. Here one finds the Shire Hall as also the Gothic Victorian Market Hill Pump, a number of timber-framed buildings, Georgian shopfronts and the Bull Hotel famous for its associations with Edward Fitzgerald and his literary circle of friends. From Market Hill, a number of quaint, narrow, medieval streets lead down to the Quay, many of the buildings adorned with Georgian facades or variously timber-framed with overhangs.

The town also boasts a couple of interesting museums. Try the **Woodbridge Museum** *(01394 380502)*, *Market Hill*, for its displays covering the natural histo

*Woodbridge Shire Hall*

ry of the area, the town's history and information on the nearby Sutton Hoo ship burial. *Open April to October. Admission charge.* Also on Market Hill is the *Suffolk Horse Museum (01394 380643)* where the exhibits are exclusively devoted to the Suffolk Punch breed of heavy working horse. The Suffolk Punch breed was originally developed in the Woodbridge area during the 15th Century and until World War II they undertook much of the heavy agricultural work on the farms as also the bulk of road freight deliveries. Special skills were necessary to handle these horses and a whole breed of suitably trained horsemen were an equally necessary part of the phenomenon. In 1960, however, the Suffolk Punch was all but extinct and only the perseverance of dedicated breeders has ensured their survival. *The Museum is open from Easter to the end of September. Admission charge.*

**Edward Fitzgerald** (1809-83) was born at nearby Bredfield House, now demolished, but spent a number of years on Market Hill and then at Little Grange, Pytches Road. Something of an eccentric scholar and socialite recluse, he is especially remembered for his *Suffolk Sea Phrases*, a collection of stories based on the tales of local fishermen and sailors, and more importantly for his translations of the 11th Century Persian poet and astronomer Khayyam and popularly published as *The Rubaiyat of Omar Khayyam*. Ten years after Fitzgerald's death, friends took a cutting of a rose flowering on Omar Khayyam's tomb in Persia and planted the same on Fitzgerald's own grave (St. Michael's at Boulge). Even today, members of the Omar Khayyam Appreciation Society gather every ten years at The Bull Hotel for a 'creative' commemorative meal; recalling the pink rose alluded to.above, everything the group orders is a variation of pink - whether salmon, strawberries, Kir or whatever else their imaginative respect can conjure up.

Also in the town is **Suffolk Larder** *(01394 386676), 17 The Thoroughfare*, known for their dry-cured bacons and hams, hot smoked meats and hand-raised pies as also for their Suffolk-spiced lamb, moist Suffolk Cyder Cake and a whole range of mustards.

Nearby is **Buttrum's Mill** built in the early 1800's by Whitmore & Binyon of Wickham Market.  This six-storey, red-brick tower mill is over 60 feet high including its cap and gallery.  Last worked in 1928, it is now preserved by East Suffolk County Council and is *open summer Bank Holidays only.*

For those looking for activities of a more sporting nature then try **Woodbridge Golf Club** *(01394 382038), Bromeswell Heath*, with its 18-hole course on a sandy heath plateau.  Visitors are welcome but do take your handicap certificate.  Alternatively, *boat trips* (with wheelchair facilities) can be taken along a ten mile wooded stretch of the River Deben via **Waldringfield Boatyard Ltd** *(01473 736260), The Quay, Waldringfield*, or there is **horse riding** at **Poplar Park Equestrian Centre** *(01394 411023), Hollesley*, and which is BHS  approved.

Nature lovers might try the Suffolk Wildlife Trust's **Bromeswell Green Reserve**, a few miles north-east of the town, and which is  rich in both woodland and wetland birdlife.  Abundant yellow-iris and marsh-marigold make it especially pretty in season, and there is a marked trail around this small Reserve.

## Food & Accommodation

**Seckford Hall** *(01394 385678), Seckford, near Woodbridge.*  Built in 1530 and set in over 30 acres of parkland, Seckford Hall Hotel is one of the county's finest Tudor buildings.  Furnished with period pieces, and retaining its original panelling, beamed ceilings and large stone fireplaces, it is as grand and splendid a place as any to stay.  The restaurant is especially popular, seafood being a speciality, and the bedroom accommodation is furnished to a high standard.  Guests can also enjoy use of a heated indoor pool, solarium, spa bath and exercise room, and there is also  trout and course fishing to be enjoyed from the lake in the grounds.

**Wine Bar** *(01394 382557), 17 The Thoroughfare, Woodbridge.*  Above the Suffolk Larder, this is a  characterful wine bar with an interesting and imaginative menu and a good creative choice of wines, many of them available by the glass.

# The Deben and Orwell Estuaries

If we follow the northerly banks of the River Deben we arrive first at **Sutton Hoo**  where excavations on four long barrows in 1938 revealed an 89 feet long skeletal ship, the resting place of a Saxon chieftain.  Most of the ships timbers had rotted away but not so the great hoard of gold, silver and enamel jewellery, an iron-standard over six feet high, a sword with jewelled mountings, shield and a  magnificent  masked  helmet.  These  treasures  can  now  be  found  in  the

*The magnificent burial helmet
unearthed at Sutton Hoo*

British Museum, London, with replicas on display at Ipswich.

It is still not clear whose grand funeral this was. Some believe it to be Aethelhere's who died fighting the King of Northumbria at Winwaed in 654 AD. Others favour Raedwald, King of the East Angles (d. 625 AD) not least because he was a Christian and two baptismal spoons with Greek inscriptions (Paulos and Saulos) were among the finds. The first known kings of East Anglia occupied a site at Rendlesham, just north of Sutton Hoo, and this perhaps adds further credence to the Raedwald theory. Whoever he was, his influence and position cannot be disputed nor can his vast trading links, his possessions variously originating from the Mediterranean (silver utensils), Merovingian France (gold coins), Rhineland (the sword blade) and Sweden (the sword hilt).

A number of additional barrows have also been excavated but have only revealed 'sand bodies' (the bodily shapes of the dead left in the sand), and evidence of habitation dating as far back as 2000 BC. The site is now closed to prevent damage to any remaining graves and visits are strictly by appointment only; unless you are an archaeologist it is not really worth the effort, as to the untrained eye there is little surface evidence that can truthfully be made out.

You will not however be disappointed by the walk outlined below which also takes in the derelict ***Methersgate Quay***. During Elizabeth I's reign, farmers in the area were interestingly enough obliged to grow hemp and the store houses for the same could once be found at this ancient Quay.

## *Walk 25: Ancient Sutton Hoo*

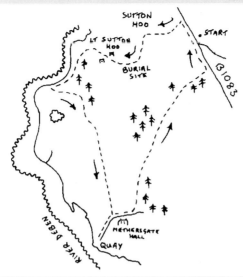

### *Directions:*

1. From your park on waste ground (near the Golf Course and close to where the B1083 to Alderton meets a minor road to Hollesley) cross the road and follow a signed footpath to Sutton Hoo Burial Site. Leave the site by descending past the site entrance, and at the bottom of this stretch go right to pass a house. Between the house and barn, go left to reach an open field and bear left along the wood edge. 2. Cross a bridge to get to the River Deben and then head left up a straight incline before dropping back down to the edge of the River. Ignore a path leading back up on your left and instead continue to a derelict hut. Follow the path round to the left as it winds its way back up the cliff. 3. Go right at a grouping of pine trees which will then take you round to the left and up a straight incline. Once at the top, bear right along another grouping of pines. 4. At the edge of this small plantation, veer slightly to your left across a field - i.e. moving away from the trees, and to a signpost. 5. Go straight over at the lane, and similarly at the next lane and continue straight ahead for approx. one mile using Methersgate Hall in the distance as your marker. 6. At the end of this stretch, go through the farm gate towards the Hall and to a lane. (If you wish to go down to the Quay and it is a decent lunch stop, head right along the lane, retracing your steps back to the Hall.) Go left along the lane, passing the Hall and at the last building on your left by the side of a belt of trees, look for a path on your left which skirts the wood. Continue along this path for approx. one mile. 7. At a junction of pathways midway along the edge of another copse go straight across to another belt of trees. Follow the path through this to a meeting of pathways. Go right here until you meet the B1083. 8. At the road, turn left to return to your starting point.

**Start: Just off the B1083 near Sutton Hoo**
**Approx. Distance: 6.5 Miles Approx. Time: 3.5 Hours**
**Map: Landranger 169**

*Ramsholt*, a little to the south, was a flourishing hamlet with much business centred around its Quay. Sailing barges delivering coal and taking on sugar beet and coprolite would once have been a familiar sight.

All Saints Church still stands above the Deben Estuary and was once probably a Saxon look-out. From the top of the tower on a clear day you can see the whole reach of the River, from Woodbridge and on right out to sea. Smugglers too would have taken advantage of the Church's elevation, using a light to advise their gangs that it was safe to land their contraband.

## Food & Accommodation

**The Ramsholt Arms** *(01394 411229), Ramsholt.* Found at the edge of a long lane and situated on a wide sweep of the River Deben, this is a beautiful and peaceful spot from which to enjoy good ales, wines, whiskies and food. Originally built as a ferryman's cottage in the mid 1700's, it has been tastefully refurbished and the bedroom accommodation is also of a good standard.

We now travel inland via Alderton and Hollesley to arrive again at the coast proper at **Shingle Street.** As its name suggests, this is literally a row of cottages built along the top of a bank of shingle, the sea to the fore and the marshes to the rear. A handful of part-time fishermen still work out of here, their punts built to ride the breakers into shore bow-on. This is a lovely and isolated part of the coast, sparse even in flora, and good for a walk northwards to the mouth of the River Ore, or indeed southwards past the Martello Towers towards Bawdsey.

There are four Martello Towers along this stretch of coast just south of Shingle Street. The idea for the Towers was originally conceived of by Sir David Dundas after a visit to Corsica where he had observed similar structures see off a succession of 'men-of-war'. The Towers built along our own coast were not quite as substantial being generally only 26 feet in diameter, 34 feet high and nine feet thick and put up quickly to offset a possible Napoleonic invasion. Nonetheless, each Tower required some 700,000 bricks (note the one to be found just south of Aldeburgh took rather more materials being slightly larger in its dimensions).

The next estuary to explore is that of the Orwell and once again we are confined, at least at the moment, to its northerly banks. Orwell Park, **Nacton,** was once the home of Admiral Vernon but is now a boys prepatory school. Although known for his capture of Portobello for George III, he is perhaps best remembered for watering down the Navy rum ration which earned him the name 'Old Grog'. Further downstream is Broke Hall (not open to the public) where an equally capable ship's commander, Sir Philip Broke, once lived. Broke was responsible for seizing the US frigate *Chesapeake* within easy sight of Boston in 1813. Memorials to the two men can be found in the Church.

Margaret Catchpole was also born at Nacton in 1773, the youngest of a labourer's six children. Her future was not so bright being obliged to enter service at an early age like many of her contemporaries. She had the misfortune to fall in love with a sailor and so desperate was she to see him that she stole her master's horse and rode the 70 miles to London to meet him. Captured and convicted in London, Margaret was sentenced to death - the penalty at that time for horse stealing. Her sentence was reduced to transportation for seven years, as a result of her employer's intervention, but before the same could commence Margaret broke out of Ipswich prison desperate to see her lover one last time. Caught and retried, the death sentence was again repealed only the transportation this time awarded for life. Aged 28, Margaret sailed for Australia where she later married a respected settler and lived a more comfortable life than she may well have enjoyed had she stayed in England. Her story was told in the famous *The History of Margaret Catchpole* (1834) based on her own writings, only elaborated upon by her former employer's son, Richard Cobbold.

# *Felixstowe*

Finally to Felixstowe and its dormitory village Felixstowe Ferry. Two-thirds of Britain's Continental trade passes through Felixstowe container port, and ferries also continue to ply passengers across the North Sea to Belgium and the Netherlands. The Landguard Fort - more about which later - seems still to almost guard sentinel the entrance to the port not only of Felixstowe but also of Harwich on the other side of the Stour and Orwell Estuaries

Situated between the estuaries of the Orwell and the Deben, the town faces south and boasts two miles of promenade bustling with boating ponds and amusement arcades. The cliffs themselves have been transformed into majestic hanging gardens, taking advantage of Felixstowe's warmer southerly aspect, it

*Felixstowe Container Port*

is after all the only seaside resort in East Anglia to face south. Of the town itself, there is little else to say save that it too claims St. Felix as its own (just as does more northerly Dunwich). To the **Landguard Fort** then, first built in 1540, rebuilt in 1624 and again in 1717 as a low polygon, and still in use during World War II. The archway is Victorian as is the interior and courtyard. It is not a place to everyone's liking, many finding it oppressive, dingy and reminiscent of some latter day camp for political prisoners or worse. Nonetheless it is impressive if only for its sheer scale and for the views it affords of the container port in full swing. Others have no doubt found more favour with it, not least Gainsborough who, unusually for him, used the Fort in one of only three seascapes he painted. Managed by English Heritage *(01394 286403)* the Fort and Museum is *open variously during the summer months and only via guided tours. Admission charge.* You can, however, see quite a bit from the perimeter fence which is accessible all year round.

The **Nature Reserve** which adjoins the Fort is much more interesting and is especially important for a number of migrant species - both bird and insect. There is also a wide variety of flora to see in this mix of shingle, shrub and woodland including sea campion, yellow-horned poppy and the rare diffander grows here in abundance.

The famous Elizabethan navigator, **Thomas Cavendish**, was born near Trinity St. Martin. In 1585, he joined Sir Richard Grenville's expedition to the newly discovered land of Virginia, and his circumnavigation of the globe followed between 1586 and 1558. A later 1591 expedition, however, was ill-fated and Cavendish died shortly after passing through the Magellan Straits. An account of his deeds is given in his own words:

> ' It has pleased the Almighty to suffer me to circompasse
> the whole globe of the world, entering in at the streight
> of Magellan and returning by the Cape de Buena
> Esperanza. In which Voyage I have discovered
> or brought certaine Intelligence of all the rich
> places of the world that ever were knowen
> or discovered by any Christian. I navigated
> along the Coast of Chilli, Peru and Nuve
> Espana, where I made great Spoiles.'

As with his contemporaries Drake and Raleigh, the Spanish must have had their fill of Cavendish's exploits not least for his destruction of so many of their vessels and the seizure of much of their new found wealth from these American colonies.

Before we leave this corner of Suffolk, a visit to **Felixstowe Ferry** is in order, but do however take care on the road as it can be hazardous. The road runs through the middle of a links course and golf balls can come hurling your way. A small ferry - operated by means of a chain and steam engine - once ran from here to Bawdsey on the other side of the Deben but not any more. Nonetheless it is an interesting shingly hamlet with its own combination of sea and tidal river, two Martello Towers, built between 1810 and 1812, and then there is the Ferry

Although no longer **Goseford** was once a huge open port along the River Deben, and once more important than either Felixstowe or Ipswich. For the Saxons. it was a major wool port, and for the Plantagenet Edward III this was where he assembled his fleet for the Calais Expedition in 1338; Calais then English owned. Goseford contributed 15 ships and over 500 men to this campaign but by the time of the Spanish Armada (1586), it had so declined that only three ships could be summoned towards the Queen's fleet.

Boat Inn which stands on a site dating back to 1181 and which was the Fish Mart at least during the 1400's. Today, fresh fish can be bought from the huts along the beach, and for the more adventurous, in the summertime, the **East Suffolk Water Ski Club** give lessons on an individual basis. Just turn up at the slipway on a Monday evening and they will arrange a boat to take you out.

# Walk 26: Felixstowe Ferry and the River Deben

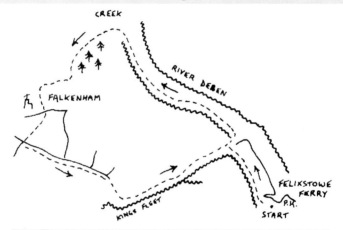

## Directions:

1. From the car park in front of the Ferry Boat Inn (Felixstowe Ferry), walk along the road to a cafe. Go left through a gap in a metal fence and follow a concrete dyke past the boatyard and then on to a more traditional dyke. At King's Fleet, cross over the Cut near an old, now derelict windpump and go right along the dyke. Continue along here for just under two miles keeping yourself midway between a drainage ditch on your left and the River Deben on your right. 2. Just before Falkenham Creek, follow the path on your left leading across the marsh i.e. now leaving the River bank. 3. At a meeting of tracks just beyond a grouping of trees keep left, and where it later reaches a T-junction of paths go to the right. At the next crossway, take the path on your left which leads to Falkenham Church. 4. At the Church, go right a few yards and cross the road to a footpath on your left. Continue along this path until you reach another lane and then go left along it to pass Deben Lodge Farm. Continue straight through over a stile to what becomes a track leading down to Kings Fleet Drainage

Cut. Follow the path round to the left to return to the derelict drainage mill seen on your outward route. Cross over the Cut to return to your starting point in Felixstowe Ferry.

**Start: Felixstowe Ferry Car Park**
**Approx. Distance: 7 Miles**
**Approx. Time: 3.5 Hours**
**Map: Landranger 169**

*Felixstowe Ferry*

# Ipswich, The Estuaries and Constable Country

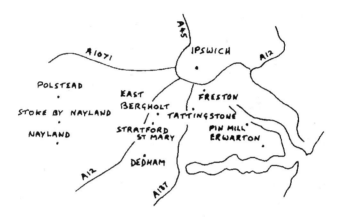

Our final Chapter sees us in Ipswich, Suffolk's county seat and still an important port. From Ipswich we explore the Orwell and Stour Estuaries before taking our last excursion through the beautiful area commonly called Constable country which is to be found on the Suffolk-Essex borders.

## Ipswich

Suffolk's county town, Ipswich, stands at the head of the Orwell Estuary. The Orwell incidentally is the easiest to navigate of all Suffolk's rivers and this enables shipping to enter the port regardless of tide or wind. Today, Ipswich is the fourth largest container facility in the country, its large Wet Dock handling vast quantities of North Sea trade.

Much of the town's architecture is Victorian, little remaining of its medieval prosperity founded on Suffolk's once lucrative cloth industry, and what there is of timber-framed buildings, most are to be found in the Quay area. Before this,

191

however, it was an ancient Anglo-Saxon settlement established circa 600 AD and called *Gipeswic*. By *Domesday* (1086), it was an important burgh and under King John it even had its own mint. The medieval castle though was destroyed by Henry II, never to be rebuilt.

It remained an important place during Henry VIII's reign attributable in part perhaps to Cardinal Wolsey's strong associations with the town. During the ensuing 17th Century, it was recognised as a notable port, served by Ipswich built colliers that had captured much of the coal trade between the North of England and London. This accomplishment was fairly short-lived though and bit by bit the trade in coals was lost to more northern competitors operating more economically out of Northumbria and County Durham. Testament to Ipswich's importance in this respect though is once again Daniel Defoe's account of 1724, but which records an earlier visit he made to the town in 1668: *'Ipswich was a town of very good business, particularly it was the greatest town in England for large colliers or coal ships employed between Newcastle and London; also they built the biggest ships and the best for the said fetching of coals of any that were employed in that trade.'* (*Tour Through the Eastern Counties.*)

Nevertheless, the building of the Wet Dock - the largest single dock in the world at that time - went ahead in the 1840's, commissioned by a collective of 72 gentlemen who constituted themselves as The River Commissioners. And still more expansion was required further downstream so that even larger shipping could be berthed. The Dock occupies an expanse of 35 acres, quite an incredible engineering feat in those early Victorian years. Alternatives to the coal trade then must have been found, not least the discovery of coprolite found in large quantities along the Orwell and Deben Peninsula during the 19th Century. Once extracted, this was ground down to form a fertiliser and in just one year alone, 1877, over 10,000 tons of this lucrative mineral was shipped out of Ipswich alone. The first artificial manure factory was built on the corner of Coprolite Street sometime during the mid 19th Century.

The **Wet Dock's** construction was the brain child of Henry Palmer, and required the cutting off of part of the existing River and the excavation of a New Cut to carry the water's of the Gipping downstream of the quays. This by-passed section was then closed off and an entrance lock built where the Harbour Master's Office now stands. This was replaced by a new lock in 1881 at the dock's southern extremity.

Ipswich also became known as one of the largest sailing barge ports along the southerly east coast, the huge milling operations of Cranfields and Pauls owning their own substantial fleets. Other prosperous industries followed the onset of the Industrial Revolution and amongst these can be counted the famous agricultural engineering works of Ransome and Rapier. Printing too has flourished here, begun as early as 1548 with the publication of John Bale's *Summary of the Illustrious Writers of Great Britain*, and continued today by the likes of Cowell's. The independent brewers, Tolly Cobbold, also operate out of Ipswich and are known for their fine traditional cask conditioned ales.

The Cornhill remains the centre of town but like the rest of Ipswich is a rather motley collection of architectural styles ranging from mock Gothic to mock Classical. Little respect at times seems to have been paid to historic buildings in the town - especially guilty of this are the Victorians - and even the Market Cross was dismantled in 1812.

Amongst those older buildings which have survived some are to be found near the quay area and include the Customs House designed by local man J.M. Clarke, built during the 1840's, and now housing the offices of the Ipswich Port Authority. A walk along Fore Street, in the same area, also reveals a number of period buildings, many of these typically Suffolk timber-framed, their backs against the River so as to facilitate the unloading of goods, and their fronts then serving as shops for the products thus supplied. Of particular note is the Malt Kiln Pub converted from 17th Century maltings, and now forming the rear of the Isaac Lord complex - formerly a merchant's house with ground floor shop, weaving sheds, warehouse and store room. Of the town's medieval churches, at one time thought to be as many as 21, little more than ten have survived and pretty well half of these are now redundant, used for a variety of secular pur-poses including the Tourist Information Centre. Finally, to the Great White Horse Inn on Tavern Street, immortalised by Charles Dickens' *Pickwick Papers* and about which Dickens unfortunately could find nothing good to say, this the place where an embarrassed Mr. Pickwick meets the lady in yellow curl papers.

The son of a butcher and merchant, **Cardinal Wolsey** (1475-1530), was born in Ipswich in a timber-framed house in Silent Street (marked by a plaque). Educated at Oxford, his first living was at Lymington in Somerset. From here he rose through the Church hierarchy occupy-ing the bishopric of Lincoln, the archbishopric of York and then the fol-lowing year appointed a cardinal (1515). The same year, he was appointed Henry VIII's Lord Chancellor and through this was able to control England's foreign policy, enjoying a ministerial position more powerful than anyone since Thomas a Becket. Although Wolsey initi-ated Henry VIII's campaign to dissolve the monasteries, the two men fell out over Wolsey's seeming evasiveness on the question of the King's divorce from Catherine of Aragon. In 1529, Wolsey was oblig-ed to surrender the Great Seal and his property was forfeited to the Crown. He died a broken man in 1530.

Only a couple of years before his death, Wolsey founded St. Mary's College in the town's Black Friar's Street and which he fully intended would rival the likes of Eton and Winchester and which would further train pupils for entry into Cardinal College (now Christ Church College), Oxford. The project was not, however, completed before his fall from grace, and today only the brick built 'Wolsey's Gateway' stands. Reference to this College for secular canons though is made in Shakespeare's *Henry VIII*:

'... *those twins of learning, Ipswich and Oxford, fell with him*
*Unwilling to outlive the good that did it.*'

# *Places to Visit*

## *Museums:*

*The Blitz Museum* (01473 251605 *during school term time only*), *Clifford Road, Ipswich.* Here you can step back in time into an underground ARP Shelter constructed in 1940 in the playground of Clifford School; this the only one of three to remain intact. Not only do you hear the sounds of wartime radio but you also experience what an air raid would have been like. *Small admission charge.*

*Christchurch Mansion* (01473 253246), *Christchurch Park, Soane Street, Ipswich.* Aside from the Ancient House, Christchurch Mansion is probably the town's most important asset. Originally built in 1548 and surrounded by a beautiful, undulating park, it holds a good collection of period furniture much of which was assembled from town houses that are no longer extant. There is even a painted and panelled Tudor Room known as the Wingfield Room where the panelling was taken from an inn in Tacket Street, and there is also Lady Drury's 'painted closet', taken from Hawstead Place, near Bury St. Edmunds. Other items of interest include a large collection of Mendlesham chairs thought to have been made in the Suffolk village of that name and an unusual and rare collection of treenware. Additionally, there is new display of china and glass which depicts changes in style - from the relatively course earthenware to the very fine porcelain - from the 18th Century onwards. Included in this is a good range of Lowestoft porcelain. In the Wolsey Art Gallery a good collection of paintings by 'local' artists can be seen including those by Constable, Gainsborough, Philip Wilson Steer and Munnings as also an interesting collection of Tudor and Stuart portraits. *Open daily. Admission charge.*

**Christchurch Mansion**

**Bronze Statue of Grandma commemorating the work of celebrated cartoonist Carl Giles**

*Ipswich Museum* (01473 213761), HighStreet, Ipswich. Suffolk's archaeology, from prehistoric to medieval times, is well documented in the Museum, plus there is a collection of ethnological and natural history exhibits from around the world. The Roman Gallery houses a reconstructed domestic interior as well as a bakery and other replicas include the respective finds at Sutton Hoo and Mildenhall. *Open daily, excluding Sunday. Admission charge.*

*Ipswich Transport Museum, Old Trolleybus Depot, Cobham Road, Ipswich.* Here you find the largest collection of transport items in the country devoted to just one town; all the exhibits were either made or used in and around Ipswich. Items on display include an 1818 hobbyhorse, a 1923 trolleybus thought to be the oldest in the world, early coffin biers, Enfield battery cars, one of the first Superstox cars, and many delivery, heavy goods and specialist vehicles. There is also a 1930's replica bicycle shop, and the original 1937 switchboard installed to supply power to trolleybuses. *Open every Sunday and also Bank Holiday Mondays, April to the end of October. Admission charge.*

*Tolly Cobbold Brewery and the Brewery Tap* (01473 231723), Cliff Road, Ipswich. For an experience of a different kind, come here to taste the malt and smell the hops of this magnificent Victorian brewery, probably the finest in the country. Guided tours take you through the complete brewing process and many brewing artefacts are on view including some dating to the operations beginnings in 1723. Items on display include a Victorian steam engine built by E.R. & F. Turner of Ipswich, two coppers dating from 1896 as well as the original Boiling Copper of 1723 thought to be the oldest such vessel in the country. At the end of all this is a refreshing pint in the Brewery Tap. *Open daily, April to September, and with reduced openings during the winter months. Admission charge.*

A **Giles Museum** seeking to demonstrate the skills of the celebrated cartoonist Carl Giles (d. 1995) is currently under consideration, much depending on the outcome of an application for lottery funding. Giles cartoons, variously depicting Grandma and the family, Stinker and Butch, Chalkie and his errant pupils, and not forgetting his masterful wartime pieces which did much to boost morale at the time, were until the artists death a regular feature in both *The Sunday Express* and *The Daily Express*. Giles worked from his Ipswich studios for many years, refusing to return what he considered the squalor of London.

## Ecclesiastical & Public Buildings:

**St. Margaret's Church,** *Soane Street,* is perhaps the most spectacular of the town's churches and enjoys an unrivalled position against the backdrop of Christchurch Mansion and the park which surrounds it. Note in particular the double hammerbeam roof, decorated to celebrate the peaceful outcome of the 1688 Revolution, and currently awaiting a cleaning programme, and the 15th Century clerestory with its closely set windows.

**St. Mary-Le-Tower** with its conspicuous 176 feet high spire is Ipswich's principal parish church and it is here that the burgesses of Ipswich met to receive King John's Charter in 1200. Built of knapped flint and employing chequered flushwork, it contains a fine pulpit, dating from around 1700 and similar in style to that in The Old Meeting House.

**The Old Meeting House**, *Friar's Street,* is a two-storey timber-framed structure and the most interesting place of worship to be found in Ipswich. Built in 1699 by Joseph Clarke for Presbyterian use, it only later became an Unitarian meeting place. Note the huge candelabra which is thought to be 17th Century Dutch, the fine pews some of which in the galleries are 'wig' pews, and the beautifully carved pulpit thought to be Grinley Gibbons work. This is one of the finest buildings of its date in the country, noted also for its windows, doorcases and double-hipped roof.

**St. Peter's Church,** *College Street,* houses the rare 12th Century Tournai marble font with its frieze of lions - just one of a small handful shipped from Flanders- as also the fine Knappe Brass of 1604 commemorating John Knappe and his family. The Church also once served as the Chapel to Wolsey's College and perhaps this accounts for Henry VIII's arms depicted on the east chancel wall.

**St. Stephen's Church**, *St. Stephen's Lane,* mostly an amalgam of 15th and 16th Century efforts, now houses the Tourist Information Centre. There are, however, some interesting bits and pieces to see including a door with the letter T in a shield (the R now lost) and representing Sir Thomas Rush, one of the Crown's dissolution henchmen. The Rush family are buried in the 1535 south-east chapel which makes use of an oak beam from their former home in Brook Street. Also look for Charles II coat of arms, and the painting of the Prince of Wales Feathers which can be dated to 1661.

*The beautifully pargeted Ancient House*

*Ancient House* is a truly wonderful  15th Century spectacle in the heart of the Buttermarket and was once the home of a wealthy family of merchants and grocers, the Sparrowe's.  The extraordinary pargeted exterior is late 17th Century and symbolises the then four known Continents: Asia with its domed structure, Africa astride a crocodile and under a sun shade, Europe with a Gothic Church and America with a tobacco pipe.  Among the many other scenes depicted are Charles II's coat of arms, Neptune, a pelican, a shepherd and shepherdess, and garlands of fruit.  Now owned by Lakeland Plastics, retailers of quality kitchenware, do take a look inside the building where you can also see a stucco ceiling of the same period and stucco reliefs from the 18th Century among them Architecture, Music, Painting and Geometry.

## Sports Venues:

*Golf: Ipswich Golf Club (01473 728941), Purdis Heath, Bucklesham Road, Ipswich,* offers both an 18-hole and a 9-hole heathland course.  Visitors are welcome but some restrictions apply and you must take your handicap certificate.

*Horse riding: Kembroke Hall Riding School (01394 448201), Newbourn Road, Bucklesham, near Ipswich and Newton Hall Equestrian Centre (01473 785616), Swilland, near Ipswich* are both BHS approved.

*Motor Sports: Ipswich Stadium (01473 254697), Foxhall Heath, Ipswich.*  This is one of the fastest oval raceways in the country and is home to various banger, stock car and hot rod events.

*Sailing: East Anglian Sea School (01473 684884), Unit 1, Fox's Marine, The Strand, Ipswich* offer RYA approved sailing and motor cruising courses. ***Note the annual South East Boat Show has now returned to Ipswich and can be found at a***

197

*new 22 acre site at Cliff Quay. This significant five-day event is held early May.*

**Ten Pin Bowling:** two facilities are available: one at *Kingpin Bowling Centre (01473 611111), Gloster Road, Martlesham Heath* and the other at *Solar Bowl (01473 241242), Sproughton Road, Ipswich.*

**Walking:** *The Gipping Valley River Path* is a 17 mile long former tow path between Ipswich and Stowmarket and runs along the banks of the River Gipping. To see the River Orwell in all its glory, follow the right hand bank from Ipswich to Shotley.

## Gardens:

**Blakenham Woodland Garden,** *Little Blakenham, near Ipswich* is a five acre woodland garden owned by Lord Blakenham and containing many rare trees and shrubs. It is especially noted for its bluebells, camellias, azaleas, rhododendrons and magnolias. *Open from the beginning of March to the end of June. Admission charge.*

# Food & Accommodation

**The Beagle** *(01473 730455), Old Hadleigh Road, Sproughton, near Ipswich.* A local favourite, this is a very comfortable, even plush, pub converted from a row of timber-framed cottages. Inglenook fireplaces and exposed beams create a warm, convivial atmosphere. Good home made food and an excellent range of ales.

**Belstead Brook Manor Hotel** *(01473 684241), Belstead Road, Ipswich.* A friendly Jacobean manor house hotel where much of the accommodation is geared towards business users being very spacious and comfortable if only a little uniform. The Restaurant here is first rate. *Note two bedrooms are especially equipped for disabled visitors.*

**Kwok's Rendezvous** *(01473 256833), 23 Nicholas Street, Ipswich.* A particularly good, family run Chinese establishment with a Pekinese and Szechuan flavour. The choice is excellent, the food always well presented and all is supported by a good wine list.

**Mortimer's on the Quay** *(01473 230225), Wherry Quay, Ipswich.* An unpretentious, busy and reliable restaurant converted from a former warehouse and enjoying a dock side setting. Fish represents pretty well all of the menu and why not when the catch can be local and sumptuously fresh. At weekends it does get very busy, so do book to avoid disappointment.

**Singing Chef** *(01473 255236), 200 St. Helen's Street, Ipswich.* Open during the evenings only, this is a French-styled bistro offering a genuine, regional menu, and where the ingredients are fresh and oozing with quality.

## Walk 27: Ipswich

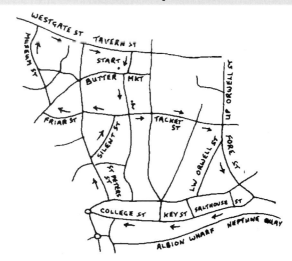

### Directions:

1. From your start at the Ancient House on the Buttermarket, go into St. Stephen's Lane.  2. Go left into Dog Head Street and continue straight on into Tacket Street and then into Orwell Place. 3. At the next junction, go right into Fore Street.  Continue along here as it joins Salt House Street and from here left into Wherry Lane taking you down to the Wet Dock. (To visit the Tolly Cobbold Brewery, go left here and then retrace your steps.)  At the Dock, turn right along Wherry, Common, and Albion Quays passing first The Home Warehouse and then The Customs House. 4. Go right into Foundary Lane and then left into College Street to pass St. Peter's Church.  Continue round College Street (keeping right) to go into St. Peter's Street over the road on your left. 5. Go right into Silent Street, left into Falcon Street and Friar's Street passing the The Old Meeting House. At the junction with Museum Street, go right passing the Gothic Methodist Church. 6. Go right into Westgate Street, then Tavern Street and then, right into Dial Street passing St. Lawrence Church before returning to your start.

**Start: The Ancient House, Ipswich**
**Approx. Distance: 2.5 Miles**
**Approx. Time: 1-2 Hours**

# The Orwell and Stour Estuaries

From Ipswich we take the southerly route along the banks of the River Orwell to *Freston*.  The village is endowed with some interesting properties not least *Freston Tower* which is barely visible from the roadside but stands just back from the banks of the Estuary.  Any effort to walk the short distance from the road is well repaid; alternatively follow the walk described below which passes the Tower.  The Tower is thought to have been built by the Latimer family (others say the Goodings) in the 1550's.  Its purpose is equally well argued, some

**Freston Tower**

saying it was a watch tower, looking out for ships inward bound up the Estuary to Ipswich. More fancifully, others say Lord Freston built it for his daughter so that she could study here. Each of the Tower's storeys being laid out for a different subject with weaving at the bottom and astronomy at the top. Whatever the truth, this fairy-tale like version remains the most popular. Other interesting snippets of village history have also survived. At the bottom of Freston Hill is Monkey Lodge built in 1861 as a Gatehouse to Woolverstone Hall. The stone monkeys on the gateposts commemorate a pet ape who alerted the owners of the property to a fire such that they were all able to escape unharmed. The tale at Latimer Cottages, Holbrook Road, is sadly much less happy for in 1910 four people were to die of the plague here; this the last known outbreak of the plague in England.

## Walk 28: Freston, Wherstead and the River Orwell

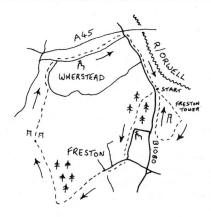

## Directions:

1. From your park (in the lay-by at the bottom of Freston Hill on the B1456) cross the road and walk a few yards north along the road towards Ipswich. Where you come to three signed footpaths on your left, take the centre path which leads along the edge of a field to a stile. Continue along the edge of another field to a second stile which will take you along a clear path through the woods. 2. Where the path forks, take the right hand path which leads to a lane at Freston Church. Go right along the lane for approx. one third of a mile until it bears sharp left. At this point ignore the road and go right onto a track leading through Freston village. 3. Continue along this track for approx. one and a half miles, through the gates towards the end of which it begins to skirt Cutler's Wood. Towards the edge of the wood. look for a gap in the trees on your right and follow the path running on your right inside the wood edge ( i.e. do not use the field). 4. At the edge of the wood, you come to a concrete track leading left away from the trees. Follow this towards the farm in front of you. 5. Once at another track, go left and almost immediate right between a barn and the house. Continue along this straight track for approx. one mile to a gate. Continue straight ahead along a lane which leads to Wherstead village. 6. Where the lane bends sharply to the left, go right instead along a track signed Wherstead Church and the River Orwell. Continue along this track until you arrive at the B1456 again. 7. Go right here following the River's edge to just before Freston Tower. Keeping the Tower on your left follow a path to a gate at the top of a slight incline. Cross the stile and continue for a short distance along the track in front of you. Where this skirts a field take the path (signed) on the right edge of the filed and on through a narrow path leading through houses. 8. At the road, go right to return to your start.

**Start: The bottom of Freston Hill  Approx. Distance: 6 Miles
Approx. Time: 2.5 Hours  Map: Landranger 169**

Now to *Pin Mill* and if possible try and time your visit to coincide with the first week in July when the colourful Barge Match, organised by the local sailing club, is staged. Don't worry if not, for there are usually a few Thames Barges moored here, proudly berthed amongst a plethora of other craft, and it is in any case such a pretty corner of the Orwell Estuary. Just to the right of the village proper is the National Trust Cliff Plantation, a large stretch of woodland badly damaged by the 1987 hurricane but substantially replanted since then.

# *Food & Accommodation*

**The Butt & Oyster** (01473 780764), Pin Mill. Situated on the banks of the Orwell, this is an old bargeman's pub appropriately decorated with model sailing ships and the like. Unchanged and unspoilt, it is a great spot to enjoy the spectacular views over the River whilst enjoying food, ale and perhaps the odd old pub game.

**The Old Boot House** (01473 787755), Main Road, Shotley. Found about a mile from the Estuary, this restaurant always has something refreshingly imaginative to offer, and the standards always well maintained. Flavours of a floral nature are quite the norm and not to be shied away from

Of the village, there is a charming group of terraced cottages in the Dell plus a small number clustered together on the Grindle. Arthur Ransome (1884-1967), the author of *Swallows and Amazons* (1931), spent much of his time here at Alme Cottage, using the skills of Harry King's boatyard for the building of the *Nancy Blackett*. Even the plot of *We Don't Mean To Go To Sea* (1938) commences at Pin Mill and the character Miss Powell was actually a local resident.

# Walk 29: Pin Mill and the River Orwell

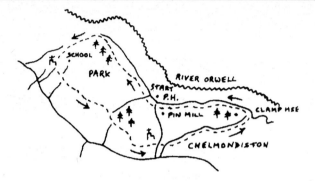

## Directions:

1. From your park at Pin Mill, bear left towards the River Orwell and the pub. Go left to cross Pin Mill Common and at a junction of paths go along the bridleway, and at the next junction go straight on a footpath which leads along the edge of a field. 2. Cross two more fields, Woolverstone Hall can be seen on your left, after which the path leads through a copse of trees and on to the River Orwell. 3. Walk in front of the Yacht Club and just after this go left on a drive (signed Woolverstone Church). Go along here to the Church, and just beyond the Church's southerly aspect take the second path on your left off a lane (this is the Chelmondiston path not the Pin Mill path). After a short distance you cross the drive to Woolverstone School and continue along the path to a stile. 4. Once over this, continue along the path until you reach Berners Lane. Keep to the left to pass a group of cottages and then go round to the right ignoring a path on your left which leads down to the River. At the end of a group of trees just a little further along, look for a bridleway on your left (Church Lane) which leads into Chelmondiston village. 5. Cross the road to get to the Church and once there continue east towards the road leading down to Pin Mill. Go straight across to the bridleway, and walk through the farm yard following the track down to Clamp House. 6. Go over a stile on your left at Clamp House to enter Pin Mill Cliff Plantation. Continue along this path until you see another path on your right which leads to the shores of the River. Continue in a westerly direction along the shore until you come to some steps just before the pub which will return you to your starting point in the village.

**Start: Pin Mill Car Park**
**Approx. Distance: 4.5 Miles**
**Approx. Time: 2 Hours**
**Map: Landranger: 169**

***Pin Mill***

# *Walk 30: The Shotley Peninsula*

## *Directions:*

1. From your start at Shotley Church (off the B1456 at Church End) car park, take the track leading slightly north-east past the Church and go right at the lane end to follow a path leading towards the River Orwell. 2. Follow the foreshore round to your right until you come to a signpost. Climb up the dyke here and follow a well worn path along the Lower Reach of the Orwell for approx. one and a half miles. 3. At Shotley Point, follow the dyke left around the marina and then use the riverside road to Shotley Gate. Once past the pub, continue along a path running against the River, now the Stour, and over a stile. Leave the foreshore by some steps in the cliff and at the top go left on a path. You will go through some woods before following waymarkers to a path which follows the edge of fields above the River Stour. 4. Cross the track at a signpost and go in front of some farm cottages to continue along the filed/riverside path. Continue along the dyke as it runs around Erwarton Bay and once over a narrow channel turn right into

a track at the signpost.  Continue along this track keeping left near the pond and so onto a lane.  5.  Go right here and at Erwarton Hall take the second left to rejoin the B1456.  At this minor road, turn left and after a short distance go right into Church Walk.  This will return you to your starting point.

**Start: Church End, Shotley**
**Approx. Distance: 5.5 Miles**
**Approx. Time: 2.5 Hours**
**Map: Landranger 169**

Heading west along what is now the Stour Estuary, we arrive in *Erwarton.* Although not open to the public, *Erwarton Hall*, rebuilt in 1575 is one of the earliest brick built country homes in the country.  It is an attractive spot built in English bond and still retaining its mullioned windows.  In line with the entrance to the Hall is a beautiful red brick tunnel-vaulted *Gateway*, with four semi-circular gables and capped with pinnacles.  Little more than a folly, a pretty one at that, it can be dated to 1549 from its heraldry.

The earlier mansion to what is seen today was owned by Sir Philip Calthorpe, uncle through his wife to Anne Boleyn.  Anne is known to have visited her relatives from time to time and story has it that after here execution her heart was buried in the village Church.  A heart-shaped casket containing a handful of dust was actually found in St. Mary's chancel wall in the 19th Century, so perhaps there is some truth to the notion after all.  Set away from the village, St. Mary's dates from the 14th Century and houses a number of monuments to past wealthy parishioners including that to Sir Philip himself.

*Erwarton Gateway*

204

*The Tattingstone Wonder*

A drive through *Tattingstone,* a traditional manorial village until the early 20th Century, is worth it to see another of Suffolk's strange buildings, probably in fact the moist peculiar and idiosyncratic of them all and endearingly know as *The Tattingstone Wonder.* It is basically a row of workmens cottages with one end built to resemble a ruined church. It was built in 1761 by the local squire as he was frustrated by his neighbours constantly wondering at nothing! His aim, which no doubt was achieved, was to give them something real to contemplate.

What is left of the rest of the village sits close to the edge of *Alton Water Reservoir*, which supports many species of waterfowl including cormorant and great-crested grebe. The lake now fits so easily into the environment that one can barely imagine the destruction of much woodland, homes and Tattingstone Hall in its original flooding.

At the south-east corner of the Reservoir, between Holbrook and Stutton, is the *Royal Hospital School*, the naval training ground for sons of Royal Navy and Royal Marine Officers. The arrangement of this vast collection of buildings is strictly axial and neo-Georgian in style. Dominated by the Clock Tower it is certainly an impressive looking set-up though one that is not truly imaginative.

# Walk 31: Stutton Ness and the Tattingstone Wonder

## Directions:

1. From your park at Alton Reservoir Car Park (off the B1080 just out-side Stutton), walk westwards along the bank of the Reservoir until you come to a seat. Go left here, over a stile, and into a lane leading into the village. 2. At the B1080, turn left and then immediate right into Church Road. Continue along the road until it bends sharp left. Here, turn right along a track (signed) which gradually becomes a path running along the edge of a field. 3. Once at a lane, turn left to pass Creeping Hall and further on a copse of trees. Continue along the track to reach the River Stour at Stutton Ness. Go right along the path above the rivers edge until you come to New Mill Creek. Follow this inlet inland towards Stutton Mill. 4. Walk along the drive to Stutton Mill keeping the house and outbuildings on your right. Go right and left with the drive to pass, approx. half a mile further on the entrance to Queech Farm. Keep on your track following it first to the right and then left and then take a track on your right skirting a belt of trees. 5. Take the first track on your left which leads to the B1080. Once at the road, go right to pass the pub and then left on a lane running alongside a belt of trees to Upper Street. Continue along this lane as it bears left and right,and then left to skirt some trees. At the end of this track fol-low the path in a north-westerly direction to Vale Farm in front of you. 6. Once near the Farm, bear right to join a drive to the right of these buildings. Turn right onto the drive and continue along here until you reach a lane. Go right at the lane and follow it for approx. one mile until you come to another lane on your left. 7. Go left here to pass the Tattingstone Wonder and then cross the road to take a path to Alton Water Reservoir. Go over a stile and onto a well used path skirt-ing the water. Keep the water on your left as you use an Anglian Water permissive path around the Reservoir to return to your start..

**Start: Alton Water Reservoir Car Park**
**Approx. Distance: 8 Miles   Approx. Time: 4 Hours**
**Map: Landranger 169**

# Constable Country

At Cattawade Bridge, the start of Constable country, we find a fine old brick arch over the River Stour. A little way upstream is an ancient tidal mill probably the last to be so worked in England. After World War II, it was used as a spice mill and is now a factory, though the wheel is no longer in operation.

Our first stop though is **East Bergholt**, meaning *wooded hill* and is derived originally from the Anglo-Saxon. East Bergholt is at the heart of Constable country for here in the centre of the village lived his parents, the house no longer evident, but their tombstones still to be found in the churchyard, as is Willy Lott's. Constable himself was born here, although he attended school in nearby Dedham, and many of his paintings capture the unique beauty of the surrounding countryside. A visit to St. Mary's Church may afford us a glimpse of the sensitivity to be found in this great painter's work, for written on a plaque in a side aisle you can read his own thoughts on the subject: '*The landscape painter must walk in the fields with an humble mind. No arrogant man was ever permitted to see nature in all her beauty*'.

Now to the churchyard to look over the peculiarly beautiful wooden bell house dating from the 16th Century; the huge bells to which are rung by hand and no doubt the peel rather deafening. It is a most eccentric building and perhaps best left to an architect to describe: '*One storey with steep pyramid roof with covered top. Heavy timbers to support the bells inside. The outside walls are a grille of timbers above a dado. The horizontal timbers woven through the vertical ones.*' Sir Nikolaus Pevsner in *Suffolk*, The Buildings of England Series, Penguin, 2nd Ed., 1971.

Story has it that every time the builders tried to erect the Church tower where the bells would normally have been housed, the Devil came along at night and cast it down. More likely is the version whereby the tower's financier, Cardinal Wolsey, lost court favour and so projects like East Bergholt were abandoned with him. The villagers themselves would not have been able to pick up the tab, their cloth industry already in decline, and hence the external structure we find in the churchyard.

That the village counted wealthy clothiers amongst its 15th Century population is clear from the period properties to be found here. Amongst these are the timber-framed Clay Cottages, and The Gables which also has octagonal chimneys. Later houses worth looking out for include the Georgian Little Court, the Victorian Abbey, and Stour House, once the home of Randolph Churchill and the place where he wrote his father's biography; the gardens here, which look over the River Valley, are usually open to the public.

It is just a short distance now to **Dedham**, nestling dignified in the valley of the River Stour, and forever immortalised by the works of Constable, Nash and Munnings. So beautiful is the Dedham Vale that it has now been designated an Area of Outstanding Natural Beauty and where the meadows are preserved as

**Dedham**

natural grazing wetlands.  But first to St. Mary's Church in the village proper, built towards the end of the 15th Century and the tower of which is evident in many of Constable's paintings.  Inside, note the tremendous display of heraldic bosses on the ceiling, including the insignia belonging to the Guild of Weavers and Millers who during their heyday richly endowed the Church.  Not least among them wool merchant Thomas Webbe.  Additionally, look out for the pew which commemorates man's first landing on the Moon.  One interesting story connected to the Church tells of the gleaner's bell - in itself a rarity - being rung between 8 a.m. and 7p.m. for a fortnight each year, and this around the turn of the 19th/20th Centuries.  The bell informed parishioners that they could glean the harvest fields between these hours.

That Dedham was once a flourishing wool town - established by Flemish weavers in the 14th Century - can be seen in the many fine houses which remain and which would once have belonged to wealthy clothiers.  Later 17th Century residences - in particular Shermans Hall with its sun dial and pilasters, and the ancestral home of the American General of the same name - have also survived, so the decline of the wool trade cannot have seen all fortunes turned. Today the village unusually is a pleasing mix of private homes, shops, art galleries together with a very necessary pub, and just outside the village proper an hotel and two restaurants.

On the outskirts is ***Castle House*** *(01206 322127)*, the former home of Alfred Munnings and now an Art Gallery displaying a good range of his paintings. Munnings who lived here from 1920 until his death in 1959 is noted for his portraits of horses; wherever there were horses, so you would find Munnings, or so they used to say.  Born in Suffolk to a miller (like Constable), Munnings graduated in 1905 from the Norwich School of Art, moving to Dedham 15 years later. One of his more well known paintings *Start at Newmarket* sold for $1.1 million in 1987.

It was also in Dedham that another painter John Nash together with Cedric Morris formed the East Anglian School of Painting. Nash spent much of his time in the Stour Valley, albeit living on the Essex side of the River, and from where he drew much of his inspiration for his mechanised agricultural landscapes for the most part devoid of people. *The Cornhill* (1918), one of his better known works, is typical of this approach. During the 1950's and 1960's, Nash also taught botanical illustration at the Field Studies Centre at Flatford Mill.

Still another painter to work from Dedham was Tom Keating, one of the world's greatest art forgers. Taking his own peculiar stand against collectors who brought paintings purely and simply for their investment potential and not for their beauty and aesthetic value, Keating was to forge the works of many great painters, among them Turner and Constable.

Now to Constable (1776-1837), born in East Bergholt in 1776 to a successful corn merchant, owner of none less than Flatford Mill itself. His father had intended John to take over his substantial business ventures once he had finished his basic schooling and only reluctantly allowed him to enroll at the Royal Academy, London, in 1799, at the relatively late age of 23. He always returned in the summers to his native Suffolk, and with sketchbook in hand recorded scenes which would later find permanence in his exquisite canvases. In 1816, he married Mary Bicknell and on her father's death, 12 years later, a decent inheritance enabled Constable to give up his portrait work in favour of his

*Flatford Mill*

**Willy Lott's Cottage**

**Flatford Lock** was originally built in 1706 and consisted of 15 locks responsible for navigability of the River Stour between Sudbury and the sea. Lighters would have been among the more regular boats to be seen along here and these frequently used for the transportation of manure from London's streets and which was spread across the fields along the banks of the Stour as additional fertiliser. Restored by the River Stour Trust, **Flatford Dock** is the only surviving dock of its time to be found along an English river.

**Flatford Mill**, built by the Constable family in 1733, continued in operation until 1846. It is now owned by the National Trust and since 1946 has been used by the Field Studies Centre in their educational programmes ranging from botany to painting and architecture. Do visit the tiny thatched **Bridge Cottage** just upstream from the Mill and which houses a display about Constable. Also managed by the National Trust *(01206 298260)*, there is also tea garden, shop and Information Centre here. Boats are also available for hire. *Open variously from the end of February to the end of November.*

beloved countryside. 1821 saw great applause in the Paris Salon for his *Haywain* (1821), and equally well received in France was his *White Horse* (1825); indeed, both received Gold Medals and are considered to have influenced the likes of Delacroix. Later years were not so happy; first the loss of his wife and then close friends, and then ill-health. He continued to paint until his death in 1837 and his work now hangs in the National Gallery and The Tate as well as in important collections the world over. By way of indication as to how valued his paintings are today, *Flatford Lock and Mill* (1812) sold in the mid-1980's for £2.64 million.

In the absence of his paintings, perhaps the best way to appreciate Constable's unique love and reverence for nature, and in which he saw spiritually divine forces, is to let him speak for himself:

*'The beauty of the surrounding scenery, the gentle declivities, luxuriant meadow flats sprinkled with flocks and herds, and well cultivated uplands, the woods and rivers, the numerous scattered villages and churches, with farms and picturesque cottages, all impart to this particular spot an amenity and elegance hardly anywhere else to be found ...'*
John Constable, 1833, 'Discourses' in *Suffolk Records Society*,
Woodbridge, 1970, Vol 14.

## Food & Accommodation

**Fountain House** *(01206 323027). Dedham Hall, Brook Street, Dedham.* This is a restaurant which also offers bedroom accommodation on a B & B Basis. The setting, overlooking the grounds of Dedham Hall, is best described as pastoral, the gardens naturally scenic, the 15th Century house characterful, the food excellent if simple - the desserts in particular are to be tried - and the prices very fair.

**Le Talbooth** *(01206 323150), Gun Hill, Dedham.* An excellent restaurant overlooking the River and where the cooking is for the most part either classical or modern British. In the evenings you pay for a sumptuous setting where every detail is taken care of but at lunch times it all seems a veritable bargain.

**Maison Talbooth** *(01206 322367), Stratford Road,* is an imposing Victorian hotel close to the road. Luxury abounds here from the very well furnished bedrooms, each named after a British poet with a piece of poetry framed and hung on the wall, to the stately but relaxing drawing room with French windows opening onto the lawn. There is no restaurant here, the owners also responsible for Le Talbooth above, so you are in any case well catered for.

**Marlborough Head** *(01206 323124), Dedham.* An 18th Century pub serving above average food and good ale. A wealth of exposed timbers and finely carved woodwork - especially in the central lounge - make for a most congenial atmosphere. Accommodation is available.

# *Walk 32: Constable and the River Stour*

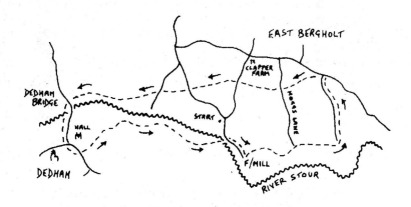

## Directions:

1. From your park at Flatford Mill Car Park, follow the signed footpath down to the River. Just before the bridge, go left along a lane to Willy Lott's Cottage. Go left again along a signed path over fields. At the end of the field, follow the signed path to your right. 2. Continue along the signed path, noting Hogg's Lane on your left which leads up to a wood. Although you do not take this lane it is nonetheless a useful marker. Instead continue along the path, over stiles, until you come to Dazeley's Lane on your left. 3. Go left along Dazeley's Lane until you reach the road leading into East Bergholt. Go left here for approx. 60 yards along the road and look for a narrow path on your left as it crosses a field to a signpost to the right of a group of trees in front of you. Go through this copse along a narrow path to a group of houses. Cross Hogg's Lane and go along the edge of two fields to get to Clapper Farm. Go right along the farm yard for approx. 20 yards to a stile 4. Once over this, head for the stile at the other end of the field. Go left a few yards to get to Flatford Road and then straight ahead into a narrow path along the edge of a field. 5. Continue along here over stiles to a lane. Go straight across the lane to a gate and stile. Once over the bridge, continue until you meet a junction of pathways. Turn right here and continue along the River's edge until you reach Dedham Bridge. 6. Go over the bridge and follow the road to a junction by the Church. Go left here and where the road bends sharp right, look for a path (to the right of a lane) which leads to the right of Dedham Hall and to the banks of the Stour. 7. Once at the River, go right along the River bank for approx. one mile. Once at Flatford Mill, cross the bridge to return to your starting point.

**Start: Flatford Mill Car Park**
**Approx Distance: 5.5 Miles**
**Approx Time: 2.5 Hours**
**Maps: Landrangers 168 and 169**

*Stratford St. Mary* along the easterly course of the River Stour was the subject of many of the great painter's works. Probably one of the better known is that depicting the Lock and Stour and entitled *The Young Waltonians*. It is an interesting village with a Tudor background - evidenced by the Weavers House which is early 16th Century, and Corner House built in 1596 - only somewhat marred today by the Water Company's pumping station. St. Mary's Church is Perpendicular with fine flushwork showing the arms of both the Chaucer's and the de la Pole's; Chaucer's granddaughter having married the first Duke of Suffolk who was a member of the de la Pole family.

Trade from the village to London flourished during the 18th and early 19th Centuries. The reason being the droves of geese and turkeys destined for the capital's markets. An interesting account of the scene is contained in Daniel Defoe's 1724 *Tour Through The Eastern Counties:*

> '... 300 droves of turkeys ... pass in one season over Stratford Bridge
> on the River Stour ... These droves ... generally contain three hundred
> to a thousand each drove ... 150,000 in all, and yet this is one of the
> least passages, the numbers which travel by ... Sudbury and Clare,
> being many more.'

North-east of Stratford St. Mary is **Little Wenham**, and although not open to the public, Little Wenham Hall, if you can catch sight of it, is of particular architectural interest as it is recorded as one of the first buildings in post-Roman times to have been built of brick, and being L-shaped was clearly built as a house instead of as a defensive keep which would have been the norm. It is thought to have been constructed for Sir John de Vallibus as early as 1270. There is also a fine 16th Century tithe barn nearby complete with brick nogging and timber-framed. All Saints Church here is home to some pretty good 14th Century wall paintings including those of the Virgin and Child, of St. Margaret, St. Catherine and St. Mary Magdalene.

Some fine buildings are to be found in nearby **Stoke-by-Nayland**. Look for the timber-framed Guildhall, The Maltings, and the old inns. The Rowley family once owned the Tendring Estate which accounts for much of the village and the lands surrounding it but this has now been covenanted to the National Trust and the Park is all that remains of Tendring Hall.

The National Trust also manage Thorington Hall, an oak framed gabled house built around 1600 and subsequently extended a hundred years later. Visits are only by prior written application to the tenant.

Set in a lovely close of Tudor buildings, is Stoke-by-Nayland's St. Mary's Church, with its 120 feet high tower. Lovers of Constable will recognise the seen it casts in a number of his paintings.

Occasionally referred to as the *Place of Pools,* **Polstead** is one of Suffolk's prettiest villages and where typically much of the property is pink-washed and tim-ber-framed. The village still has a pool or artificial lake to be found at the bot-tom of the hill, and this is where witches would have been 'swum' during those intermittent purges against their likes.

St. Mary's Church is unusual in Suffolk not only for its stone spire but also for the brick arches in the chancel and nave; the Normans were not  ones for employing brick in their buildings and this is in any case a very early example of their use. Those interested in the colonisation of new lands should look to the Church archives which lists those parishioners who sailed aboard *The Mayflower* in search of a brighter future.

The village's real claims to fame though are twofold: it was once home to an annual Cherry Fair held on the village green in mid-July and known through-out the county for its Polstead Blacks, and it was also the place where, in 1827, Maria Marten was murdered by William Corder. The cottage where Maria lived in Marten Lane still stands but the Red Barn, the scene of the murder, went up in flames in 1842.

Many relics relating to the crime can be found in Moyses Hall Museum, Bury St. Edmunds. By way of recap though for those who are unfamiliar with the story, let us begin by saying that William Corder was the son of a wealthy farmer and he and Maria, a mole catcher's daughter, were having an affair. Although they had a child together, William, the son, died shortly after he was born. Maria was nevertheless persuaded by Corder that they would marry and in order to effect the same she was to meet in him in the Red Barn, change into men's cloth-ing, and off they would go away from the village and no-one the wiser.

Maria indeed was never seen again, but Corder did leave, later writing to the girl's parents advising that he and Maria were married. Maria's mother, how-ever, regularly had dreams about the Red Barn and about one spot in particular. Persuading her husband to investigate, they uncovered Maria's body, beaten and shot, in the very place she had pictured. Corder was subsequently arrest-ed in Brentford where he had married a wealthy woman and where they man-aged a school for young ladies.

He was convicted of murder by a Bury St. Edmunds Court in 1828, and hung in front of a crowd of 10,000 spectators in August that year. The hangman sold the rope from which Corder dangled for a guinea an inch and perhaps even more macabre was the prison doctor's action in flaying the body; the skin later being used to bind a book about Corder's trial and just one of the relics on view in Moyses Hall Museum.

## Walk 33: The Box Valley and Polstead

### Directions:

1. From your park near Polstead Church, take the road leading up to the village proper. Look for a path on your right (signed) between some houses and over a field to a lane. 2. At the lane, go left to walk through Bell's Corner. After approx. one mile, where the road goes left, follow it instead round to the right. Where another lane joins in after approx. half a mile from the right, continue straight on instead. Where the road sweeps round to the left, take a track on your right leading down to Welands Farm. At the barn, follow the bridleway down to another lane and turn right into Torrington Street. 3. Once over the bridge, look for a grassy track on your right between some cottages and on to a meadow. Keep left when the track forks and head for a path beside the River Box. Keep left at Valley Farm buildings but instead of continuing left on the track, cross a stile ahead of you to go over a field to another stile and round the right side of another field. 4. Walk diagonally up hill across a field. Once at the top, follow the field edge behind some gardens and then right into a footpath leading to Scotland Street (To explore Stoke-by-Nayland, go left here and then retrace your steps.) 5. Go right at the lane and near a house called 'Oak Beams' go left over a stile to a path and leading to the bottom of the valley. 6. Continue along here until you get to the lane at Mill Street where you go right along the road. 7. Just before the last property on your left, go through a kissing gate to follow the path back to Polstead Church in front of you.

**Start: Polstead Church**
**Approx. Distance: 7 Miles**
**Approx. Time: 3 Hours (Allow longer if you intend to explore Stoke-by-Nayland)**
**Map: Landranger 155**

Our final visit is to ***Nayland***, a delightful village on the Stour's banks and once an important wool trade and cloth making centre. Former weaver's cottages, locks, a watermill, timber-framed and pargeted buildings abound. The 15th Century Alston Court has a canopied hood doorway, mullioned windows and a beautiful 16th Century nine-light window. Overlooking the central village square is the former Guildhall thought to have been built for the Brotherhood Fraternity of the Guild of our Lady of Nayland in the 15th Century. It later found use as the local judiciary, then a bakery, dairy and now a private home. Fen Street has the mill stream running along side it together with many attractive cottages reached across tiny little bridges. And bordering the Stour is a large tract of common land known as 'The Fens.' Then there is Abel's Bridge, a brick built hump of the 16th Century (renovated in the late 1950's) and financed by a wealthy clothier John Abel, so that barges carrying essential corn for the mill could navigate their way along this part of the River Stour. Finally, to St. James' Church where one of only two religious works by Constable can be seen, namely *Christ Blessing the Bread and Wine* (1809).

## *Food & Accommodation*

**The Angle Inn** *(01206 263245), Polstead Road, Stoke-by-Nayland.* This is a very popular eating establishment, especially with the locals and who can blame them with the choice on offer. Dating from the 18th Century, heavy beams and huge fireplaces are an inevitable part of The Angel's charms but there is also an air of sophistication to find here too, attributable in part to the many antique pieces of furniture and the use of warm colour schemes. Accommodation is also available.

**Martha's Vineyard** *(01206 262888), 18 High Street, Nayland..* An unpretentious restaurant which takes much influence from America in its bright, colourful decor and its menus which are fixed price and represent very good value for money. The baking is especially good, most notably the breads, and in all other respects the kitchen is both inventive and usually well-timed. It can get very busy, so do book.

# *Tourist Information Centres*

**Aldeburgh** *(01728 453637), The Cinema, High Street, IP15 5AU*

**Beccles** *(01502 713196), The Quay, Fen Lane NR34 9BH and The Library (01502 714073), Blythburgh Gate*

**Bury St. Edmunds** *(01284 764667), 6 Angel Hill IP33 1UZ*

**Diss** *(01379 650523), Meres Mouth, Mere Street IP22 3AG*

**Felixstowe** *(01394 276770), Undercliff Road West IP11 8AB*

**Hadleigh** *(01473 822922), Toppesfield Hall, IP7 5DN*

**Ipswich** *(01473 258070), St. Stephen's Church, St. Stephen's Lane IP1 1DP*

**Lavenham** *(01787 248207), Lady Street CO10 9RA*

**Lowestoft** *(01502 523000), East Point Pavilion, 1 Royal Plain NR33 OAP*

**Newmarket** *(01638 667200), 66 The Rookery CB8 8HT*

**Southwold** *(01502 722366), Town Hall, Market Place IP18 6EF*

**Stowmarket** *(01449 676800), Wilkes Way IP14 1DE*

**Sudbury** *(01787 881320), Town Hall, Old Market Place CO10 6TL*

**Woodbridge** *(01394 382896), The Library, New Street*

# *Chronology of Monarchs*

### Anglo-Saxon & Danish Kings
Egbert 802    Ethelwulf 839    Ethelbald 855
Ethelbert 860    Ethelred I 865    Alfred the Great 871
Edward the Elder 899    Athelstan 924    Edmund 939
Edred 946    Edwy 955    Edgar 959
Edward the Martyr 975    Ethelred II the Unready 979    Edmund II Ironside 1016
Canute 1016    Harold 1035    Hardicanute 1040
Edward the Confessor 1042    Harold II 1066

### Norman Kings
William I 1066    William II 1087    Henry I 1100
Stephen 1135

### House of Plantagenet
Henry II 1154    Richard I 1189    John 1199
Henry III 1216    Edward I 1272    Edward II 1307
Edward III 1327    Richard II 1377

### House of Lancaster
Henry IV 1399    Henry V 1413    Henry VI 1422

### House of York
Edward IV 1461    Edward V 1483    Richard III 1483

### House of Tudor
Henry VII 1485    Henry VIII 1509    Edward VI 1547
Mary I 1553    Elizabeth I 1558

### House of Stuart
James I 1603    Charles I 1625

### The Commonwealth  1649-60

### House of Stuart (restored)
Charles II 1660    James II 1685    William III & Mary II 1689
Anne 1702

### House of Hanover
George I 1714    George II 1727    George III 1760
George IV 1820    William IV 1830    Victoria 1837

### House of Saxe-Coburg
Edward  VII 1901

### House of Windsor
George V 1910    Edward VIII 1936    George VI 1936
Elizabeth II 1952

# Index

Principal references are in **bold** type

*King (later Saint) Edmund*